No Nonsense

Merijn Oudenampsen is a political scientist and teaches at the University of Amsterdam. For his PhD, he studied the ideas behind the rise of right-wing populism in the Netherlands. It was published as *The Rise of the Dutch New Right* and won the Choice Outstanding Academic Titles Award. Together with the historian Bram Mellink he wrote the book *Neoliberalisme: Een Nederlandse geschiedenis*, which traces the history of neoliberalism in the Netherlands all the way back to the 1930s. He writes a column for the Dutch weekly *De Groene Amsterdammer*.

No Nonsense

A History of the Dutch Neoliberal Turn

Merijn Oudenampsen

VERSO

London • New York

First published by Verso 2026

The manufacturer's authorized representative in the EU for product safety (GPSR)
is LOGOS EUROPE, 9 rue Nicolas Poussin, 17000, La Rochelle, France
contact@logoseurope.eu

1 3 5 7 9 10 8 6 4 2

Verso
UK: 6 Meard Street, London W1F 0EG
US: 207 East 32nd Street, New York, NY 10016
versobooks.com

Verso is the imprint of New Left Books

ISBN-13: 978-1-80429-419-2
ISBN-13: 978-1-80429-420-8 (UK EBK)
ISBN-13: 978-1-80429-421-5 (US EBK)

British Library Cataloguing in Publication Data
A catalogue record for this book is available from the British Library

Library of Congress Cataloging-in-Publication Data
A catalog record for this book is available from the Library of Congress

Typeset in Minion by Hewer Text UK Ltd, Edinburgh
Printed and bound by CPI Group (UK) Ltd, Croydon CR0 4YY

Contents

Acknowledgements

This is the first study of the Dutch neoliberal turn to appear, and it sometimes feels like it should have been written decades ago. A popular saying, attributed to the German poet Heinrich Heine, is that everything in the Netherlands happens fifty years late. In that light, this book is still timely. After the global financial crisis of 2008, there was a renewed impulse to understand the free market ideas that had led to the crash. Scholars began exploring the historical origins of neoliberalism, its main thinkers and the policies inspired by this worldview in a wide range of countries.

In the Netherlands, however, the debate on neoliberalism never really took off. In the years after the financial crisis, a number of popular Dutch books appeared on the remarkable dominance of market-based policies in the Netherlands. The authors all described the sensation of a sudden awakening. With a shock, they had realized that the Netherlands had ideologically transformed into a (more) neoliberal country. How this happened remained something of a mystery to them. The dominant self-image of the Netherlands at the time was that of a highly pragmatic, sober and level-headed country, where ideology had been as good as banished from public life. The assumption was that neoliberal ideas had entered the Netherlands by a subtle form of osmosis, as part of a pragmatic adjustment to a more neoliberal global economy. As a small country with an open economy, 'all we can do is adjust to a world market that is becoming ever more neoliberal in character due to the hegemony of the United States', the philosopher Hans Achterhuis wrote. As a result, neoliberalism remained a rather elusive Zeitgeist in the Netherlands, which seemed to take on solid form only in other countries – especially the United States. In the Dutch universities, 'neoliberalism' was widely seen as a polemical term, unfit for academic research.

Dissatisfaction with this state affairs prompted me to start the research for this book, which has lasted seven years, and has taken me from Amsterdam to Berlin, from the jungle of Papua New Guinea (my partner is a tropical doctor) to Brussels and Florence. It all began with the research project Market Makers, funded by an open competition grant from the Dutch Research Council (NWO). As part of the project, I worked as a postdoc at the University of Amsterdam, from 2018 to 2021. Then I continued my research as a Marie Curie fellow at the Université Libre de Bruxelles, from 2021 to 2023.

My largest intellectual debt in writing this book is to my close friend and former colleague Bram Mellink, with whom I collaborated very closely on the Market Makers project. Together, we wrote a series of research papers and a widely read Dutch-language book on the history of neoliberalism in the Netherlands. Mellink worked on the earlier period, from the 1930s to the 1960s, while I charted the later period, from the 1970s to the 1990s. Even though this book is an individual effort, it builds on the research I carried out with Bram and could not have been done without him. This book presents my section of the research and extends that into the period of the Third Way coalitions of the 1990s and the Eurozone crisis in the 2010s. I would also like to thank my other former Market Makers colleague, Naomi Woltring, who wrote her PhD on the market-based reforms of the Dutch welfare state in the 1990s. The three of us formed a tight research group, sharing our nerdy enthusiasm for sifting through technocratic and oft-forgotten debates.

My gratitude also goes out to Ewald Engelen and Ido de Haan, who oversaw the Market Makers project. I fondly remember the lively conversations and brainstorms we had at Café de Ysbreker in Amsterdam, or at Ewald Engelen's home during the coronavirus pandemic. A crucial role was played by Dieter Plehwe and Hagen Schulz-Forberg, who helped set us on this path by inviting Bram Mellink and me to the Berlin conference More Roads from Mont Pelerin in March 2016. Here we became properly acquainted with the field of neoliberalism studies. At the time we were still novices in the subject, and our presentation must have seemed somewhat sketchy. Their enthusiasm was crucial in kick-starting the project. Ana Teijeiro Fokkema, as a student assistant, helped to schedule the expert interviews conducted as part of my research project. Another range of expert interviews on the subject of the Eurozone crisis was conducted with the journalist Koen Haegens, initially for a journalistic essay on austerity in the Dutch weekly *De Groene Amsterdammer*.

My knowledge of Dutch economic policy debates was greatly improved through interviews and correspondence with economic policymakers, senior civil servants, economists and politicians. I would like to thank Bart le Blanc, Eduard Bomhoff, Wouter Bos, Elco Brinkman, Ferd Crone, Chris Driessen, Jaap van Duijn, Mariëtte Hamer, Bas Jacobs, Wouter Koolmees, Pieter Korteweg, Dick van der Laan, Paul van Leeuwe, Rob Mulder, Rick van der Ploeg, Jo Ritzen, Onno Ruding, Diederik Samsom, Jarig van Sinderen, Paul Tang, Roel in 't Veld, Bert de Vries, Nout Wellink, Gerrit Zalm and Arie van der Zwan for their time and hospitality.

This book would not have existed, however, without the help of Daniel Zamora Vargas. At his suggestion, I applied for a Marie Curie fellowship at the Université Libre de Bruxelles. The resulting European grant (H2020-MSCA-COFUND-2017) has allowed me to write this book. I have fond memories of our Brussels reading group with Daniel Zamora, Anton Jäger, Jouke Huijzer, Helmer Stoel and Jens van 't Klooster, where we shared food and our ongoing research. I would like to thank Monica Minneci for her administrative assistance in getting me started in Brussels. And I should also mention Anton Hemerijck, who hosted me at the European University Institute in Florence. Despite our disagreements on Dutch consensus politics, Anton was intellectually generous and supportive.

Finally, many thanks to Sebastien Budgen and the people at Verso for their interest in the project and for their editorial assistance.

Introduction: How to Depoliticize Things and Influence People

'Holland isn't a country, it's a business at best', writes Michel Houellebecq in his bleak 2019 novel *Serotonin*.[1] Neither do its inhabitants, styled as 'a race of opportunist polyglot tradespeople', find much favour with the infamous French author. Of course, cultural tropes of the Dutch as stingy capitalists are as old as the country itself; they date at least as far back as the seventeenth century. Jean-Jacques Rousseau once wrote, 'In Holland, it is said that people demand payment for telling the time or giving directions.'[2] Similarly, the American diplomat and founding father Benjamin Franklin complained that the Dutch Republic was 'no longer a nation but a great shop', with 'no other principles or sentiments but those of a shopkeeper'.[3] But in contemporary times, the reputation of the Netherlands as a frugal nation of hard-nosed businessmen is a much more recent development.

In the 1960s and 1970s, Dutch politicians of various political persuasions built one of Europe's most generous welfare states, with high wages, a large social housing stock and high taxation levels. In the late seventies, the *Financial Times* observed that the Dutch had succeeded in establishing 'one of the world's most prosperous and enlightened welfare

---

1 Michel Houellebecq, *Serotonin* (New York: Farrar, Straus & Giroux, 2019), 24.

2 Jean-Jacques Rousseau, cited in Nelleke Noordervliet, 'Een volk van nomaden met een rijtjeshuis', *NRC Handelsblad*, 20 October 1994.

3 Benjamin Franklin, *The Complete Works of Benjamin Franklin*, vol. 7 (New York: G. P. Putnam's Sons, 1888), 283.

states, with minimum wages higher than in any other industrial society'.[4] Not much later, the *Economist* noted sardonically that 'if somewhere must be found to ride out the recession, Holland must be the comfiest place to choose'.[5]

Much has changed since then. Of all OECD countries, the Netherlands has retrenched its welfare state the most.[6] It sold large parts of its social housing stock, became the European leader in flexible employment and acquired a reputation as a global tax haven.[7] The share of national income allocated to wages decreased from its historic peak of almost 81 per cent in 1980 to 69 per cent in 2023. Meanwhile, a long-standing privatization drive has touched everything from the postal service to energy and transportation, from youth and elderly care to kindergarten facilities, the latter now largely owned by private equity.[8] This transformation has extended to the political realm. In the past decade, the right-wing liberals (Volkspartij voor Vrijheid en Democratie, VVD) have grown to become the country's leading political force.[9] Gradually, the

---

4   Cited in Jelle Visser and Anton Hemerijck, *'A Dutch Miracle': Job Growth, Welfare Reform and Corporatism in the Netherlands* (Amsterdam: Amsterdam University Press, 1997), 119.

5   Ibid., 9.

6   Christoffer Green-Pedersen, *The Politics of Justification: Party Competition and Welfare-State Retrenchment in Denmark and the Netherlands from 1982 to 1998* (Amsterdam: Amsterdam University Press, 2002).

7   Diederik Stadig, 'Ruling the Dutch Tax Haven: How the United States Drove the Rise and Fall of the Ruling Practice of the Netherlands', *Politics of the Low Countries* 6, no. 2 (2024): 103–23; Naomi Woltring, 'De marktconforme verzorgingsstaat: 1989–2008' (PhD diss., Utrecht University, 2023), 99–100.

8   Bart Stellinga, *Dertig jaar privatisering, verzelfstandiging en marktwerking* (Amsterdam: Amsterdam University Press, 2012); Mirjam de Rijk, *Gekaapt door het kapitaal: Zorg, onderwijs, wonen en kinderopvang* (Amsterdam: Pluim, 2024); Roelof Kuiper, *De terugkeer van het algemeen belang: Privatiseringsverdriet en de toekomst van Nederland* (Amsterdam: Van Gennep, 2014).

9   The Dutch context, due to its proportional voting system, has always had a dizzying number of political parties. Historically, the main three currents are the Christian democrats, the social democrats and the right-wing liberals. The Christian democrats were originally organized in three main parties: the Catholic People's Party (Katholieke Volkspartij, KVP), the protestant Anti-Revolutionary Party (Anti-Revolutionaire Partij, ARP) and the protestant Christian Historical Union (Christen-Historische Unie, CHU). After 1980, they combined to form the Christian Democratic Appeal (Christen-Democratisch Appèl, CDA). The social democrats were represented by the Dutch Labour Party (Partij van de Arbeid, PvdA). The right-wing liberals by the People's Party for Freedom and Democracy (Volkspartij voor Vrijheid en Democratie, VVD).

Netherlands has turned into an economically liberal country. Of course, it is still far from a free market utopia. By international standards, the Netherlands continues to have a low level of income inequality and a relatively generous welfare state. But it has undergone a significant neoliberal transformation.

On the international stage, the Netherlands has made a name for itself as Europe's staunchest advocate of austerity and structural reform. It was no accident that Jeroen Dijsselbloem, the Dutch social democratic finance minister, came to embody the European austerity drive in a dramatic clash with his Greek counterpart Yanis Varoufakis. In marked contrast to the earlier commentaries from the 1970s, the *Financial Times* and the *Economist* now depicted the Netherlands as a 'prosperous Calvinist country', 'committed to austerity' and 'a famously thrifty people' with 'Calvinist attitudes' – as if a penchant for belt-tightening were somehow an ingrained quality of the Dutch national character, rather than a newfound political imperative.[10]

How has this change occurred? Who were the main actors and ideas behind this transformation? This book traces the historical roots of this political transformation back to the 1980s, when Dutch politics underwent a neoliberal turn. The Netherlands, of course, was not the only country to experience a political transformation of this kind. The iconic examples are the rise of Margaret Thatcher and Ronald Reagan, who together pushed through a free market revolution amid a fierce 'battle of ideas' with Keynesian policy elites and a polarizing confrontation with the trade unions. Over the past twenty years, a large and sophisticated literature has emerged on the rise of neoliberalism in a wide range of countries.[11] The Netherlands, though, remains a relatively blank space

---

10   Matt Steinglass, 'Dutch Mood Shifts Against Austerity and the EU', *Financial Times*, 8 August 2013; 'Not So Calvinist Anymore', *Economist*, 3 October 2013.

11   Some key titles: Quinn Slobodian, *Globalists: The End of Empire and the Birth of Neoliberalism* (Cambridge, MA: Harvard University Press, 2018); Philip Mirowski and Dieter Plehwe, eds, *The Road from Mont Pèlerin: The Making of the Neoliberal Thought Collective* (Cambridge, MA: Harvard University Press, 2009); Angus Burgin, *The Great Persuasion: Reinventing Free Markets Since the Depression* (Cambridge, MA: Harvard University Press, 2012); Cornel Ban, *Ruling Ideas: How Global Neoliberalism Goes Local* (Oxford: Oxford University Press, 2016); William Davies, *The Limits of Neoliberalism: Authority, Sovereignty and the Logic of Competition* (London: Sage, 2016).

on this map.[12] The country has long been considered an exception to the rule.

The Dutch, it has long been argued, pursued market-based reform in a more reasonable and pragmatic fashion, through consensual politics and corporatist compromise. The political scientist Peter Katzenstein was the first to make this argument. In his 1986 classic *Small States in World Markets*, he discussed economic policy in small western European countries. Katzenstein contended that small states with open economies were vulnerable to shocks but could not enact protectionist measures, nor could they push through policies in a polarized and authoritarian manner.[13] Instead, policymakers relied on a corporatist strategy: enlisting the cooperation of trade unions and business associations to secure broad support for market-oriented reforms. According to Katzenstein, this helped smooth the process of economic adjustment. Published during Ronald Reagan's presidency, *Small States* was as much an exercise in comparative political economy as a criticism of the polarized nature of American politics.

Roughly ten years later, Dutch social scientists Jelle Visser and Anton Hemerijck drove home Katzenstein's point in their landmark study '*A Dutch Miracle*'.[14] It appeared at a fortuitous moment: the Dutch economy was experiencing a strong economic recovery in the mid-1990s,

---

12   For indirect treatments of Dutch neoliberalism, see Jeroen Touwen, *Coordination in Transition: The Netherlands and the World Economy, 1950–2010* (Leiden: Brill, 2014); Petrus Willem Zuidhof, 'Imagining Markets: The Discursive Politics of Neoliberalism' (PhD diss., Erasmus University, 2012); Bastiaan Van Apeldoorn, 'A National Case-Study of Embedded Neoliberalism and Its Limits: The Dutch Political Economy and the "No" to the European Constitution', in Bastiaan Apeldoorn, Jan Drahokoupil and Laura Horn, eds, *Contradictions and Limits of Neoliberal European Governance* (New York: Springer, 2009), 211–31. Non-academic Dutch books on neoliberalism include Hans Achterhuis, *De utopie van de vrije markt* (Rotterdam: Lemniscaat, 2010); Marc Chavannes, *Niemand Regeert* (Amsterdam: Nieuw Amsterdam, 2009); Maarten van Rossem, *Kapitalisme zonder remmen: opkomst en ondergang van het marktfundamentalisme* (Amsterdam: Nieuw Amsterdam, 2011); Marcel van Dam, *Niemands land: biografie van een ideaal* (Amsterdam: De Bezige Bij, 2009); Gerard Driehuis, *De daders en de meelopers: wie is wie in de kredietcrisis* (Amsterdam: Balans, 2009); and, more recently, Duco Hellema and Margriet van Lith, *Dat hadden we nooit moeten doen: De PvdA en de neoliberale revolutie van de jaren negentig* (Amsterdam: Prometheus, 2020).

13   Peter J. Katzenstein, *Small States in World Markets: Industrial Policy in Europe* (Ithaca, NY: Cornell University Press, 1985).

14   Jelle Visser and Anton Hemerijck, '*A Dutch Miracle*': *Job Growth, Welfare Reform and Corporatism in the Netherlands* (Amsterdam: Amsterdam University Press, 1997).

after a decade of austerity and market-based reform. The Dutch economic model began to acquire international fame. The *Wall Street Journal* praised the Netherlands as the only European country to cut back its welfare state, while central bankers Hans Tietmeyer and Jean-Claude Trichet held up the Dutch reforms as an example for Germany and France.[15] Not to be outdone, US President Bill Clinton lauded the Dutch economic model as an inspiration for the Third Way.[16] 'Dutch Take Third Way to Prosperity', the *New York Times* wrote, upholding the Dutch approach as a model for Europe.[17]

In their book, Visser and Hemerijck argued that the Dutch consensual approach was a superior alternative to the polarizing politics of Reagan and Thatcher. Central to their account was the 'Wassenaar Accord' of 1982, in which Dutch trade unions and employers agreed to moderate private-sector wages to combat the economic crisis. Visser and Hemerijck depicted this agreement as the return of corporatist consensus in the Netherlands, providing support for a series of austerity measures and supply-side reforms. 'A broad consensus over central policy goals', they noted, rendered 'policy elites sufficiently autonomous from partisan pressures . . . to formulate and implement policies based upon efficiency, expertise, and professional rationality rather than political expediency'.[18] They stressed, in particular, the role of the Dutch trade unions and 'the possibility that under specific institutional preconditions, comprehensive interest groups might have learned from failure and feel themselves under a sense of urgency "to make things better" and support reforms against the short-term interests of some of their constituency'.[19]

This focus on consensus and pragmatism as drivers of Dutch market-based reform quickly became the scholarly norm.[20] 'A remarkable aspect

---

15   'The Dutch Exception', *Wall Street Journal*, 24 April 1997, 8.

16   Luchien Karsten, Kees van Veen and Annelotte van Wulfften Palthe, 'What Happened to the Popularity of the Polder Model? Emergence and Disappearance of a Political Fashion', *International Sociology* 23, no. 1 (2008): 53.

17   Marlise Simons, 'Dutch Take "Third Way" to Prosperity', *New York Times*, 16 June 1997, 6.

18   Visser and Hemerijck, '*A Dutch Miracle*', 74.

19   Ibid., 62.

20   See Anton Hemerijck and Martin Schludi, 'Sequences of Policy Failures and Effective Policy Responses', in Fritz W. Scharpf and Vivien A. Schmidt, eds, *Welfare and Work in the Open Economy*, vol. 1, *From Vulnerability to Competitiveness in Comparative Perspective* (Oxford: Oxford University Press, 2000), 125–228; Hans Keman, 'Explaining

of the rather radical change in government policy is that it was shared by all major parties involved', wrote Jan Luiten van Zanden in his standard work on Dutch economic history. 'In the early 1980s, a new consensus emerged in Dutch politics.'[21] The renowned European studies scholar Erik Jones declared that policy changes in the Netherlands were 'more practical than ideological': 'Neo-liberal outcomes were accepted, not because they were neo-liberal but because they were necessary.'[22]

While internationally, the neoliberal turn developed into the dominant narrative of the changes in economic policy of the 1980s and 1990s, the Dutch success story of the 'polder model' buried that of neoliberalism. Naturally, this notion of consensus and pragmatism has always been a somewhat self-congratulatory narrative: while politicians elsewhere were engaged in heated ideological brawls, the Dutch resolved things in a calm and professional manner. Critics have shown that the degree of consensus has been overstated, while the role of corporatist institutions was surprisingly inconsequential for most of the 1980s. The Canadian political scientist Steven Wolinetz was among the first of these critics. After conducting a series of expert interviews, he concluded that the Dutch case did not really fit Katzenstein's thesis of smooth adjustment. The market-based shift, Wolinetz noted, did not originate in the Wassenaar Accord or in corporatist institutions. Instead, he pointed to 'the relatively autonomous role of the government in determining policy'. The Dutch government had consciously decided to 'circumvent corporatist structures in order to orchestrate a response to economic change', while the Dutch trade unions were allowed 'scant influence on

---

Miracles: Third Ways and Work and Welfare', *West European Politics* 26, no. 2 (2003): 115–35; Vivien A. Schmidt, 'How, Where and When Does Discourse Matter in Small States' Welfare State Adjustment?', *New Political Economy* 8, no. 1 (2003): 127–46. Other scholars pointed to a party-political consensus on economic policy as central to Dutch welfare state retrenchment. See Frank Hendriks, *Polder Politics: The Re-Invention of Consensus Democracy in the Netherlands* (Routledge, 2017); Green-Pedersen, *Politics of Justification*; Robert Henry Cox, 'The Social Construction of an Imperative: Why Welfare Reform Happened in Denmark and the Netherlands but Not in Germany', *World Politics* 53, no. 3 (2001): 463–98.

21   Jan Luiten van Zanden, *The Economic History of the Netherlands 1914–1995: A Small Open Economy in the 'Long' Twentieth Century* (London: Routledge, 1998), 170.

22   Erik Jones, 'The "Monetarist" Turn in Belgium and the Netherlands', in Bernard H. Moss, ed., *Monetary Union in Crisis: The European Union as a Neo-Liberal Construction* (London: Palgrave Macmillan, 2005), 247. See also Erik Jones, *Economic Adjustment and Political Transformation in Small States* (Oxford: Oxford University Press, 2008).

government policy'.[23] In the decades that followed, Wolinetz's critique was taken up by a series of Dutch scholars and politicians, who argued that Dutch labour relations could be better described in terms of 'dominance' and 'acquiescence' rather than consensus.[24]

Among these politicians was Bert de Vries, the former Christian Democratic minister of social affairs. He complained in his memoirs that the idea of the polder model had taken on 'mythological proportions'.[25] A key player in the clashes of the time, De Vries stressed that the common notion that 'Dutch economic restructuring took place in great corporatist harmony' was 'decidedly wrong'.[26] Of course, it was true that the Dutch government did not wage war on the trade unions like Thatcher and Reagan did. Still, the Dutch trade unions strongly opposed the 1980s market-based reforms and were politely ignored by politicians and policymakers as a result. The Social and Economic Council, the major corporatist public policymaking body, remained divided over the reforms of the 1980s and was largely bypassed and discounted.[27]

23   Steven B. Wolinetz, 'Socio-Economic Bargaining in the Netherlands: Redefining the Post-War Policy Coalition', *West European Politics* 12, no. 1 (1989): 90, 95; Rudi Andeweg, 'From Dutch Disease to Dutch Model? Consensus Government in Practice', *Parliamentary Affairs* 53, no. 4 (1 October 2000): 697–709.

24   Uwe Becker, 'A "Dutch Model": Employment Growth by Corporatist Consensus and Wage Restraint? A Critical Account of an Idyllic View', *New Political Economy* 6, no. 1 (2001): 19–43; Jaap Woldendorp, *The Polder Model – from Disease to Miracle? Dutch Neo-Corporatism 1965–2000* (Amsterdam: Rozenberg, 2005); Andeweg, 'From Dutch Disease to Dutch Model?'; Jaap Woldendorp and Hans Keman, 'The Polder Model Reviewed: Dutch Corporatism 1965–2000', *Economic and Industrial Democracy* 28, no. 3 (2007): 317–47; Uwe Becker, 'An Example of Competitive Corporatism? The Dutch Political Economy 1983–2004 in Critical Examination', *Journal of European Public Policy* 12, no. 6 (2005): 1078–102; Uwe Becker, ' "Miracle" by Consensus? Consensualism and Dominance in Dutch Employment Development', *Economic and Industrial Democracy* 22, no. 4 (2001): 453–83; Wiemer Salverda, 'The Dutch Model: Magic in a Flat Landscape?', in *Employment 'Miracles': A Critical Comparison of the Dutch, Scandinavian, Swiss, Australian and Irish Cases Versus Germany and the US* (Amsterdam: Amsterdam University Press, 2005), 39–64.

25   Bert de Vries, *Ontspoord kapitalisme: Hoe het kapitalisme Ontspoorde en na de coronacrisis hervormd kan worden* (Amsterdam: Prometheus, 2020), 238.

26   Ibid.

27   Anthonie Knoester, *Economische politiek in Nederland* (Leiden: Stenfert Kroese, 1989), 167; Ad Geelhoed, 'Making a Difference: De beleidsagenda en AEP', *Tijdschrift Voor Politieke Economie* 24, no. 1 (2002): 60–72; B. J. P. van Bavel, Rogier Overman and Pieter Webeling, *SER 1950–2010: zestig jaar denkwerk voor draagvlak advies economie en samenleving* (Amsterdam: Boom, 2010).

This book builds on these critiques and aims to deconstruct the consensus narrative that has been erected around Dutch economic policy. Dutch market-based reforms were not simply the result of 'professional rationality' and objective expertise. That was, as we will see, the official government line. But, on a deeper level, the policy shift had an obvious ideological character. When we consider the ideas behind the reforms, we find that they were inspired by very similar ideas as those in the Anglo-American context. Senior Dutch economic policymakers referred to neoliberal economists such as Milton Friedman, James Buchanan, Martin Feldstein, Robert Lucas and Robert Barro to plead for more market, less government. In other words, the Netherlands was far from immune from the wave of free market ideology sweeping the globe. The scholarly use of the Dutch case as a contrast to the Anglo-American trajectory seems to have obscured the overarching parallels.

No Nonsense

It was the Christian Democrat Ruud Lubbers, Dutch prime minister from 1982 to 1994, who forcefully broke with Keynesian prescriptions and embarked on a neoliberal agenda of austerity, tight monetary policy, labour market liberalization, deregulation and privatization. On the occasion of an official visit to Washington, *Time* magazine portrayed Lubbers glowingly as 'Ruud Shock', who had 'transformed the Netherlands from one of Western Europe's freest-spending welfare states into its leading belt tightener'.[28] The *Time* article featured a reverential quip by Margaret Thatcher while on an earlier state visit to the Netherlands: 'Mr. Lubbers, are you really intending to cut the salaries of your public employees by more than 3%? That's a disaster. I am supposed to be the toughest in Europe. You are going to ruin my reputation as the Iron Lady.'

The 1982 government, which comprised Christian Democrats (CDA) and right-wing liberals (VVD), enacted far-reaching austerity measures and cut public sector wages and unemployment benefits. As a leading Dutch economist wrote, it was 'the first government in the post-war

---

28   'The Netherlands: Ruud Shock', *Time*, 23 January 1984, 29.

period to make a wholesale break with the Keynesian ideas that have long been such an important influence on economic policy'.[29]

The Lubbers government certainly did not conceal its pro-business leanings. In keeping with the spirit of the above Houellebecq quote, Ruud Lubbers and his cabinet literally referred to the Netherlands as a business enterprise. Many of the ministers had been recruited from the Dutch business elite and proudly presented themselves to the public as hard-headed 'business managers' in politics, charged with downsizing an ailing company. They proclaimed that they were running the 'BV Nederland' or 'the Netherlands Inc.' The metaphor signalled that the restoration of business profitability had become the leading political priority. What was good for Dutch business was good for the nation. After a decade defined by leftist social movements and trade union militancy, business had returned to the heart of Dutch political life.

In sharp contrast, however, to the grand ideological rhetoric of Thatcher and Reagan, the Dutch Prime Minister Ruud Lubbers carefully depoliticized the reforms as 'no-nonsense policies', presenting them as an objective necessity decreed by technocratic policy elites. Lubbers had obvious reasons for doing this. The Dutch Christian democrats, the dominant force in Dutch politics for most of the post-war period, had nothing to gain by using polarizing language. As a centrist party, they had to accommodate their centre-left flank and trade union wing to push reforms through parliament. For this reason, it was essential to present the policy shift in a depoliticized manner. Hans van der Voet, head of communications during the Lubbers cabinets, made this point explicitly:

This is a frugal policy, and it is better to present it in a business-like and depoliticized manner. It will seem somewhat corporate, but you shouldn't loudly proclaim that it is your holy mission to fire so many teachers and care workers.[30]

Depoliticization, it is argued, involves displacing a contentious issue from the political sphere to 'quasi-public bodies and to officials who can

---

29   Knoester, *Economische Politiek in Nederland*, 159.

30   Cited in Max van Weezel and Joop van Tijn, *Inzake het kabinet-Lubbers* (Amsterdam: Sijthoff, 1986), 254.

present them as purely technical matters'.[31] This was certainly a central part of the strategy. The first Lubbers cabinet outsourced the initiative to senior officials at the Ministries of Finance and Economic Affairs. As the political parties were internally divided over economic policy, the task of hammering out a neoliberal supply-side policy was left to civil servants. 'The bureaucrats have come up with the solutions, and then it's our turn to implement them', explained the Christian Democratic minister of welfare, public health and culture.[32] It was Max Weber's classic theory of state bureaucracy turned on its head.[33] The result was an exceptionally technocratic and ideologically muted neoliberal turn, in which the senior civil servants at the Ministries of Finance and Economic Affairs played an outsized role.

In a more general sense, depoliticization involves the framing of a politically contentious issue in terms of fate and necessity.[34] This is also something that has clung to the Dutch reforms. In the 1980s and early 1990s, the 'no-nonsense' policies and austerity measures were mired in controversy, their effectiveness often put in doubt. In 1988, the OECD observed in its *Economic Outlook* that the Netherlands had been one of the worst-performing OECD countries in the 1980s. Economic growth was structurally 1 per cent lower and unemployment 5 per cent higher than the OECD average. Public debt had risen steeply, from 50.6 per cent of GDP in 1980 to 72.6 per cent of GDP in 1990, while both public and private investment lagged behind.[35] In fact, as the Ministry of Finance noted anxiously, the Netherlands had experienced the lowest per capita GDP growth of all OECD countries from 1980 to 1993.[36] In this common indicator for a country's prosperity, the Dutch had fallen behind Germany, France, the United Kingdom, Belgium and Italy.

Yes, business profitability had been restored, wages had been moderated and public spending was curtailed, but no one celebrated the austerity of the 1980s as a big success. The larger picture was one of

---

31   Colin Hay, *Why We Hate Politics* (Cambridge: Polity, 2007), 81.

32   Elco Brinkman cited in Weezel and Tijn, *Inzake het kabinet-Lubbers*, 161.

33   Max Weber, *From Max Weber: Essays in Sociology*, transl. Hans H. Gerth (London: Routledge & Kegan Paul, 1970).

34   Hay, *Why We Hate Politics*, 79.

35   OECD, *Economic Outlook* 44 (December 1988).

36   Jeroen J. M. Kremers, *Inspelen op Europa: Uitdagingen voor het financieel-economische beleid van Nederland* (Schoonhoven: Academic Service, 1993), 1. See also Eduard Bomhoff, *Een Haagse lente?* (Schoonhoven: Academic Service, 1994), 44.

worrying stagnation. Deep-seated conflicts about the depth of austerity and market reform dominated the political debate. Social democrats and trade unions alike bitterly denounced the 'neo-liberal approach' of the right-wing government.[37] In exchange, they were sidelined from the policymaking process and reduced to organizing a series of fruitless mass protests.

It was a polarized standoff, but that changed in 1989, when Lubbers changed tack and formed a centre-left government with the Dutch Labour Party (Partij van de Arbeid, PvdA). The ideological tide was turning. In fits and starts, a new compromise emerged between neoliberal reform and corporatist social democracy – a Dutch Third Way. In the mid-1990s, buoyed by a great rise in female part-time employment and a credit-fuelled housing market boom, the Dutch economy experienced an impressive recovery. This cleared the way for a new, shared understanding of the recent past. The 'no-nonsense' austerity policies of the 1980s and wage moderation agreed in the 1982 Wassenaar Accord were now widely celebrated as the root cause of the recovery and achieved the uncontroversial status of a historic necessity. Deep conflicts and ideological divisions over economic policy were soon ignored or forgotten. The Dutch 'polder model' became an international cause célèbre, proof of the blessings of consensual politics and a market-minded left.

This revised understanding of the 1980s fundamentally reshaped the Dutch perspective on how to respond to an economic crisis. It became the basis for the political belief in expansionary austerity, which defined the Dutch position during the Eurozone crisis. 'It's not about what Brussels wants,' the Dutch right-wing liberal Prime Minister Mark Rutte underlined at a Euro Summit in Brussels in March 2012. 'I value fiscal discipline because I think it's important. It's the lesson of the 1980's.'[38] In the most significant fiscal policy document, the government's Budget Memorandum, the 1980s were presented as proof that one could cut one's way to growth:

---

37 Wim Kok, 'Volledige werkgelegenheid: Uitdagingen voor de jaren tachtig', *Socialisme en Democratie* 45, no. 7/8 (1983): 3–7.

38 Cited in Coen Teulings, *Over de dijken: Tien jaar na het uitbreken van de financiële crisis* (Amsterdam: Prometheus, 2018), 103.

The Dutch experiences of the 1980s showed that while consolidation can indeed hurt, it can also provide the basis for economic recovery. The government decided to intervene vigorously: industrial subsidies were halted; unemployment benefits lowered; public sector wages cut. With the Wassenaar Accord, the social partners and the government agreed to moderate wages in the private sector. This contributed in subsequent years to a lower inflation and the recovery of Dutch competitiveness.[39]

Similarly, in a 2011 book on the Eurozone crisis, the most influential Dutch economic think-tank, the Central Planning Bureau (CPB), held up the Dutch 1980s reforms as an inspiration: 'Experience teaches that often a large crisis is necessary before far-reaching reforms can be implemented to boost growth. The Netherlands has successfully implemented such a policy in the 1980s and 1990s and is now reaping the benefits. Before that could occur, our country had to bite the bullet.'[40] In other words, the lesson drawn from the 1980s by Dutch policymaking elites was that one should never waste a good crisis.

During the Eurozone crisis, subsequent coalition governments led by Prime Minister Mark Rutte implemented an ambitious austerity programme, amounting to an estimated €50 billion in budget cuts and tax increases, which is now widely believed to have deepened the crisis. A coalition of right-wing liberals (VVD) and social democrats (PvdA) who governed from 2012 till 2017 were responsible for the lion's share of these measures, which included controversial and painful cuts in social security, education and social care. At the end of their term, the Labour Party was punished with the single largest electoral defeat in Dutch history, losing twenty-nine of its thirty-eight seats in parliament. Since then, the broader bloc of the Dutch left has dwindled electorally to its lowest vote score of the entire post-war period.

But the legacy of the 1980s has also cast its shadow over the political right. The pro-business party VVD became the leading political force in a highly fragmented political landscape. After assuming the leadership of the VVD, Mark Rutte expressed his admiration for Friedrich Hayek,

---

39   Parliamentary records, HTK, 2010–2011, 32 500, no. 1, 37.
40   Coen Teulings et al., *Europa in Crisis: Het Centraal Planbureau over schulden en de toekomst van de eurozone* (Amsterdam: Balans, 2011), 147.

describing *The Road to Serfdom* as 'essential reading for liberals'.[41] When, as prime minister, he assembled his first government, he declared in parliament: 'The Netherlands suffers from administrative obesity, and it's about time we put the state on a diet. Bureaucracy is a tax on growth. Society itself can do things better if the government steps back.'[42] In public lectures, Rutte presented his policies as a reiteration of the 1980s, a period he remembered glowingly as the first time the state had been forced back. But the neoliberal reforms of the 2010s only deepened the crisis; in his last coalition government, Rutte was forced to change tack and repair some of the damage done to the Dutch public sector. As the longest-serving prime minister in Dutch history, Rutte oversaw a period of declining trust in government and elites and waning support for free market recipes. In 2024, the VVD tried to win the elections by focusing on immigration instead – inadvertently setting the stage for the victory of Geert Wilders' right-wing populist Freedom Party. Mark Rutte had by that time left Dutch politics to become secretary-general of NATO.

The Consensus School

This book takes issue with what I call the 'consensus school' in Dutch historiography and social science. Due to its proportional voting system and its coalition governments, Dutch politics is of course more consensual than the majoritarian Anglo-American models. But I contend that there is a dominant scholarly tendency to overstate the degree of consensus in Dutch politics and society and to reduce historically existing disagreement to mere obstacles on the road to consensus.

In the United States, the term 'consensus school' emerged to refer to a style of historiography that emphasizes harmony and basic agreement in society and that downplays conflict, especially class conflict. The term was coined by the historian John Higham in his classic 1959 essay, 'The Cult of the American Consensus'. Higham took aim at a dominant trend in American historiography in the 1940s and 1950s, epitomized by

---

41 Mark Rutte, 'Betutteling: Politiek van wantrouwen', *Elsevier Weekblad*, 11 August 2007.

42 Parliamentary records, HTK, 2010–2011, Regeringsverklaring minister-president Rutte, 26 October 2010, no. 13, 4.

authors like Richard Hofstadter, Louis Hartz and Daniel J. Boorstin. By contrast with the 'progressive historians' of an earlier generation, who 'painted America in the bold hues of conflict', the authors of the consensus school emphasized continuity, institutional stability and unity of purpose. Consensus historians replaced the dualisms of progressive history (labour versus capital, people versus elites, and so on) with a more monistic approach, championing the basic harmony of the American national character and its continuity over time. In his essay, Higham derided it as 'a massive grading operation to smooth over America's social convulsions', warning that it had 'a deadening effect on the historian's ability to take a conflict of ideas seriously'.[43] While the American consensus school was dominant up to the mid 1970s, it has since been eclipsed by other currents.[44] In the present era of intense political partisanship, its appeal has obviously diminished.

I would argue that a similar consensual scholarly tendency exists in the Netherlands, but, unlike in the United States, it remains a rather dominant force. It is generally not even referred to as a particular school of thought but tends to pass for mainstream thinking. The roots of the Dutch 'consensus school' arguably lie with the Dutch-American political scientist Arend Lijphart and his work on Dutch consensus democracy.[45]

The Dutch argument on consensus started out differently from its US counterpart. For a large part of the twentieth century, Dutch society was deeply divided between a series of socio-religious subcultures: the Catholic, Protestant, socialist and liberal 'pillars' that organized Dutch society in segmented groups. Each pillar had its own schools, newspapers and radio and television stations, its own trade unions, housing corporations, leisure organizations and so forth. In short, the whole of Dutch civil society was segmented in this way. On top of the pillars sat the political parties. According to Lijphart, it was the fear of social disintegration that gave rise to a culture of consensus and proportional power-sharing among the elites of these parties. This elite culture formed the

---

43   John Higham, 'The Cult of the American Consensus', *Commentary* 28 (1959): 93.

44   See Leo P. Ribuffo, 'What Is Still Living In "Consensus" History and Pluralist Social Theory', *American Studies International* 38, no. 1 (2000): 42–60.

45   See Merijn Oudenampsen, *The Rise of the Dutch New Right: An Intellectual History of the Rightward Shift in Dutch Politics* (London: Routledge, 2021), 21–40.

metaphorical 'roof' uniting the pillars in a common structure. Consensus culture began with the Great Pacification of 1917, in which the various parties reached a historic compromise to subdivide the Dutch public school system along religious lines.[46] Lijphart wrote of prudent elites whose courageous compromises, business-like style and depoliticizing tactics prevented Dutch society from falling apart. In the United States, consensus was believed to follow from the unity of the national character. In the Netherlands, in contrast, consensus referred to an elite culture that served as a counterweight to a divided national character.

A fundamental prerequisite for Lijphart's consensus democracy was a strongly hierarchical relationship between the leaders and the led, giving elites a large degree of autonomy to make compromises on behalf of their socio-religious constituencies. As a conservative liberal, Lijphart was quite explicit that his elitist model of consensus democracy was not just a descriptive theory of how Dutch society was supposed to work but also a normative ideal that prescribed how democracy *ought* to work in countries with large ethnic, religious or linguistic divisions. Democratic stability was best achieved by containing democratic participation, taking key decisions behind closed doors, quelling class antagonism and depoliticizing the most divisive issues. Lijphart's theory was in fact highly contested, but it nonetheless exerted a powerful influence on scholars and Dutch political elites alike.[47]

Published in 1968, Lijphart's theory of consensus politics became an emblem of the 'pillarized' order in the Netherlands. Due to rapid secularization and the youth revolts of the 1960s, this *ancien régime* was quickly eroding. In the 1970s, the left sought to democratize Dutch politics by pursuing a politics of dissensus and politicization. The hope was that politicization of socioeconomic issues would drive a wedge through the Christian democratic power bloc, moving Christian workers to the left. In 1975, Lijphart wrote of the 'breakdown of the politics of accommodation'.[48] Dutch politics seemed to take on the more adversarial character of the majoritarian Westminster model.

---

46   Arend Lijphart, *The Politics of Accommodation: Pluralism and Democracy in the Netherlands* (Berkeley: University of California Press, 1968).

47   M. P. C. M. Van Schendelen, 'Consociational Democracy: The Views of Arend Lijphart and Collected Criticisms', *Political Science Reviewer* 15 (1985): 143.

48   Arend Lijphart, *The Politics of Accommodation: Pluralism and Democracy in the Netherlands*, 2nd edn (Berkeley: University of California Press, 1975).

By the end of the 1970s, however, the fragmented Christian democrats successfully reconstituted themselves in a new unified party. The Christian Democratic Appeal (CDA) would become the major driver of the neoliberal turn of the 1980s. When it entered power in 1982, in a coalition with the right-wing liberals of the VVD, it brought a return of the depoliticizing style of old. Observing the sober, technical rhetoric of the new government, journalists spoke of the 'new business-like style'. This referred to the work of Lijphart, who had identified pragmatic, 'business-like politics' as one of the core elements of the Dutch politics of accommodation. In response to this development, Lijphart wrote in 1989 that political culture in the Netherlands had not changed all that much after all.[49] Critics such as Peter Mair were less convinced and showed that, by Lijphart's own metrics, the Netherlands had an 'average' or 'run-of-the-mill' score on consensual politics since the 1960s.[50]

Lijphart's theory proved fairly resistant to critique. The idea of the Dutch 'polder model' that emerged in the late 1990s was Lijphart's basic framework applied the field of socioeconomic policy. In *Small States in World Markets*, Katzenstein explicitly presented his work as an extension of Lijphart's theory.[51] His argument was that small European states like Belgium, the Netherlands, Switzerland and Austria had developed 'distinctive political structures' in which 'groups are held together by pragmatic bargains struck by a handful of political leaders'.[52] This allowed them to remain competitive on world markets while preventing the polarization of the Anglo-American context. While Katzenstein's argument had its merits, it also confounded matters. Cases as ideologically diverse as Austro-Keynesianism in Austria and the neoliberal supply-side policies of Switzerland and the Netherlands were all reduced to consensual pragmatism.

It was the Netherlands that ultimately became the poster child for this consensus argument. In no small part, this was due to the success of Dutch social scientists Jelle Visser and Anton Hemerijck and their book *A Dutch Miracle*. Published in 1997, it has garnered close to 2,000

---

49   Arend Lijphart, 'From the Politics of Accommodation to Adversarial Politics in the Netherlands: A Reassessment', *West European Politics* 12, no. 1 (1989): 139–53.

50   Peter Mair, 'The Correlates of Consensus Democracy and the Puzzle of Dutch Politics', *West European Politics* 17, no. 4 (1 October 1994): 97–123.

51   Katzenstein, *Small States in World Markets*, 35.

52   Ibid.

citations. Their argument that the Dutch approach was superior to the Anglo-American trajectory under Reagan and Thatcher owed much to Arend Lijphart. The Wassenaar Accord of 1982 was presented by Visser and Hemerijck as a socioeconomic sequel of Lijphart's Great Pacification of 1917, the historic deal subdividing the Dutch school system.[53] Their idea that trade union and political elites, when freed from partisan pressures, 'developed policies based upon efficiency, expertise, and professional rationality' was a restatement of Lijphart's central idea that the elites of the Dutch pillars were able to make business-like decisions due to their substantial autonomy from their political bases.[54]

During the economic boom of the second half of the 1990s, the 'polder model' soon became part of the national imaginary – as Dutch as windmills, clogs and dikes. The term had been coined in 1995 by Evert Rongen, the former president of the Dutch chemical giant DSM.[55] The contention was that this model could be traced all the way back to the illustrious Dutch Golden Age. Hence the invocation of 'polder', referring to the seventeenth-century system of governance of Dutch polders and dikes, in which local citizens and farmers had to achieve a workable consensus to keep the water out. The idea took hold that Dutch water management had been highly egalitarian and democratic, providing the cultural roots of the Dutch 'polder' model of the nineties.

Due to the economic recovery and the revival of Dutch corporatism in the nineties, the term caught on. Third Way social democrats began promoting the polder model as a successful middle course between top-heavy continental welfare states and the social polarization of Anglo-American neoliberalism. Soon politicians, businessmen, journalists and historians all hailed the polder model as an inherent part of a centuries-old Dutch national character. Of course, this was more foundational myth than respectable historical genealogy, but it was too good a story to check.[56] Historians specialized in the Dutch water boards responded to the hype by pointing to the deeply oligarchic and often conflictual

---

53   Visser and Hemerijck, 'A Dutch Miracle', 57.

54   Ibid., 74.

55   Karsten, Van Veen and Van Wulfften Palthe, 'What Happened to the Popularity of the Polder Model?', 46.

56   Marjolein 't Hart, 'Polderen en ploeteren: Een debat over geschiedenis, continuïteit en Nederlandse identiteit', in Jasper van der Steen and Hans Cools, eds, *Vroegmoderne geschiedenis in actuele debatten* (Leuven: Leuven University Press, 2020), 17–38.

nature of water management in the seventeenth-century Dutch Republic. 'It seems that the less people know of the history of the water boards, the more they are prone to believe in the Dutch polder model', one specialist observed drily.[57]

The hype surrounding the polder model gave rise to a cottage industry of academic research in Dutch (economic) history, political science, sociology and public administration.[58] Academic and popular historians boldly declared that the striving towards consensus was indeed the red thread running through Dutch history. 'The desire for consensus is so cherished by the Dutch, that they will never depart from it,' one historian noted. 'After all, the end of the culture of deliberation would be nothing less than the end of Dutch national identity.'[59] Another historian wrote in an op-ed: 'Whoever is against the polder model is against the Netherlands.'[60] The two leading economic historians of the Netherlands even traced the 'polder model' back through a thousand years of Dutch consensual mores, portraying it as the fount of Dutch prosperity. Their book was a consensual manifesto of sorts, claiming that the history of all hitherto existing Dutch society was the history of pragmatic consensus-building.[61]

57   Milja van Tielhof, 'Op zoek naar het poldermodel in de waterstaatsgeschiedenis', *Tijdschrift voor Geschiedenis* 122, no. 2 (1 January 2009): 148.

58   See Hendriks, *Polder Politics*; Maarten Keune, *Nog steeds een mirakel? De legitimiteit van het poldermodel in de eenentwintigste eeuw* (Amsterdam University Press, 2016); Joost Jonker, ed., 'The Netherlands and the Polder Model' – 'Nederland en het poldermodel', special issue, *BMGN – Low Countries Historical Review* 129, no. 1 (March 2014): 88–133; Touwen, *Coordination in Transition*, 1950–2010; Woldendorp, *The Polder Model – from Disease to Miracle?*; Ian Bruff, *Culture and Consensus in European Varieties of Capitalism*, vol. 7 (Basingstoke: Palgrave Macmillan, 2008); Dennis Bos, Henk te Velde, and Maurits Ebben, eds, *Harmonie in Holland? Het poldermodel van 1500 tot nu* (Amsterdam: Bert Bakker, 2007); P. de Rooy and H. te Velde, *Met Kok* (Amsterdam: Wereldbibliotheek, 2018); Robin Fransman, Jenny Kossen and Frank Kalshoven, *Het Nederlandse consensusmodel: De succesfactoren van het poldermodel in kaart gebracht* (Amsterdam: Argumentenfabriek, 2019).

59   Jona Lendering, *Polderdenken: De wortels van de Nederlandse overlegcultuur* (Athenaeum-Polak & Van Gennep, 2005), 134.

60   W. Kieskamp, 'Wie tegen het poldermodel is, is tegen Nederland' [Who is against the polder model, is against the Netherlands], *Trouw*, 9 April 2005. I include English translations of Dutch news article titles since these help support my argument.

61   Maarten Prak and Jan L. Van Zanden, *Nederland en het poldermodel: Sociaaleconomische geschiedenis van Nederland, 1000–2000* (Amsterdam: Bert Bakker, 2013).

Lijphart and Katzenstein were the first to argue that consensus politics needed 'an ideology of social partnership'.[62] This 'ideology of social partnership', one is tempted to remark, has at times been a more forceful presence than the actual social partnership itself. Here it is pertinent that the dominant twentieth-century ideology in the Netherlands has been Christian democratic organicism, which opposed the rising Dutch labour movement by reference to visions of social harmony and consensual class relations.[63] The polder model narrative, then, fits seamlessly with a historically dominant strain of ideological thought. That Marxism, with its focus on class conflict, has an ideological character is often seen as self-evident in the Netherlands; but that the same might apply to its consensual counterpart is generally overlooked.

It is hard to overstate how central the idea of the polder model has become to Dutch self-perception. In the catalogue of the Dutch public library, a search for 'polder model' turns up an illustrative video from the Schooltv website, made for Dutch high schools.[64] It begins with a teacher talking about Dutch corporatist institutions such as the Social and Economic Council (SER): 'The SER is an advisory council that advises the government on the terrain of labour and income. But the SER is also very Dutch. It is rooted in our cultural identity to aim for consensus together.' The image shifts to a high school class gathered in a collective meeting. The teacher asks the children how they would like the other children to behave in class. Together, they write down a list of rules. At the end the teacher asks: 'Now what have we achieved?' 'Consensus!' the children answer obediently.

Yet few scholars from the consensus school seem to have gone through the effort of scrutinizing whether there really was a consensus in the relevant periods. Most academic studies in this genre tend to focus on policy outcomes, but not on the ideas held by the relevant actors, public debate or the contested process of political decision-making. On closer examination, one finds that the assumption

---

62   Arend Lijphart, *Patterns of Democracy: Government Forms and Performance in Thirty-Six Countries* (New Haven, CT: Yale University Press, 1999), 159; Katzenstein, *Small States in World Markets*, 32.

63   Kees van Kersbergen, *Social Capitalism: A Study of Christian Democracy and the Welfare State* (London: Routledge, 2003).

64   'Het Nederlandse poldermodel: Overleggen tot er een consensus is', Schooltv, 17 June 2010), schooltv.nl.

of consensus as a driver of Dutch reform is not really tested in the academic literature itself; it serves as an underlying axiom. The problem with the consensus view is that there is little evidence in the Dutch 1980s for a 'broad consensus over central policy goals', whether in corporatist institutions or among political parties.

One can define consensus in layman's terms, as a form of general agreement. Or one can consider consensus-democracy, following Lijphart, as an institutional process of decision-making that 'aims at broad participation in government and broad agreement on the policies the government should pursue'.[65] This of course is counterposed to (Anglo-American) majoritarian systems where minority opinions can be ignored by vote-winning majorities. In both senses, the Dutch controversies over economic policy in the 1980s do not correspond with the idea of consensus. The policy shift in that decade involving fiscal constraint, public sector cutbacks and social security reform was inherently controversial and was pushed through in majoritarian fashion.

An additional problem is that the assumption of consensus has, as Higham contended, a deadening effect on one's ability to take a conflict of ideas seriously. When history is reduced to a series of pragmatic compromises, power relations and ideological conflict remain outside of our purview. When political decisions that benefit some more than others – and negotiations in which one party is dominant and another compliant – are recast as consensual and proportional, it becomes hard to make an analysis of power relations. The same goes for ideas that become hegemonic versus alternatives that peter out. Due to its normative celebration of elite pragmatism, the Dutch consensus school is ill-equipped to assess ideological change.

This book challenges this dominant consensus narrative. Building on the work of institutionalists such as the political economist Mark Blyth and the recent literature on the rise of neoliberalism, it shows that the Dutch economic crisis of the 1970s and 1980s saw similar ideological divisions on economic policy in the Netherlands as those that pertained internationally.[66] Admittedly, these conflicts were less explicit than in

---

65 Lijphart, *Patterns of Democracy*, 2.

66 Mark Blyth, *Great Transformations: Economic Ideas and Institutional Change in the Twentieth Century* (Cambridge: Cambridge University Press, 2002); Monica Prasad, *The Politics of Free Markets: The Rise of Neoliberal Economic Policies in Britain, France, Germany, and the United States* (Chicago: University of Chicago Press, 2006); John L.

the Anglo-American context, as a result of the Dutch coalition system and its tradition of depoliticization, but they were nonetheless clearly present. In the footsteps of Blyth, I treat ideas as the instruments and banners of various socioeconomic coalitions, with social democrats and trade unions on one side and business and the right on the other, while Christian democrats were split between both camps.

Blyth argues that a situation of economic crisis is a time of 'Knightean uncertainty', when agents become unsure about their interests and the best means of pursuing them.[67] In such a context, policy entrepreneurs come to the fore who contest the existing policy paradigm and offer alternative solutions to the crisis. A crisis is not a self-evident phenomenon but rather something that various camps argue over, in a contest to impose their specific interpretation of events. As a result, there is a greater role for ideas in crisis situations, in particular economic ideas, since they determine how a 'crisis' is defined and when a given situation can be described as one. The political declaration of a crisis, institutionalists argue, determines to a large extent what response will emerge.[68]

As this book shows, the writings of Dutch economic policymakers in the 1980s uphold the notion of 'Knightean' insecurity and ideational conflict, rather than the 'broad consensus' and self-evident 'professional rationality' presupposed by consensus scholars. Perhaps needless to say, the Keynesian and supply-side paradigms use different conceptions of how the economy functions, resulting in different notions of what 'efficiency, expertise, and professional rationality' concretely entail. An illustrative example is that of Frans Rutten – as head of the Ministry of Economic Affairs (1973–90), the single most influential economic policymaker in the country at the time. Rutten described the situation in the 1980s as a 'deadlock' rather than a 'consensus'.[69] Since the erosion of the dominant Keynesian paradigm in the mid-1970s, the field of

---

Campbell and Ove K. Pedersen, *The Rise of Neoliberalism and Institutional Analysis* (Princeton, NJ: Princeton University Press, 2001); Hay, *Why We Hate Politics*; Vivien A. Schmidt, *The Futures of European Capitalism* (Oxford: Oxford University Press, 2002); Peter Hall, 'Policy Paradigms, Social Learning, and the State: The Case of Economic Policymaking in Britain', *Comparative Politics* 25, no. 3 (1993): 275–96. See also note 11.

67   Blyth, *Great Transformations*, 9.

68   See also Colin Hay, 'Narrating Crisis: The Discursive Construction of the "Winter of Discontent"', *Sociology* 30, no. 2 (1 May 1996): 253–77.

69   Frans Rutten, *Zeven kabinetten wijzer: de nieuwe zakelijkheid bij het economische beleid* (Groningen: Wolters-Noordhoff, 1993), 96.

economic policymaking had devolved into an ongoing series of skirmishes between the rival schools of neoclassical economics and neo-Keynesianism. The intensity of their continuing disagreement, Rutten suggested, was due to the clear political implications of the debate: 'The opposition between neoclassicals and neo-Keynesians can run parallel to that of liberal champions of the free market and socialist advocates of detailed government regulation.'[70]

I contend that Dutch developments of the 1980s lend more support to the Blythian model than one positing a policy consensus. A state-led supply-side coalition enforced a turn in economic policy in majoritarian fashion, while social democrats and trade unions were first sidelined and later accommodated. The fundamental disagreements between Keynesians and neoliberals extended to Dutch corporatism and consensus politics itself. Many on the right and in Dutch business were convinced that consensus politics and corporatist institutions were major obstacles to a more competitive Dutch economy. Political conflicts over these issues lasted well into the mid-1990s. Neoliberals derided consensus democracy as 'the sluggish state' and pleaded for a Dutch Margaret Thatcher to squash the public sector unions. This demonstrates that consensus and corporatism are not necessarily inherent qualities of the Dutch political system but rather the outcome of often subtle – though sometimes not-so-subtle – power relations and political struggles.

This is not to say that the Dutch case is all that similar to Anglo-American developments. They should be situated somewhere halfway between the open ideological contestation of the Anglo-American cases and the idyllic consensual mores described in the polder-model discourse: neither an all-out conflict nor a harmonious peace, but more of an 'armed truce'. In the Anglo-American context, a lot of research on neoliberalism has centred on free market think-tanks, particularly the Mont Pelerin Society, a prominent international network of neoliberal economists and businessmen, founded by the Austrian economist and philosopher Friedrich Hayek in 1947. Other scholars have focused on specific economic currents with close links to the Mont Pelerin Society and a large influence on the neoliberal turn of the 1980s: monetarism,

---

70   Frans Rutten, *Verval, herstel en groei: lessen voor het economisch beleid gelet op het leergeld van twintig jaar* (Utrecht: Lemma, 1995), 26.

public choice theory, neoclassical economics and supply-side economics.[71] The Dutch context is challenging to research with such an ideational approach, since there is no private think-tank infrastructure to speak of.[72] Instead, the intellectual work on policy development generally takes place within the various ministries and within affiliated bureaucratic think-tanks and advisory councils, staffed by economists. As a result, the tone of Dutch economic debate is much more technocratic and depoliticized than in the Anglo-American context. As P. W. Zuidhof has shown in his study of the neoliberal discourse of bureaucratic think-tanks in the Netherlands, 'the strategy of many reports is to depoliticize the idea of the market'.[73]

This does not mean that the 'battle of ideas' between Keynesians and neoliberals did not take place in the Netherlands. Rather, the Dutch neoliberal turn has been obscured by layers of technocratic and depoliticizing language. To reconstruct the neoliberal turn in the Netherlands, I have identified the key neoliberal concepts and authors from the international literature and examined their reception in the major Dutch economic policymaking debates. In this I have relied on the Dutch economic policy literature, newspaper archives, political biographies, parliamentary minutes, archival sources, political party publications and forty in-depth interviews with Dutch politicians and senior economic policymakers that I conducted. On that basis, I have been able to identify ideological debates and controversies in the Netherlands that strongly resemble those that have taken place internationally.

Let us now turn to an overview of the chapters that follow. Chapter 1 introduces the Dutch context and explains the late development of a Keynesian welfare state. Like Germany, the Netherlands was initially an exception to the post-war dominance of Keynesian ideas. It developed a market-led, export-oriented strategy, combining wage restraint with modest social services. This model collapsed with the wage explosions of the mid-1960s, and governments led by Christian democrats then

---

71   Prasad, *Politics of Free Markets*; Blyth, *Great Transformations*.

72   John L. Campbell and Ove K. Pedersen, 'Knowledge Regimes and Comparative Political Economy', in Daniel Beland and Robert Henry Cox, eds, *Ideas and Politics in Social Science Research* (Oxford: Oxford University Press, 2011), 14; Zuidhof, 'Imagining Markets', 210.

73   Zuidhof, 'Imagining Markets', 212.

attempted to induce wage restraint by 'wage deferral', resulting in a rapid expansion of the Dutch welfare state.

Chapter 2 focuses on the leftist Den Uyl government, which entered power in 1973. By this date, the Netherlands had transformed from a welfare laggard into one of Europe's most generous welfare states. Den Uyl sought to contain the stagflation crisis of the 1970s by Keynesian conjunctural policy and by offering trade unions enhanced workplace democracy and wage-earner funds in exchange for continued wage restraint. It prompted a strong response from employers and from an emerging coalition of economists at the ministries and the Dutch Central Bank, who warned that Den Uyl was leading the country towards economic dictatorship.

Chapter 3 shows how public choice theory and monetarism played an important role in underpinning the turn to austerity in the late 1970s and early 1980s. Initially, critiques of Keynesianism came in two dominant forms. There was the Dutch public choice tradition, which had first emerged around the Dutch Ministry of Finance in the 1950s and 1960s. Senior civil servants and academic economists argued that pressure groups had taken over Dutch democracy, while vote-maximizing politicians had caused public spending to spiral out of control. The proposed solution was to devise new budgeting norms and strengthen the power of the Ministry of Finance. At the same time, the 1970s saw a revival of monetarism. Economists around the Dutch Central Bank had long espoused their own tradition of 'Dutch monetarism'. In the 1970s, Dutch monetarists hardened their resolve against Keynesian public spending, inspired by Friedman's monetarist counter-revolution and the monetarist turn of the West German Bundesbank.

The rise of supply-side economics is the subject of Chapter 4. After the election of Ronald Reagan, the term was suddenly everywhere in Dutch economic policy circles. Known in the Netherlands as *aanbodeconomie*, it referred to a shift in focus to the improvement of the investment climate. Rather than propping up effective demand, the government had to secure a competitive environment for Dutch business. Important in this respect was the powerful Wagner committee, set up by the Ministry of Economic Affairs and chaired by Gerrit Wagner, the former CEO of the Anglo-Dutch oil company Shell. This expert committee had officially been tasked by the centre-right Van Agt cabinet (1977–81) to advise on a new industrial policy. In reality, the committee proposed a general overhaul of Dutch economic policy, including wage liberalization, labour market flexibilization, welfare cuts and the marketization of the public sector. When, in 1982, the first Lubbers cabinet entered power, it adopted almost all of the recommendations of the Wagner committee. Lubbers lowered public sector wages and unemployment benefits by 3 per cent and continued a large-scale process of privatization, deregulation and state restructuring. But this policy shift was sold to the public as a largely apolitical development. Lubbers spoke of a 'no-nonsense policy'. Frans Rutten, the powerful head of the Ministry of Economic Affairs, later described the new policy paradigm as the 'new business-like politics', inspired by Milton Friedman.

Chapter 5 focuses on the Labour Party, which had been in opposition for much of the 1980s. By the end of the decade, however, the austerity policies of the Lubbers cabinets had lost much of their forward momentum. While Lubbers had succeeded in reducing public spending, both unemployment and budget deficits remained stubbornly high. Wim Kok, the new leader of the Dutch Labour Party, accused the Christian Democrats of being in thrall to neoliberal ideas, neglecting the Dutch tradition of consensus politics and failing to implement an active employment policy. Inspired by the Swedish model, the Labour Party proposed increasing public investment and creating an 'active welfare state'. The Christian Democrats were sensitive to the critique and accepted a centre-left coalition with the PvdA after the 1989 elections. When the new government entered power, the economic climate worsened. The Labour Party was forced to backtrack on its election promises and implemented drastic austerity measures. The large cuts to the disability allowance proved especially controversial, plunging the PvdA into an existential crisis. Having barely survived, Wim Kok emerged purified.

Chapter 6 explores the so-called 'Purple' or Third Way cabinets. From 1994 to 2002, the PvdA (red) and the VVD (blue) formed a historic coalition government together with the small progressive-liberal party Democrats '66 (D66). Never before had the left (PvdA) and right (VVD) governed together without the Christian Democrats. Dutch politics in the nineties was marked by a feverish debate on globalization. Organized business and senior officials at the Ministry of Economic Affairs warned that the country was not yet ready for the European single market and the globalization of trade under the WTO. The technocratic Purple cabinets embarked on a series of projects to make the Dutch economy and labour market more market-friendly. An amended neoliberal settlement emerged. On both the left and right flanks, the Purple comprise was seen as deeply flawed. The disheartened neoliberal Pim Fortuyn emerged in the 1990s as a populist critic of the Dutch corporatist welfare state. He proposed to abolish permanent contracts, to 'emancipate' Dutch citizens from the welfare state and to dismiss half of all Dutch civil servants. He combined these free market views with a critique of Islam and immigration and became the founding father of Dutch right-wing populism.

Chapter 7 turns to 2008, when the Lehman Brothers bank collapsed and the global financial crisis broke. Leading left-wing authors proclaimed the end of neoliberalism. In reality, however, Dutch policy-makers soon fell back on the prescriptions of the 1980s. A powerful expert committee from the Ministry of Finance advised an extensive austerity programme to reduce the budget deficit and promote 'structural reform'. A government of right-wing liberals and social democrats adopted the advice and explicitly based its agenda on the policies of Ruud Lubbers. On the international stage, the social democratic finance minister, Jeroen Dijsselbloem, captured headlines as the president of the Eurogroup clashing with the Greek Finance Minister Yanis Varoufakis over the Greek austerity programme. With the help of expert interviews, this chapter offers a detailed reconstruction of the Dutch austerity debate and traces its roots to the establishment of European Monetary Union.

1

A Keynesian Intermezzo (1963–73)

On a Saturday afternoon in the late 1950s, Joop den Uyl wandered into a bookstore in the Amsterdam city centre.[1] As director of the think-tank of the Dutch Labour Party (PvdA), Den Uyl was responsible for the ideological renewal of the party. At the time this was an influential position, in close coordination with the party leadership. Den Uyl, who was to become an iconic leader of the Labour Party in the 1970s, was looking for new ideas. 'With the self-assuredness one still has at that age, I went to the bookshelf and saw a new American book by John Kenneth Galbraith,' he remembered later.[2] The book provided the inspiration for a new ideological programme. The sober socialism of post-war reconstruction felt increasingly outdated, and the Labour Party began to embrace the Keynesian welfare state.

To understand the rise of Dutch neoliberalism in the 1970s and 1980s properly, it is essential to recognize what it concretely opposed – what rival project, as it were, it sought to displace. That was the idea of the Keynesian welfare state, as espoused by left-leaning Keynesians.[3] The

---

1 This chapter was written with Bram Mellink.

2 Joop Den Uyl, 'Om de kwaliteit van het bestaan: Een postume voordracht', *Socialisme en Democratie* 2 (1995): 51.

3 There were of course various currents within Keynesianism. There was a more moderate and mainstream version that favoured conjunctural policy, but with limited government and modest social services. There was also a more left-leaning tendency, called left-Keynesianism or post-Keynesianism, that favoured a high level of redistribution and a larger role for the state. This is the current introduced in this chapter.

ways in which that political project emerged in the Netherlands – and eventually failed – are important to explain the neoliberal turn that followed. Very little has been written on Dutch Keynesianism; its existing historical imaginary has been heavily shaped by the critiques and caricatures of its opponents. That is why it is necessary to retrace its rough contours here.

Arguably the most influential left-Keynesian was John Kenneth Galbraith, whose strapping figure has often been contrasted with the modest build of his foremost opponent and critic, Milton Friedman. During the Second World War, Galbraith had worked as a planner in the Office of Price Administration in the United States. After the war, he became an economics professor at Harvard University and served as economic adviser to John F. Kennedy. His most famous book, *The Affluent Society* (1958), discussed the problem of private affluence and public squalor.[4] In the book, Galbraith criticized the American consumer society, in which citizens were compelled by advertising to buy ever more expensive cars, televisions and fridges. Meanwhile, public goods such as roads, housing, environmental protection, education and healthcare were neglected. In forceful and evocative prose, Galbraith asked why the accumulation of private goods was celebrated as a momentous achievement, while the expansion of public services was still considered to be a burden on citizens. What use were cars without a proper public infrastructure? How could innovation happen without schools and universities to train engineers and technicians? Consumer society set the wrong priorities and confused wellbeing with purchasing power.

Galbraith's book was received warmly by Dutch Keynesian economists. The Netherlands had always imported its ideas from abroad. After the Second World War, Dutch elites turned away from Germany, looking increasingly to the United States (and the United Kingdom) for the latest policy ideas. In an enthusiastic column in 1960, the leading Keynesian economist Jan Pen predicted 'a politics à la Galbraith'. The reason for his enthusiasm was not merely the persuasive power of the Canadian-American economist, but the concrete practicality of his ideas. 'Politics is not directed from the pages of books, not even when it's bestsellers sold all over the world,' Pen

---

4   John Kenneth Galbraith, *The Affluent Society* (London: Pelican, 1958).

observed. 'But still – ideas have legs. In addition, Galbraith's ideas have hands and feet.'[5]

The economic reality in the United States and the Netherlands, however, were not completely comparable. After the Second World War, the Netherlands followed an export-oriented economic strategy. Like Germany, it formed an initial exception to the Keynesian 'post-war compromise', comprised of generous wages and high taxes, while business profited from a stable domestic market to sell its products.[6] The Keynesian compromise focused on wage-led growth, while the Dutch had an export-led growth strategy. This was a supply-side approach, aimed at offering business the best investment conditions and helping to build up capital stock. Under the 'guided wages policy', the Dutch government, employers and trade unions together agreed to keep Dutch wages below the market price.

This corporatist arrangement, combined with low taxes, sparse regulation and modest social services, gave the Dutch export sector a formidable competitive edge on world markets. As a senior civil servant at the Dutch Ministry of Economic Affairs stated in 1949: 'On the world market, it ultimately comes down to the question who is the cheapest. We have to make sure we become the country with the lowest production costs.'[7] The Netherlands had a small but influential neoliberal movement in the 1950s that campaigned against economic planning and pushed for market-based post-war reconstruction.[8] It was intellectually far less developed than German neoliberalism but nonetheless made its mark on post-war Dutch economic policy. At the other end of the political spectrum, the social democrats and trade unions agreed to this market-oriented policy because they prioritised employment over higher wages. It formed an alternative route to full employment.

5   Jan Pen, 'Een politiek à la Galbraith' [A policy à la Galbraith], *Hollands Weekblad*, 16 November 1960, 3.

6   Christopher S. Allen, 'The Underdevelopment of Keynesianism in the Federal Republic of Germany', in Peter A. Hall, ed., *The Political Power of Economic Ideas: Keynesianism Across Nations* (Princeton, NJ: Princeton University Press, 1989), 263–89.

7   Minutes from Hoofdcommissie voor de Industrialisatie, 3 October 1949, nr. 1328, 12, HEEMAF archive, Historisch Centrum Overijssel, Zwolle.

8   Bram Mellink, 'Towards the Centre: Early Neoliberals in the Netherlands and the Rise of the Welfare State, 1945–1958', *Contemporary European History* 29, no. 1 (2020): 30–43.

As a result of wages being kept artificially low, private consumption in the Netherlands lagged far behind that of similar countries. Consequently, the 1950s were an austere period of hard work and low pay. Even though, on paper, the economy grew with exceptional vigour, Dutch citizens did not feel like they were living in an 'affluent society'. By 1960, only a quarter of Dutch households owned a black-and-white television, and even fewer owned a fridge.[9] The Netherlands was also frugal in terms of public spending. During the 1950s, the level of Dutch public spending as a proportion of GDP had barely increased.[10] The Dutch government adhered to a strict budgeting norm that prevented public spending from rising more than GDP. Internationally, this made the country into a 'welfare laggard'.[11] In the 1950s, Dutch social democrats and trade unions still shared a commitment to this principle of frugality. 'Not everything is possible, and certainly not everything at the same time', was the watchword of Willem Drees, the frugal social democratic prime minister of the 1950s, who favoured balanced budgets.[12]

Table 1.1 The Netherlands as a 'welfare laggard'. Social transfers as a percentage of GDP (1930–80)

	1930	1950[a]	1960	1970	1980
Belgium	0.6	9.6[b]	13.1	19.3	30.4
Germany	5.0	12.4	18.1	19.5	25.7
UK	2.6	5.7	10.2	13.2	16.4
France	1.1	11.3	13.4	16.7	22.6
Italy	0.1	9.3[c]	13.1	16.9	21.2
Denmark	3.4	5.8	12.3	19.1	27.4
(1) Unweighted average	2.1	9.0	13.4	17.5	24.0
(2) Netherlands	1.2	6.6	11.7	22.5	28.3

Source: Jan Luiten van Zanden, *The Economic History of the Netherlands 1914–1995: A Small Open Economy in the 'Long' Twentieth Century* (London: Routledge, 1998), 55.
[a] As a share of GNP. [b] 1953. [c] 1955.

9   Hans Righart, *De eindeloze jaren zestig: Geschiedenis van een generatieconflict* (Amsterdam: Amsterdam University Press, 2006), 102.

10   Hans Daalder and Jelle Gaemers, *W. Drees. Premier en elder statesman. De jaren 1948–1988* (Amsterdam: Balans, 2014), 102.

11   Jelle Visser and Anton Hemerijck, '*A Dutch Miracle': Job Growth, Welfare Reform and Corporatism in the Netherlands* (Amsterdam: Amsterdam University Press, 1997), 119.

12   Hans Daalder, *Het socialisme van Willem Drees* (Amsterdam: Bert Bakker, 2000), 40.

As a result of this growth strategy, Keynesian ideas did not predominate in the Netherlands. The Keynesian argument, developed during the Great Depression of the 1930s, was that the private sector was reluctant to spend and invest in the economy in times of crisis, which increased unemployment and deepened the crisis. Public spending in times of crisis had a flywheel effect: the wages that public investment provided for were subsequently spent on all sorts of products, giving a boost to the economy. This was the fiscal multiplier effect. In times of elevated economic growth, the opposite should occur: the government should either curtail spending or raise taxes. 'The boom, not the slump, is the time for austerity at the Treasury', Keynes famously remarked.[13] In the Keynesian view, the principal objective of public finances was not to balance the budget but rather to balance out the economy through countercyclical spending. The expansion of the welfare state was an expression of this logic: welfare spending went up during a crisis while it receded during a boom. Internationally, the Keynesian revolution became a crucial intellectual support for the left.

The Netherlands had long been renowned for its conservative fiscal tradition, focused on balanced budgets and sound money. It was one of the last countries in the Western world to ditch the Gold Standard and try deficit spending in the 1930s. While views on state finances had modernized somewhat after the Second World War, Dutch policymaking elites continued to have a conservative stance on public spending. When the aforementioned economist Jan Pen gave his inaugural lecture as professor of economics in Groningen in 1956, he lamented that the country had still not 'picked the fruits of the tree that Keynes planted in 1936'. He spoke from experience: Pen had worked as a senior official at the Ministry of Economic Affairs in the years before. In Dutch public opinion and among policymaking elites, the old-fashioned 'bookkeeper mentality' that abhorred public debt and public investment still prevailed, according to Pen.[14]

Indeed, Dutch policymaking institutions were resistant to Keynesian ideas. The Dutch Ministry of Finance was a bulwark of fiscal

13   John Maynard Keynes, *Collected Writings of John Maynard Keynes*, vol. 21 (Basingstoke: Palgrave Macmillan, 1983), 390.

14   Jan Pen, *Duwen en trekken in de conjunctuurpolitiek* (Leiden: Universiteit Leiden, 1956), 30.

conservatism that positioned itself as a watchdog against spendthrift politicians; the Ministry of Economic Affairs, the principal architect of post-war industrialization, adhered to a supply-side philosophy; and the Dutch Central Bank was home to a monetarist school of thought, which saw Keynesianism as prone to causing inflation.[15] Even declared socialists, such as the Nobel Memorial Prize–winning economist Jan Tinbergen, were sceptical of Keynesian precepts such as deficit-spending and the fiscal multiplier.[16] Tinbergen, a world-leading econometrist who pioneered large macro-economic models, was the intellectual godfather of the Dutch Central Planning Bureau (CPB). The name of this influential bureaucratic think-tank, which resided under the Ministry of Economic Affairs, as of today still alludes to the original intention of social democrats to plan parts of the Dutch economy. In response to intense opposition to economic planning from Dutch business and the neoliberal right, however, the CPB became an economic forecasting agency, not unlike the Congressional Budget Office in the United States.

Changing Tides

The low-wage growth strategy soon became a victim of its own success. Rapid economic growth and a shortage of workers brought the system to the brink of collapse. By 1962, there were only 32,000 unemployed and more than 73,000 vacancies in the Netherlands.[17] Companies started to pay workers extra under the counter to keep them from going to competitors. At the request of desperate employers, wages were liberalized in 1963, resulting in the so-called 'wage explosions'. In 1963, wages rose by 9 per cent, in 1964 by 15 per cent and in 1965 by 11 per cent.[18] In a matter of just a few years, the Netherlands was transformed into a

<hr>

15   Martin Fase, 'The Rise and Demise of Dutch Monetarism; or, the Schumpeter-Koopmans-Holtrop Connection', *History of Political Economy* 26, no. 1 (1 March 1994): 21–38.

16   Erwin Dekker, *Jan Tinbergen (1903–1994) and the Rise of Economic Expertise* (Cambridge: Cambridge University Press, 2021), 220.

17   Parliamentary records, HTK, 1961–1962, 14 March 1962, 3723.

18   Cees Schuyt and Ed Taverne, *1950. Welvaart in zwartwit* (The Hague: SDU Uitgevers, 2000), 274.

consumer society. At the same time, the government saw its tax income rise in large jumps. When the exploitation of large reserves of natural gas was added to this, the overall picture changed completely in the 1960s. In this new context, Galbraith's argument was suddenly highly relevant. What to do with this newfound wealth?

Politically, there were essentially two answers to this question. On one side stood the proponents of small government. They championed a property-owning democracy as a market-based alternative to the welfare state. This idea, popular on the right and in business circles, held that the state should support citizens in acquiring their own private property. Right-wing Christian democrats were inspired by the German neoliberal Wilhelm Röpke, who argued that individual property helped educate workers in personal responsibility.[19] Having their own houses, private insurance and savings made workers independent and less reliant on the state. Taxes could remain low and government small. 'Who does not own property . . . is someone's property', the Catholic People's Party proclaimed in the election campaign of 1963.[20] The party had even created a state secretary for 'private property promotion'.

The left and the trade unions wanted to move in the opposite direction. They sought to finance public services from a reduction in private purchasing power through higher levels of taxation. The emancipation of the worker was better served by an expansion of social security, healthcare, social housing and education, rather than by keeping taxes low and boosting private consumption. With abundant economic growth and the newfound power of labour under full employment, the left broadened its political horizons and raised its political ambitions.

Den Uyl's intellectual attraction to Galbraith – his opponents in the Labour Party scornfully called him 'professor Uylbraith' – was reinforced by this development. Den Uyl edited a series of social democratic reports, 'For Quality of Life', which translated Galbraith's vision to the Netherlands. 'In the tolerant numbers of the national income', Den Uyl wrote in 1963, 'the electric toothbrush counts as much as nursing care,

19   Wilhelm Röpke's book *Civitas Humana* was translated into Dutch and was well known at the time. Wilhelm Röpke, *Civitas Humana* (London: William Hodge, 1948). Röpke visited the Netherlands repeatedly in the 1950s to give lectures. See Mellink, 'Towards the Centre'.

20   Hans Bornewasser, *Katholieke volkspartij 1945–1980*, vol. 1, *Herkomst en groei (Tot 1963)* (Nijmegen: Valkhof Pers, 1995), 113–14.

advertising expenses for the ultimate sedative as much as entry tickets to the theatre, the manager's bonus as much as the blind person's allowance.'[21] But these were not of equal value. Because politicians and economists only had eyes for GDP growth, they had ignored the need for public services, which remained underdeveloped:

> Consumer durables, which suggest a certain standard of living, are often housed in hovels. There are major shortages in care for the sick and disabled, which feels all the more outrageous when there is an abundant supply of goods to satisfy luxury needs. Public transport has lagged far behind the development of private car traffic.[22]

This controversy over the size of the Dutch public sector cut straight through each of the major political parties – a result of the religious cleavages in the Netherlands. The Christian parties, both Catholic and Protestant, that dominated Dutch politics for much of the twentieth century were internally divided on socioeconomic issues. They traditionally comprised a left-leaning 'social' wing, formed by the Christian trade unions and civil society organizations, and a fiscally conservative employers' wing.

Even within the Dutch Labour Party, there was substantial controversy over expanding the welfare state. An influential fiscally conservative current within the party saw the sober regime of post-war reconstruction as the political ideal. Willem Drees, the frugal social democratic prime minister from 1948 to 1958, was the face of this tendency. He favoured a 'guarantor state' that provided an absolute minimum and left the rest to the personal responsibility of individuals.[23] Willem Drees soon clashed with Den Uyl over his proposals for welfare state expansion. 'People have a different mentality', he said at a meeting of the party executive in 1963, 'they don't want that from the government, at least not if they have to pay taxes for it. They have other desires than all those beautiful things – education, housing, healthcare – Den Uyl wants to give them.'[24] When the social democrats lost the elections of 1963, it was blamed on Den Uyl and the

---

21   J. M. den Uyl, *Om de kwaliteit van het bestaan*, part 1, *De besteding van de groei van het nationaal inkomen* (Amsterdam: Partij van de Arbeid, 1963), 11.

22   Ibid., 14.

23   Daalder and Gaemers, *W. Drees*, 118.

24   Den Uyl, 'Om de kwaliteit van het bestaan', 57.

proponents of a welfare state. A broad leftist front in favour of a Keynesian welfare state failed to materialize in the Netherlands. For most of the 1960s, the Netherlands would be ruled by centre-right Christian–liberal coalitions.

And yet, in this same period, the Netherlands saw an impressive expansion of public services. The sociologist Bram de Swaan once described the rise of the Dutch welfare state 'in terms of a firework, as a long hiss and a late bang'.[25] After a period of relative stagnation, the Dutch welfare state was built up at a rapid pace, with legislation on family allowances (1963), unemployment benefit (1965), disability insurance (1966), sickness benefits (1967) and the minimum wage (1969). Expenditure on the aforementioned 'beautiful things' – education, healthcare and housing – increased rapidly. It is the major paradox of the Dutch welfare state: it was largely constructed by centre-right Christian–liberal coalitions that had long vowed to oppose the rise in public spending. What caused this turnaround?

The Deferred Wage

Existing explanations of the rise of the Dutch welfare state have centred on a Dutch peculiarity. The conventional argument is that rapid secularization and depillarization weakened the religious cleavages that prevented Christian workers from voting for the social democratic party. In the ensuing electoral competition for workers' votes, the Christian parties moved left.[26] It sounds plausible, except for the fact that secularization and depillarization largely occurred *after* the expansion of the welfare state, in the late sixties and early seventies. And we should not forget that social democrats, too, had been opposed to increased public spending.

The central problem facing Dutch policymakers in the 1960s was that of rapidly rising wages. The wage explosions were observed by elites

---

25   Abram de Swaan, *In Care of the State: Health Care, Education and Welfare in Europe and the USA in the Modern Era* (London: Oxford University Press, 1988), 215.

26   Jan Luiten van Zanden, *The Economic History of the Netherlands 1914–1995: A Small Open Economy in the 'Long' Twentieth Century* (London: Routledge, 1998), 63–4; Harold Wilensky, 'Leftism, Catholicism, and Democratic Corporatism', in Peter Flora and Arnold J. Heidenheimer, eds, *The Development of Welfare States in Europe and America* (New Brunswick, NJ: Transaction, 1981), 345–82.

with a mood of heightened anxiety. 'We are being hurried along by rising prosperity and often feel more a victim than beneficiary thereof,' complained the liberal Finance Minister (and future IMF director) Johan Witteveen in 1964.[27] The fear was that this would price out Dutch products in world markets and lead to an inflationary spiral. As companies paid out higher wages, they increased their prices to cover the costs. Higher prices meant that workers saw the real value of their existing wages decline, again provoking higher wage claims. In this way, a negative wage-spiral could develop, making inflation endemic. The problem for the right was that their ideal of a property-owning democracy provided little in the way of a solution. In fact, the wage explosions could be seen as the fulfilment of the proposed expansion of private property.

There were few palatable options on the table. Dutch employers tried to attract guest-workers from abroad, but that was not nearly enough to relieve wage pressures. Another option was austerity – a deflationary policy to increase unemployment and stop the economy from overheating, but this was a hard sell politically. The secular and Catholic trade unions offered a way out. They tabled a new grand bargain: the unions would rein in their wage claims in exchange for an expansion of social services. This formed part of a broader international trend: that of the 'deferred wage'.

As Gosta Esping-Andersen famously explained in *The Three Worlds of Welfare Capitalism*, almost all advanced economies in the 1960s were confronted with the problem of how to dampen prices and labour costs. The 'deferred wage' or 'social wage' was a promise to improve future social benefits and services, in return for present wage restraint.[28] It led to a tremendous expansion of the public budget in a large range of countries, seemingly irrespective of the party in power. In the US, it was the Nixon administration that gave the social-wage strategy full prominence, legislating large increases in social security benefits at the end of the 1960s.[29] In the Netherlands, too, it was centre-right coalition governments that did most to expand social services. The Dutch welfare state

---

27   ' "Door welvaart voortgejaagd". Tekort betalingsbalans al 300 miljoen gulden' ['Hurried along by wealth': Shortage balance of payments 300 million guilders], *De Volkskrant*, 27 May 1964.

28   Gosta Esping-Andersen, *The Three Worlds of Welfare Capitalism* (Princeton, NJ: Princeton University Press, 1990), 172–3.

29   Ibid., 175.

was something of a cuckoo's egg: originally conceived by the trade unions and the social democrats, but hatched in a right-wing nest.

Also crucial were the internal divisions within the largest party in the land: the Catholic People's Party. The employers' wing of the party had long presided over economic policy. But its trade union wing, emboldened by the situation in the labour market, broke ranks with the party leadership over the welfare state. Two ministers emerged from the left of the party who were responsible for vital additions to the Dutch welfare state: Gerard Veldkamp of the Ministry of Social Affairs and Public Health and Marga Klompé of the Ministry of Social Work. Veldkamp, whose father had been a Catholic mechanic, had financed his economics education by playing the organ. He was a combative minister, unpopular in his party and in the governments he served, though celebrated by the unions. He oversaw a veritable spree of social legislation: child support was made universal (1962) and unemployment benefits were extended (1964), while he introduced the disability allowance (1966), long-term health insurance (1968) and minimum wage legislation (1969).[30] Klompé, who was from a family of small entrepreneurs, became the first female government minister in the Netherlands. She professionalized social work, which had largely been the domain of voluntary (and religious) initiative. Poor relief, still based on the 1854 Poor Law, was replaced with modern social assistance in 1965, a shift that Klompé dubbed 'from mercy to social right'.[31] Veldkamp and Klompé were not unopposed, however.

As late as 1966, budget hawks in the Catholic People's Party forced the fall of the government over rising public spending. Even so, the right failed to muster the necessary political support for a deflationary course. In 1967, a new centre-right coalition government led by the very same Catholic People's Party realized the largest post-war expanse of social services in a single governing term. Without batting an eyelid, the Catholic Prime Minister Piet de Jong declared in the government policy statement:

30   Jan Willem Brouwer and Jan Ramakers, eds, *Het kabinet-Drees IV en het kabinet-Beel II, 1956–1959: Het einde van de rooms-rode coalitie* (Amsterdam: Boom, 2007), 121–2; Johan van Merriënboer and Carla van Baalen, *Polarisatie en hoogconjunctuur. Het kabinet-De Jong 1967–1971* (Amsterdam: Boom, 2013).

31   Ido de Haan and Jan Willem Duyvendak, eds, *In het hart van de verzorgingsstaat. Het ministerie van Maatschappelijk Werk en zijn opvolgers (CRM, WVC, VWS), 1952–2002* (Zutphen: Walburg, 2002).

'One of the most important questions we are currently faced with is how to make use of growing affluence. The rapid growth of prosperity strengthens the need to vigorously expand all sorts of public services.'[32]

To appease the right wing of his party, De Jong added the disclaimer that this growth would be 'bound to clear limits'. But that proved to be easier said than done. In the decade that followed, the Netherlands built one of the most generous of European welfare states. Its largesse was the paradoxical result of its late conception, in a time of full employment. The centre-right reluctantly accepted the Keynesian welfare state not as an objective in itself, but as an instrument for achieving wage moderation. This implied that, if this instrument failed to accomplish its purpose, support would quickly be reconsidered.

Fissures in the Keynesian Coalition

The mid-1960s formed the beginning of a Keynesian intermezzo in Dutch economic policymaking. Dutch developments closely mirrored those in Germany, where there was a 'Keynesian interlude' under Chancellor Willy Brandt and Finance Minister Karl Schiller.[33] The Keynesian ideas that had long found a lukewarm reception in the Netherlands were now being picked up and propagated by a new generation of progressive economists. But the shift away from neoclassical precepts had taken place not out of conviction but through force majeure: an example of Galbraith's dictum that ideas 'yield not to the attack of other ideas but . . . to the massive onslaught of circumstance with which they cannot contend'.[34] Within the institutions, Keynesianism remained fragile. It provided an uneasy fit with the Dutch export-oriented growth strategy and never settled into a dominant policy paradigm.[35] Austerity was never really off the table.

---

32   Parliamentary records, HTK, 1966–1967, no. 3, 18 April 1967, 24.

33   Fritz Scharpf, *Crisis and Choice in European Social Democracy*, transl. Ruth Crowley and Fred Thompson (Ithaca, NY: Cornell University Press, 1991), 117–57; Julian Germann, *Unwitting Architect: German Primacy and the Origins of Neoliberalism* (Stanford, CA: Stanford University Press, 2021), 90.

34   Galbraith, *Affluent Society*, 26

35   Jonne Harmsma, 'Reverting to Restraint: A Keynesian Intermezzo and Neoliberalism in the Netherlands (1971–1977)', *Contemporary European History*, 12 July 2023, 1–17.

Dutch Keynesianism rested on a fragile coalition comprising the political left – both within the Dutch Labour Party and on the social wing of Christian parties – and the trade unions. The social democrats had originally been opposed to the liberalization of wages. It had been introduced at the behest of Dutch employers, who wanted more freedom to differentiate in pay. The Keynesian economist and social democratic parliamentarian Hans van der Doel contended that the liberalization 'disallowed any substantial levelling of incomes'.[36] It was not that the Dutch left favoured the low wages of the 1950s. Rather, they saw the centralized wage policy as a crucial tool for left-wing politics. Once liberalization was a fact, they feared it would be hard to turn back the clock. As Van den Doel wrote in 1965,

> People, once they have learned to take what they can get, will not want to go back to a system in which not their material, but immaterial interest is the priority. Something has been messed up for years to come. The last instrument that could structurally reform our economic order has been jettisoned. The liberalization of wages is therefore a betrayal of the dream of a better society.[37]

Of course, the trade unions saw matters differently. In a context of full employment, the absence of a wage policy gave them a powerful negotiating position. In the 1950s it was the spectre of unemployment that had compelled the unions to agree to wage moderation in exchange for jobs. Now that the fear of unemployment had dissipated, the trade unions shook off their former subservience. They were the main force behind the new social contract: wage restraint in exchange for expansion of the welfare state.

Again, in 1970, the trade unions presented an action programme offering such an exchange. The question was, however, whether the trade unions could make good on their promise. The union leadership was challenged from below by increased labour militancy. From the other end, right-wing critics attacked the trade union leadership for being afraid to contradict their restless base. 'The majority of workers

---

36   Hans van der Doel, *Lastig links: Socialistische dilemma's* (Utrecht: Spectrum, 1976), 13.

37   Ibid., 14–16.

has come to consider wage increases of 5 to 10 per cent per year as a right', the liberal newspaper *NRC* complained.[38]

While the left wanted to clamp down on private consumption, workers were not so easily persuaded. They wanted to ensure their income was not going to be eroded by inflation and higher taxes. Leftist intellectuals began criticizing workers for being in thrall to consumer society. In 1964, the Frankfurt School theorist Herbert Marcuse published *One-Dimensional Man*.[39] Marcuse contended that advanced industrial society created false needs. The workers, once the class that would usher in a better society, had been seduced by the lure of consumer society. The combined power of mass production, modern mass media and advertising techniques integrated the worker into the capitalist system. Rejecting the worker as revolutionary subject, Marcuse placed his hope in minorities, outsiders and the radical intelligentsia.

In the Netherlands, Marcuse's theory was taken up by the Provo movement, an anarchist youth movement that exemplified the Dutch spirit of '68. It sought to bring down the Dutch conservative social order through endless provocation. Roel van Duijn, the movement's main figurehead, popularized a simplified version of Marcuse's ideas as the *klootjesvolktheorie* (or 'hoi polloi theory'). The term referred to the materialistic, hardworking, authoritarian petty bourgeois – in the words of Roel van Duijn: 'The masses who we can't and barely want to convince'.[40] Next to paternalistic and conservative Dutch elites, the *klootjesvolk* were the declared adversary of the radical youth revolt of the 1960s.

In his book *Bericht aan de Rattenkoning* (Message to the rat king), a homage to the Provo movement, the celebrated author Harry Mulisch wrote in capital letters of the AUTO and the TEEVEE as semi-religious institutions that numbed the class consciousness of the workers. 'Their parents sat on fridges and washing machines, watching their TEEVEE with their left eye and with their right the AUTO in front of the door, a

---

38   'Regering moet kiezen of delen' [Government must take it or leave it], *NRC*, 21 May 1966, 13.

39   Herbert Marcuse, *One-Dimensional Man* (London: Sphere, 1968).

40   Roel van Duijn, 'Inleiding tot provocerend denken' [Introduction to provocative thought], *Trouw*, 10 July 1965. See also James Kennedy, 'Building New Babylon: Cultural Change in the Netherlands During the 1960s' (PhD diss., Iowa University, 1995).

mixer in one hand, [right-wing newspaper] *De Telegraaf* in the other, while the kids went to the Spui' – the last being the name of the iconic Amsterdam square where the Provos gathered to stage performances and provoke the authorities.[41]

Meanwhile, workers themselves seemed out to disprove Marcuse's theory. A long wave of labour militancy swept across the country. Increased labour unrest culminated in a weeks-long wildcat strike at the Rotterdam harbour in 1970, led by young communists. It was the single largest strike of the post-war period.[42] The workers eventually won, and Dutch employers were so intimidated that they reached a central agreement with the trade unions to grant each worker a lump sum of 400 Dutch guilders – at that time almost a monthly wage. Quite a few companies refused to honour the agreement, provoking yet another wave of strikes.

That same year, Dutch sociologists convened to discuss the labour unrest. In response to the strikes, Rotterdam sociologist Pieter ter Hoeven argued that workers channelled their social discontent into demands for money, and employers were assuaging deeper problems with wage increases.[43] Surprisingly, the labour unrest of the time had a Janus face: on the one hand a communist-led protest against capitalism, on the other a further step in the ongoing integration of the working class within capitalism. As Ter Hoeven contended, workers had an increasingly instrumental relationship to work, which they perceived as hard and boring. The challenge for unions and the left, he said, was to channel widespread discontent in such a way that it would manifest itself in an expansion of collective services and the improvement of immaterial conditions (such as worker control within the company).

The controversy over wages came to a head during the so-called 'wage debate' of 1970. In that year, the Wage Formation Act had been passed by the centre-right De Jong cabinet.[44] It formally buried the guided

---

41   Harry Mulisch, *Bericht aan de rattenkoning* (Amsterdam: De Bezige Bij, 1966), 62.

42   Sjaak van der Velden, *Stakingen in Nederland: Arbeidersstrijd 1830–1995* (IISG, 2000), 155–6.

43   Harry Lockefeer, 'Sociologen over onrust in beraad' [Sociologists deliberate over unrest], *De Volkskrant*, 2 januari 1971; Pieter ter Hoeven, *Breukvlakken in het arbeidsbestel* (Alphen aan den Rijn: Samsom, 1972), 46–7.

44   Van Merriënboer and Van Baalen, *Polarisatie en hoogconjunctuur*, 459.

wage policy of the 1950s, ushering in free wage negotiations. Responsibility for wages and working conditions now fell squarely in the hands of the social partners. But the government kept one foot in the door: in exceptional situations, it could still decree a wage limitation to curb excessive increases. Spooked by the wildcat port strike and the subsequent inflationary wage increase, the government made immediate use of the exception clause. It unilaterally proclaimed a wage-control measure, refusing to negotiate with the unions. In the first two quarters of 1970, wages were not allowed to increase beyond inflation. The trade unions reacted with great indignation. The National Confederation of Trade Unions (NVV), the largest and secular Dutch trade union, organized a general political strike. Hundreds of thousands of workers stopped working for an hour.[45] The left-wing opposition, in turn, castigated the cabinet in a parliamentary debate that was broadcast live on Dutch public television.

On the right, commentators reacted with scorn. Weren't the unions and the left the ones who wanted to moderate wages and curb consumer society? *De Telegraaf* wrote sarcastically that the government, with its wage-control measure, 'had dealt a heavy blow to the puffy face of consumer society'.[46] The newspaper duly noted that the unions and left-wing parties all had wage restraint in their programmes and favoured public provision over private consumption. They should have been in favour of the government measure. Yet 'the fiercest opponents of our nauseating consumer society' voted against it and even managed to put the government on the defensive.[47] In reality, *De Telegraaf* concluded, the leftist opposition should have been in the stand, because they wanted to deprive the workers of everything, from their cars to their purchasing power.

To the surprise of many, it was the Keynesian economist Jan Pen who came to the defence of the government's wage measure. It was a painful moment, since Pen was a card-carrying social democrat who had proposed 'a politics à la Galbraith' in the years before. It was not that Pen

---

45   Van der Velden, *Stakingen in Nederland*, 156.

46   Jacques Fahrenfort, 'Het omturnen van de consumptiemaatschappij' [The battle against consumer society], *De Telegraaf*, 12 December 1970.

47   Jacques Fahrenfort, 'Met het treiteren van de eigen ministers behaalt men geen verkiezingswinst' [You do not win elections by tormenting your own ministers], *De Telegraaf*, 19 December 1970.

had changed his mind. He wrote that such a left-wing politics was only possible if the government put a brake on rising wage claims, since the unions proved unable to do so. Pen charged that the hundreds of thousands of striking workers were simply wrong if they thought they were in danger of losing out in real terms. It was inflation that was eating up their wages. 'The leftist parties and the leftist newspapers do not fight the workers' misconceptions', Pen wrote sharply. 'They do not give honest information because it could be interpreted as support for the right-wing cabinet. Instead, in a manner close to deception, they stiffen the most vindictive worker in his most vindictive delusion.'[48] Ultimately, Pen contended, the left had shot itself in the foot. Workers, strengthened in their discontent, would turn against their unions and political parties.

The response from social democratic leader Joop den Uyl came swiftly. In a rejoinder titled 'Pen Contra Pen', Den Uyl noted that the economics professor was contradicting himself.[49] Had not Pen himself written recently that wages could only be controlled within the framework of a broader wage policy? Had he not argued that the government could not move too far from market realities? Private investment was up by 10 per cent, and employers were chasing workers to make their investments profitable. Under those circumstances, guided wages were 'a joke'. Effective government intervention was only possible with a relationship of trust between politicians and unions. But the right-wing administration had thoroughly undermined that very trust with its unilateral wage measure. Den Uyl himself had travelled to Rotterdam to convince the striking dockworkers of the importance of wage moderation. He had not encountered Pen there 'informing' the workers, he coolly noted in his response.

The Birth of Dutch Public Choice Theory

Meanwhile, Keynesian ideas and rising public spending provoked opposition. At the Ministry of Finance, public officials had been sounding the

---

48   Jan Pen, 'Schouwspel in de Kamer was beschamend' [Performance in parliament was shameful], *Het Parool*, 17 December 1970, 4.

49   Joop den Uyl, 'Pen Contra Pen', *Het Parool*, 23 December 1970, 4. For Pen's reply, see Jan Pen, 'Laat links zich op de waarheid toeleggen' [The left should focus on the truth of the matter], *Het Parool*, 29 December 1970, 4.

alarm over the increase in public spending. One of its key figures was Willem Drees Jr, the son of post-war social democratic Prime Minister Willem Drees, who had led four cabinets from 1951 to 1958. Like his father, Drees Jr would acquire an almost legendary reputation for his personal frugality. In 1956, he had been appointed director of the budget at the Ministry of Finance, serving as right-hand man to the finance minister. For a senior civil servant, Drees was remarkably outspoken, becoming one of the most vocal critics of the expansion of the Dutch welfare state. At a much-discussed annual meeting of the Dutch Economic Association in 1963, Drees warned that ministers and parliamentarians had been captured by societal pressure groups, above all the trade unions. Pleas by politicians for higher social benefits were bluntly dismissed by Drees as 'claptrap' and 'gibberish'.[50] In the eyes of the young Drees, the Netherlands owed its post-war economic recovery to its sober, market-based policy, with low wages and minimal social services. In a fiery 1965 lecture, Drees stated that the Ministry of Finance was 'virtually the taxpayer's only friend, because it is the only one that constantly tries to curb spending'.[51]

The claim that Dutch politics had been captured by pressure groups was not an isolated observation. In the early 1950s, while working at the Finance Ministry, Drees had written his dissertation on the role of pressure groups and self-interested politicians and bureaucrats in driving up spending. It became a foundational text in Dutch public finance – a new discipline in economics that focused on state finances. Titled *On the Level of Government Expenditure in the Netherlands After the War* (1955), Drees's dissertation focused on the relationship between the Dutch Ministry of Finance and the other ministries. At its core, Drees's argument was that public spending continued to increase because the Ministry of Finance had lost out to the combined power of the other ministries, which were solely interested in maximizing their budgets and pleasing the pressure groups in their sectors.[52] As a rule,

---

50　'Bezinning nodig op overheidsuitgaven' [Reflection needed on public expenditures], *Telegraaf*, 25 November 1963.

51　'Pressiegroep nodig tegen verhoging rijksuitgaven' [Pressure group needed against increased government spending], *Nieuwsblad van Het Noorden*, 18 November 1965.

52　Willem Drees Jr, *On the Level of Government Expenditure in the Netherlands After the War* (Leiden: Stenfert Kroese, 1955), 62.

ministers of spending departments supported the budgetary demands of their colleagues, in exchange for support for their own budgetary claims.[53] Lacking a veto in budgetary matters, the minister of finance faced combined pressure from all spending departments in government. Finally, parliament also failed to control spending, because the specialists in the various political parties strongly identified with their respective sectors – a form of loyalty that transcended ideological divisions.[54]

Drees's academic work strongly resembled the rational choice and public choice theory being developed in the United States at the time. This was probably not an accident. Drees had worked at the International Monetary Fund in Washington, DC, for some time in the late 1940s, and it is likely that he kept himself informed of American debates in economics. Public choice theory would grow to become an important intellectual pillar of the international neoliberal turn of the 1970s and 1980s.[55] Key works by early advocates, such as Duncan Black (1948), Kenneth Arrow (1951), Anthony Downs (1957) and James Buchanan and Gordon Tullock (1962), were written in reaction to the post-war dominance of welfare economics and the idea of market failure.[56] It was argued that markets failed whenever the price system could not sustain desirable activities or impede undesirable ones. This referred to public goods such as defence, public parks, welfare, education, healthcare and infrastructure, which could not be effectively denied to people. Because the bill for such services could not be based on individual use, they had to be provided collectively. There were also 'public bads': costs that could be ignored by companies and passed on to the public, such as

---

53   Willem Drees Jr, *Gespiegeld in de tijd: De nagelaten autobiografie, Willem Drees*, ed. Johanna Marijke Drees and E. Schoorl (Amsterdam: Balans, 2000), 117.

54   Drees, *On the Level of Government Expenditure*, 65.

55   Melinda Cooper, *Counterrevolution: Extravagance and Austerity in Public Finance* (Princeton, NJ: Princeton University Press, 2024); Colin Hay, *Why We Hate Politics* (Cambridge: Polity, 2007); Eamonn Butler, 'Public Choice: A Primer', Institute of Economic Affairs Occasional Paper 147 (2012).

56   Duncan Black, 'On the Rationale of Group Decision-Making', *Journal of Political Economy* 56, no. 1 (1948): 23–34; Kenneth J. Arrow, *Social Choice and Individual Values* (New Haven, CT: Yale University Press, 1951); Anthony Downs, *An Economic Theory of Democracy* (New York: Harper, 1957); James M. Buchanan and Gordon Tullock, *The Calculus of Consent: Logical Foundations of Constitutional Democracy* (Ann Arbor: University of Michigan Press, 1962).

pollution. As a result, it was believed that there was a wide mandate for government intervention.

In response to the theory of market failure, public choice theorists developed what Nobel Memorial Prize–winner James Buchanan described as a 'theory of government failure'.[57] They sought to contest the post-war consensus that an expansion of government intervention was desirable. Their challenge consisted of turning the debate on its head by analysing the state as if it were a market. Public choice theorists based their analyses on the neoclassical axiom that, in the marketplace, individual behaviour is motivated by rational self-interest. They expanded that logic by assuming similar behaviour in the political and bureaucratic spheres. Politicians, civil servants and voters were not driven by lofty ideals or some sort of public ethos but pursued their own rationally conceived self-interest.

While this self-interested behaviour panned out well in the marketplace, it made the political sphere a severely dysfunctional system. Political institutions were plagued by perverse incentives, while voters had little motivation to inform themselves properly about politics, since the costs of casting an informed vote far outweighed the benefits. Lacking perceptive voters focused on the public interest, pressure groups of organized minorities decided the fate of elections. Since the primary interest of politicians was to maximize votes and win elections, they spent as much of their energy as possible courting interest groups by increasing spending. Finally, civil servants tended to drive up spending even further, since it was in their own self-interest to maximize the budgets of their departments. As a result of these combined dynamics, democracies had a natural tendency to overspend.

For Drees, who laid out similar arguments in one of the first textbooks on Dutch public finance, this was not only an academic argument.[58] He sought to act upon his ideas. In 1969, he had been promoted to treasurer-general, the highest position at the Ministry of Finance. The department

---

57   James M. Buchanan, 'The Achievement and the Limits of Public Choice in Diagnosing Government Failure and in Offering Bases for Constructive Reform', in Hanusch Horst, ed., *Anatomy of Government Deficiencies* (Berlin: Springer, 1983), 15–25.

58   Willem Drees Jr, Cees Goedhart and Louk de Mast, *De Nederlandse overheidsuitgaven, Preadviezen / Vereniging voor de Staathuishoudkunde* (The Hague: Martinus Nijhoff, 1963).

had become more politicized, as the struggle to contain inflation and wages ploughed on. The ministry, Drees declared militantly, 'takes up a front position' and 'fights a battle against those groups that want (too much) money from the treasury'.[59] As part of that effort, Drees had proposed the creation of 'a pressure group against rising public spending' that would serve as a counterweight to the trade unions.

Later that year, together with his public finance colleagues Theo Stevers and Cornelis Goedhart, he founded the Institute for Research on Public Spending (Instituut voor Onderzoek van Overheidsuitgaven). It served as a watchdog against rising expenditure and published a leading Dutch journal on public finance. Like Drees, Stevers and Goedhart were influential neoclassical economists, founders of the Dutch discipline of public finance and believers in small government. In their leading textbooks, Stevers and Goedhart developed a trenchant critique of Keynesianism, arguing that the expansion of social security, rather than containing inflation, led to higher wage claims and an inflationary spiral.[60]

One year later, Drees entered politics. Conservative social democrats had created a right-wing breakaway party from the Labour Party, named Democratic Socialists '70, or DS '70. It was founded in protest against the leftward turn of the Labour Party under Den Uyl and the sixties youth movements. Drees was invited to become the new party's political leader. Praised in the press as 'stiff, but disciplined', he exemplified the frugality of the 1950s that DS '70 wanted to return to. According to one famous anecdote, Drees timed his private calls at the department with a stopwatch, so he could pay back the costs to the department. When invited by the queen after the elections, he asked the other members of the new government to share a ride and save costs.[61]

As the economic outlook worsened and the government proved unable to stem rising inflation, a turn to austerity seemed imminent. In the election campaign of 1971, Drees exploited his frugal image. With

---

59   'Thesaurie werkt op drie fronten' [Treasury works on three fronts], *Het Parool*, 21 October 1969.

60   Theo Stevers, *Openbare financiën en ekonomie: De openbare financiën als instrument van ekonomische politiek* (Leiden: Stenfert Kroese, 1971); Cornelis Goedhart, *Hoofdlijnen van de leer der openbare financiën* (Leiden: Stenfert Kroese, 1967).

61   Pieter Sijpersma, *Hans Wiegel: De biografie* (Amsterdam: Atlas Contact, 2020), 177.

DS '70, he aimed to 'recover the virtues that the Labour Party had relinquished ever since the 1950s', he declared to the press. 'We want to look like the social democrats back then: sober, austere, hard-working. We are a Victorian party, without talk of drugs and sex, but with discipline, strictness and dedication.'[62] He connected the rise in public profligacy with a broader loosening of morality. The expansion of social services formed part of what Drees criticized as the 'pleasure-seeking qualities' of the swinging sixties.[63] He proposed to rein in public spending and discipline the trade unions.

It was a political triumph: DS '70 won eight seats and was promptly invited to join the centre-right government of Christian democrat Barend Biesheuvel. When it took office in 1971, however, instilling discipline proved difficult. Negotiations with the unions failed, as the NVV refused to accept a wage freeze while the government raised VAT. The government instead opted for austerity, proposing to cut back public investments by nearly one-quarter, while castigating the 'unreasonable' trade unions for having caused the crisis.[64] But such levels of austerity required more unity than the coalition could muster. Less than a year later, the government collapsed over internal disagreements on where to cut back. Now the initiative fell to the Dutch left. In the election battle that followed, the Labour Party joined forces with two new progressive parties: Democrats 66 (D66) and the left-Christian splinter party Political Party of Radicals (PPR). They had written a shared election manifesto, *Turning Point '72*, which captured the spirit of '68 and the New Left. The manifesto attributed the failure of past governments to stem inflation to their conservative and authoritarian character:

> The fall of the Biesheuvel cabinet is more than an incident. It is the conclusion of a period characterized by a political style in which political decisions were taken over people's heads. It is a signal that the tide of emerging democratization, the doing away with existing power relations, can no longer be ignored. It is the collapse of an order based on

62   NRC Handelsblad, 'DS '70: Met Drees een eigen Zijlstra' [With Drees another Zijlstra], *NRC Handelsblad*, 14 April 1971.

63   Martin van Amerongen, 'De memoires van Willem Drees Jr: "Tegen de genotzuchtige aspecten"', *De Groene Amsterdammer*, 8 December 2000; Drees Jr, *Gespiegeld in de Tijd*.

64   Harmsma, 'Reverting to Restraint'.

the perpetuation of inequality between people. The theme of the 1972 elections is the reduction of this inequality, the realization of democratization, the implementation of essential reforms in our social structure. They can be a turning point and open the way to a NEW POLICY, a NEW POLITICAL SYSTEM, a NEW DEMOCRACY.[65]

The elections that followed led to a left-wing victory, but not a majority. The most left-wing government in Dutch history, with Joop den Uyl as its iconic prime minister, was still dependent on the support of the Christian democrats, who also supplied some of the ministers. This was said to be the government that had brought 'the imagination to power', after the famous '68 slogan. But that buoyant vision soon evaporated in the face of a deepening stagflation crisis.

---

65   PvdA, PPR and D66, *Keerpunt '72: Regeerakkoord van de progressieve drie* (Amsterdam: PvdA/PPR/D66, 1972), 4.

2

The Crisis of Keynesianism (1973–77)

The Den Uyl cabinet had only been in place for a few months when the Yom Kippur War broke out in the Middle East. In protest at Western support for Israel, Arab countries decided on an oil embargo in October 1973. The price of oil quadrupled in a few months, in what came to be known as the first oil crisis.[1] Prime Minister Joop den Uyl addressed the country on radio and television. Sitting in front of a sober grey curtain and wearing thick, horn-rimmed glasses that gleamed under the studio lights, Den Uyl delivered a historic speech. In a sombre tone, he declared:

> the world from before the oil crisis will not return. We will have to permanently adjust to a way of life with a more economical use of raw materials and energy. This will change our way of life. Certain perspectives will fade away. But our existence need not become unhappier for it.[2]

The 1973 oil shock would prove to be a historic turning point, but not for the reasons Den Uyl had anticipated. The oil supply was never really in danger, and the use of raw materials and energy would only further increase in the following decades. The higher price of oil did trigger a global economic shock, however. The roaring engine of economic

---

1   Today, the Suez crisis of 1956 is seen by many as the real 'first oil crisis'.

2   Binnenhof NL, 'Toespraak premier Den Uyl – Oliecrisis 1973 (NOS)', 30 January 2021, youtube.com.

growth that the rich, industrialized nations had come to take for granted began to falter. Inflation, unemployment and stagnation, long considered phenomena from the distant past, now re-emerged. The following years were marked by 'stagflation', the joint occurrence of stagnation and inflation. Against this background, neoliberalism gained momentum, first within the discipline of economics and then in politics. A sign of the times was that the neoliberal economist Friedrich Hayek won the Nobel Memorial Prize in Economic Sciences in 1974, and his colleague Milton Friedman was accorded the same privilege in 1976.[3]

In 'These Times Shall Not Return', a speech given at the end of his premiership, Den Uyl looked back and concluded that the 1973 oil crisis had marked 'the end of an era'.[4] It heralded the end of the 'golden age' of capitalism, the post-war period of heady economic growth. Some historians have portrayed 1973 as the Waterloo of Keynesianism, but that is getting ahead of ourselves.[5] For the actors involved, it was far from clear what political conclusions could be drawn from this rupture. In the conventional view on the Dutch 1970s, the folds of history have often been smoothed out, and the idea has retroactively emerged that there was great unanimity on the cause of the crisis. 'We all knew what was wrong: too much government, too little individual freedom,' said Chris van Veen, the leader of the largest Dutch employer's federation

---

3   What is commonly referred to in the press as the 'Nobel Prize in Economics' is not an actual Nobel Prize funded from Alfred Nobel's estate but a prize awarded by the Swedish central bank that was added later under the name 'Sveriges Riksbank Prize in Economic Sciences in Memory of Alfred Nobel'. The underlying motivation was to enhance the prestige of economic science to better safeguard the autonomy of central banks. The prize became an important element in the rise of free market thinking. No fewer than eight MPS members would win the 'Nobel Prize in Economics': Friedrich von Hayek (1974); Milton Friedman (1976), George Stigler (1982), James Buchanan (1986), Maurice Allais (1988), Ronald Coase (1991), Gary Becker (1992) and Vernon Smith (2002). Peter Nobel, great-grandson of Alfred Nobel's brother Ludvig, called the prize a 'PR coup', designed to give profit maximization a respectable appearance. Philip Mirowski, 'The Neoliberal Ersatz Nobel Prize', in Dieter Plehwe, Quinn Slobodian and Philip Mirowski, eds, *Nine Lives of Neoliberalism* (London: Verso, 2020), 219.

4   Joop den Uyl, 'Die tijd komt nooit meer terug', in *Inzicht en uitzicht: Opstellen over economie en politiek* (Amsterdam: Bakker, 1978), 204–15.

5   See, for example, Herman de Liagre Böhl, 'Consensus en polarisatie: Spanningen in de verzorgingsstaat, 1945–1990', in *Land van kleine gebaren. Een politieke geschiedenis van Nederland 1780–1990* (Amsterdam: Boom, 2013), 324.

(VNO), of the crisis.[6] The only thing lacking, in his view, was the political courage to take unpopular decisions. The turn to the market was thus given an aura of inevitability – as if the political response was already contained in the crisis itself.

By extension, Den Uyl's Keynesian views have frequently been dismissed as a historical anachronism. There is an oft-cited anecdote from Fons van der Stee, who shortly served as secretary of state for finance in 1973. The story goes that he gently informed the social democratic finance minister, Wim Duisenberg, that he harboured the suspicion that 'Joop [Den Uyl], in terms of economic theory [was] ten, fifteen years behind'. To which Duisenberg responded by banging his fist on the table, replying: 'What, are you completely crazy! He's at least thirty years behind!'[7] Keynesian economists like Den Uyl, this implied, were stuck in the 1930s.

This has become part of the common perception of the crisis of the 1970s – as if it were only a question of bringing one's economic views 'back up to date'. Temporal concepts such as 'ahead' and 'behind' do not do justice to the situation, however. They implicitly assume that a new economic consensus existed in the 1970s that had not nearly arrived by then. Leading institutions such as the OECD, the IMF and the European Council were still working within a largely Keynesian framework, and even the right-wing US President Richard Nixon stated in 1971 that he was now 'in an economic sense, a Keynesian'.[8] Seen in this light, Den Uyl really was an economist of his time.

In reality, a fundamental controversy arose among economists and politicians worldwide over the correct interpretation of the crisis. It is a well-known fact that an economic crisis is often accompanied by a crisis in economic thinking. In a crisis, the macro-economic models that normally enable policymakers to look ahead and make economic trade-offs cease to make sense. A fundamental economic uncertainty takes hold of society, and policies are decided on in a thick fog. Nobody can say with certainty what the economic effect of a certain policy measure

---

6   Chris Van Veen, 'Meer markt, minder overheid: Terug naar de onderneming', in A. Knoester, ed., *Lessen uit het verleden: 125 jaar Vereniging voor de Staathuishoudkunde* (Leiden: Stenfert-Kroese, 1987), 289.

7   Peter Bootsma and Willem Breedveld, *De verbeelding aan de macht: Het kabinet-Den Uyl 1973–1977* (The Hague: SDU Uitgevers, 1999), 117.

8   Reuters, 'Nixon Reportedly Says He Is Now a Keynesian', *New York Times*, 7 January 1971.

will be, whether the crisis is cyclical or structural, whether unemployment is permanent or whether recovery is at hand. This is how it was in the 1970s. Den Uyl observed, in retrospect, that 'stagnation in the economy and deadlock in economic thinking go hand in hand'.[9] Referring to the British post-Keynesian economist Joan Robinson, Den Uyl spoke of a 'second crisis of economic theory', following the crisis of the interwar period that had ushered in the Keynesian revolution.[10]

A crisis requires a theory: what exactly the economic crisis is, and what caused it, is never a foregone conclusion.[11] There is a struggle between opposing socioeconomic coalitions, which come up with their own analyses and solutions. A coalition first has to make its interpretation of the crisis dominant before a policy response can be hashed out. History shows that this goes hand in hand with the development of a 'simplifying ideology' that can convince wider sections of the population of the remedy offered.[12] Two interpretations of the stagflation crisis vied for precedence: one that located the crisis in the market economy and saw increased planning as the solution, and one that focused on the state and saw the free market as the solution. The global ideological polarization of the 1970s was the result of this struggle.[13] The Netherlands was certainly no exception to that trend.

Two Perspectives on the Stagflation Crisis

On one side stood the Keynesian coalition, which saw in the crisis a validation of its perspective. Stagflation was not an entirely new

---

9   Den Uyl, 'Die tijd komt nooit meer terug', 204.

10   Robinson's complaint was that economists had not satisfactorily solved the first crisis (the unemployment problem), while a second crisis now made itself felt. Economists had never thought about the quality of economic growth, and externalities on issues such as the environment, global inequality and militarism. Joan Robinson, 'The Second Crisis of Economic Theory', *American Economic Review* 62, no. 2 (1972): 1–10; Mary Wrenn, James Ronald Stanfield and Michael Carroll, 'Galbraith and Robinson's Second Crisis of Economic Theory', *Journal of Economic Issues* 42, no. 1 (1 March 2008): 5–11.

11   Mark Blyth, *Great Transformations: Economic Ideas and Institutional Change in the Twentieth Century* (Cambridge: Cambridge University Press, 2002), 9–10.

12   Colin Hay, 'Narrating Crisis: The Discursive Construction of the "Winter of Discontent"', *Sociology* 30, no. 2 (1 May 1996): 253–77.

13   Duco Hellema, *The Global 1970s: Radicalism, Reform, and Crisis* (London: Routledge, 2018).

phenomenon. The first signs were already visible in the late 1960s. As a concrete consequence of the wage explosions, inflation and unemployment had started to rise together. Labour costs had risen precipitously, and Dutch post-war industries built on low wages (textiles, leather, shipbuilding) were in trouble. All this had not gone unnoticed on the left. The *Turning Point '72* manifesto with which the left parties went into the 1972 elections has been remembered mainly for its immaterial themes: the idea of democratization and the final reckoning with the authoritarian politics of the 1950s.[14] But that agenda was intertwined with an economic programme that has since been somewhat forgotten. For instance, the fight against stagflation is the very first theme mentioned in *Turning Point*:

> Successive governments of a conservative nature have failed to respond to the issues of the day: continuing inflation, rising unemployment, the challenge of environmental issues, inequality of incomes, wealth, democratic participation, etc. The root cause of this failure is that effective public policies cannot be implemented unless one involves the affected people in developing them.[15]

The authors of *Turning Point* believed that a left-wing government held better cards to fight stagflation because it enjoyed the trust of the trade unions and had something concrete to offer them.[16] The text referred to a new 'social contract'.[17] In exchange for wage moderation, public services and workers' control would be expanded through the strengthening of works councils and the introduction of wage-earner funds. This agenda was thus built on the social-wage strategy and the ideas of John Kenneth Galbraith. Wage moderation was intended to create room for the expansion of undervalued public services, thereby increasing quality of life. As Den Uyl proclaimed in the government statement: 'For socio-economic policy, [this means] slowing down the growth of private consumption in order thereby to create space for improving the housing

---

14 Henk te Velde, *Stijlen van leiderschap: Persoon en politiek van Thorbecke tot Den Uyl* (Amsterdam: Wereldbibliotheek, 2002), 208.

15 PvdA, PPR and D66, *Keerpunt '72*, 4.

16 Wil Albeda, 'Loonvorming in de periode van neergang tot beginnend herstel 1973–1987', in Knoester, *Lessen uit het verleden*, 305–18.

17 PvdA, PPR and D66, *Keerpunt '72*, 23.

and living environment.'[18] The problematic of the oil crisis fitted well into this thinking. Den Uyl's statement that 'our existence need not become unhappier for it' was entirely in the spirit of Galbraith.

Keynesianism, long half-heartedly professed in the Netherlands, grew into an explicit policy philosophy under Den Uyl. Supporters of this thinking were to be found among a new generation of economists, among social democrats and progressive Christian democrats, among trade unions and the new social movements. Left-leaning social democrats such as Willy Brandt, Bruno Kreisky and Olaf Palme acted as international standard-bearers.[19] In their view, the moderate Keynesian order that had emerged in the mid-1960s had become unsustainable. The government had to start intervening more actively in wages and prices, providing housing, redistributing labour, democratising the workplace and guiding investment decisions so that they would serve the community. In short, in response to the oil crisis, a new type of economic planning would have to emerge, in line with the New Left's democratization agenda.

Another major influence on progressive thinking in the 1970s was *The Limits to Growth*, the influential Club of Rome report.[20] Using the latest in computer modelling, a team of scientists from the Massachusetts Institute of Technology had calculated how long existing resource stocks would last, given the exponential growth of the economy and population. The report predicted that, if nothing was done to make the economy more sustainable, the economic system would reach its limits in the second half of the twenty-first century due to resource depletion. In the Netherlands, this message landed like a bomb: it was front-page news before the report was even published. 'Disaster Threatens World', warned the newspaper *NRC Handelsblad* in a headline, after seeing a draft version of the report in August 1971.[21] The Dutch paperback edition of

18   Frans Becker, 'De jaren 1970–1994', in Maarten Brinkman, Madelon de Keizer and Maarten van Rossem, eds, *Honderd jaar sociaal-democratie in Nederland 1894–1994* (Amsterdam: Bert Bakker, 1994), 249.

19   See Willy Brandt, Bruno Kreisky and Olof Palme, *La social-démocratie et l'avenir* (Paris: Gallimard, 1976). See also Adam Przeworski, 'Revolution, Reformism, and Resignation', in Maya Adereth, ed., *Market Economy, Market Society: Interviews and Essays on the Decline of European Social Democracy* (New York: Phenomenal World, 2021), 16–31.

20   Donalla Meadows, Jorgen Randers and William Behrens, *The Limits to Growth: A Report for The Club of Rome's Project on the Predicament of Mankind* (London: Pan, 1972).

21   Arie de Kool, 'Ramp bedreigt wereld' [Disaster threatens world], *NRC Handelsblad*, 31 August 1971.

the report eventually sold 350,000 copies. In progressive circles, the recent decline in economic growth was read through the lens of the Club of Rome report. As *Turning Point* explained,

> The time of production for the sake of production is definitely over. An economic growth that leads to more and more goods that have to be renewed ever faster, to more cars on ever bigger roads, involves an ever-greater assault on our limited space and environment. At the same time, resources are at risk.[22]

Turning Point and the policies of the Den Uyl government have often been described as offshoots of the economic optimism of the 1960s. The oil crisis then brought a change of sentiment, when 'suddenly it appears that trees don't grow to the sky'.[23] But the radicalism of Den Uyl's programme was more a consequence of growing doubts about the sustainability of economic growth. It explains the newfound importance of planning. The loss of employment had to be absorbed by increased redistribution and expansion of the public sector. And because the free market did not correctly price all sorts of things – from public services to the environment – it was up to the government to steer investments in a social and sustainable direction. This effort would take shape under the Den Uyl government in the form of the Selective Growth policy and the Investment Account Act (WIR) – an attempt to use targeted subsidies to steer private investments in the direction of desired social goals (employment, innovation, environment, regional development).

It is not that the left's ambitions waned in response to 1973, as some have argued.[24] Rather, these aspirations only assumed full force in response to the crisis.[25] Not for nothing did the industrial sector union of the Dutch Trade Union Confederation (FNV) publish a controversial pamphlet in 1974, in which the union called for a socialist society.[26] Den Uyl made a similar gesture in a renowned lecture at the annual meeting of the Christian employers' association. In exchange for wage

---

22   PvdA, D66 and PPR, *Keerpunt '72*, 6.

23   Bootsma and Breedveld, *De verbeelding aan de macht*, 129.

24   De Liagre Böhl, 'Consensus en polarisatie'.

25   On this point, see Duco Hellema, *Nederland en de jaren zeventig* (Amsterdam: Boom, 2012), 11–21.

26   Industriebond FNV, *Fijn is anders* (Amsterdam: Industriebond FNV, 1974).

moderation, he demanded 'workers' control over investment decisions', inspired by the Swedish Meidner Plan. Den Uyl presented this as an important step in the transition to socialism: an arrangement 'in which those who are employed in different ranks of the production process jointly organize capital and the opposition between employers and workers is overcome'.[27]

At the same time, the radicalism of Den Uyl's policies should not be exaggerated. Because the left-wing parties fell short of a majority and were dependent on the support of Christian democratic parties, political rhetoric often diverged from policy realities. Ruud Lubbers, the Catholic minister of economic affairs under Den Uyl, turned the public-invest-ment strategy into a generous and almost unconditional subsidy spree from which the largest Dutch corporations benefited most. A senior offi-cial at Economic Affairs later concluded that the WIR 'had been given a business-friendly from'.[28] Lubbers also described it as the task of Economic Affairs to 'resist the anti-growth virus stemming from the Club of Rome ideas'.[29] Den Uyl himself had already stated in his employers' lecture that 'Lubbers comes from the North Pole, and I come from the South Pole, and even so, we're content to shake hands at the equator'.[30]

Still, Den Uyl's radical programme explains some of the ferocity of the response. At the other end of the political spectrum stood the market-oriented coalition, which saw the state not as the solution but rather as the main culprit: the government, with its spending frenzy, was eroding profits and fuelling inflation. The main exponent of this view in the Netherlands was Jelle Zijlstra, former Christian democratic minister of finance and economic affairs and then president of the Dutch Central Bank. Whereas Den Uyl saw the expansion of collective provisions as a prerequisite to getting the unions to agree to wage moderation, Zijlstra asserted that the causal relationship was in the opposite direction. In the 1973 annual report of the Dutch Central Bank, Zijlstra argued that a

27   Joop den Uyl, 'Socialisme en vrije ondernemingsgewijze productie', in *Inzicht en uitzicht*, 195.

28   Frans Rutten, *Zeven kabinetten wijzer: de nieuwe zakelijkheid bij het economis-che beleid* (Groningen: Wolters-Noordhoff, 1993), 25.

29   Ruud Lubbers, 'De economische politiek in Nederland vanaf de jaren '60', in Jarig van Sinderen, ed., *Het sociaal-economisch beleid in de tweede helft van de twintigste eeuw* (Groningen: Wolters-Noordhoff, 1990), 17.

30   Den Uyl, 'Socialisme en vrije ondernemingsgewijze productie', 196.

higher tax burden would in turn trigger higher wage demands, which would come at the expense of profits and investment and therefore employment.[31] It was a classic supply-side view: the collective sector had to be cut back to give business more breathing space.

Consequently, the close connection that the Den Uyl government had with the trade unions was not seen as a benefit but rather as a major source of concern. The fear was that the radicalizing trade union movement would secure too much influence, further driving up wages and public spending. Would Den Uyl be able to halt rising inflation, VVD leader Hans Wiegel wondered following the government policy statement, or would wage negotiations under Den Uyl's leadership resort to 'just listening to a diktat?'[32] DS '70 leader Willem Drees warned in *De Telegraaf* that Den Uyl was opening the floodgates to a 'tidal wave of pressure'.[33] The push for democratization that was such an integral part of progressive politics in that period was seen in a very different light on the right. Under the influence of public choice theory, economist and politicians saw politics as increasingly controlled by pressure groups. As a result, the government risked losing power over public spending, and the country was fast becoming ungovernable.

This analysis could be heard among employers, right-wing politicians such as the Christian democrat Dries van Agt and the right-wing liberal Hans Wiegel, of the VVD, and among economic policy-makers in the ministries and the central bank. The solution they identified was less state intervention and regulation: the market mechanism had to be restored. Internationally, Milton Friedman and his Chicago school of economics emerged as the main intellectual exponents of this vision. Like the left, this camp wanted a fundamental restructuring of the economic order. The economic role of the state and the power of the labour movement had to be fundamentally reduced, so as to restore the eroding profits of business. Some Dutch economists and politicians even argued that Den Uyl's policies threatened to result in totalitarianism.

---

31   Jelle Zijlstra, *Gematigd monetarisme: 14 jaarverslagen van De Nederlandsche Bank* (Leiden: Stenfert Kroese, 1985), 197.

32   Parliamentary records, HTK, 1972–1973, 28 May 1973, 1580.

33   Edo Brandt and Kees van der Wild, 'Den Uyl had pressiegroepen kunnen intomen' [Den Uyl could have contained pressure groups], *De Telegraaf*, 20 October 1973, 51.

The Peak of the Keynesian Wave

'Keynes squared' – that is how the Den Uyl government has gone down in history.[34] But this reputation is partly due to the oil crisis. Initially, the Den Uyl cabinet did not intend to pursue a strongly expansionist policy.[35] The Dutch parliament even insisted on spending cuts. Soon after the government took office, central bank president Jelle Zijlstra called for 'shock therapy' to bring inflation down. This was to be implemented through a rigid price freeze, wage moderation and a revaluation of the guilder. Only when this policy was well and truly in place could 'some expansion of spending take place to combat unemployment'.[36] In this stance, Zijlstra was supported by the Ministries of Economic Affairs (Lubbers) and Finance (Duisenberg), as well as a significant part of the Dutch parliament.

But the oil crisis changed everything. Experts worldwide soon realized that the crisis would cause a major drop in demand. As a result of the higher oil prices, a lot of capital accumulated in the oil-producing countries. Since those countries could not possibly spend all that money immediately, large amounts of capital were effectively withdrawn from the global economy. Adding a bout of austerity on top of that could trigger a deflationary spiral. The international response to the crisis therefore took the form of an expansionary policy: governments that had the ability to do so were encouraged to substantially increase public spending to maintain effective demand. The Netherlands, with its gas exports and balance-of-payments surplus, was one of the few countries that had the fiscal space to do so. 'The IMF and the OECD called on the Netherlands and Germany to expand,' recalls the senior finance official and later central bank director Nout Wellink. 'They begged us to increase our budget. Otherwise, the world economy would flatline.'[37] In this way the oil crisis 'again gave a wide berth to Keynesian, countercyclical thinking', recalled then–Minister of Economic Affairs Ruud Lubbers.[38]

---

34   Bruno de Haas and Cees van Lotringen, *Wim Duisenberg: Van Friese volksjongen tot Mr. Euro* (Amsterdam: Business Contact, 2003), 90.

35   Jonne Harmsma, 'Reverting to Restraint: A Keynesian Intermezzo and Neoliberalism in the Netherlands (1971–1977)', *Contemporary European History*, 12 July 2023, 1–17.

36   Jonne Harmsma, *Jelle zal wel zien: Jelle Zijlstra, een eigenzinnig leven tussen politiek en economie* (Amsterdam: Prometheus, 2018), 327.

37   De Haas and Lotringen, *Wim Duisenberg*, 84–5.

38   Lubbers, 'De economische politiek in Nederland vanaf de jaren '60', 17.

When the Den Uyl cabinet decided to embark on an ambitious stimulus policy in the spring of 1974, it was able to count on widespread support. Some 3.5 billion guilders (at the time, roughly $1.5 billion) was spent to protect purchasing power and employment, followed by a similar amount the following year.[39] This expansionary response was combined with controls on wages and prices. Initially, Den Uyl's crisis policy was moderately successful.[40] Even the top civil servant at the Ministry of Economic Affairs, Frans Rutten – a declared opponent of Keynesian cyclical policies – praised 'the strong cyclical policy in 1974–1975' that had helped the Netherlands weather the crisis better than nearby countries.[41] The assessment of Den Uyl's main opponent – central bank chief Zijlstra – was also positive, although he had hoped for more tax relief and less spending.[42]

The Dutch economy recovered somewhat, and the nightmare scenario of a global crash ebbed away. However, in 1975 it became increasingly clear that the stagflation crisis was not just a momentary pause, after which the old growth pattern of the 1950s and 1960s would resume. The crisis turned out to be structural: a significant part of industrial employment was steadily moving away from advanced economies as a result of automation and competition from emerging industrial countries. Private investment slumped. Politics had long revolved around how to share the spoils of growth; now parties haggled over who would have to cut back.

The new 'social contract' proposed by the Den Uyl government in response to the crisis was blocked from two sides. Dutch business vehemently opposed wage-earner funds and the strengthening of works councils. Business leaders mobilized openly against the left-wing government. The president of the Employer's Federation VNO, Chris van Veen, warned that the reforms were 'completely irreconcilable with the continued existence of the free enterprise system'. In a famous full-page advertisement in the major Dutch newspapers, VNO sounded the

---

39   Nout Wellink, 'De ontwikkelingen in de jaren zeventig en tachtig en enkele daaruit te trekken lessen', in Knoester, *Lessen uit het verleden*, 333–65.

40   Later on it would increasingly be seen as a fiasco. It is an image that was propagated above all by VVD leader Hans Wiegel. He presented himself as a 'clearer of debris' after the Den Uyl cabinet. However, the subsequent Van Agt/Wiegel cabinet fared worse in terms of fiscal prudence. See Anthonie Knoester, *Economische politiek in Nederland* (Leiden: Stenfert Kroese, 1989), 147–53.

41   Rutten, *Zeven kabinetten wijzer*, 25.

42   Zijlstra, *Gematigd monetarisme*, 217.

alarm about the state of Dutch business.[43] It was followed shortly by 'The letter from the nine', in which the CEOs of the nine largest Dutch multinationals lambasted the policies of the Den Uyl government. They accused the cabinet of pursuing social change based on 'a one-sided and dogmatic vision', breaking the 'vital laws' of capitalism.[44] The wage-earner funds and the strengthened works councils were obstructed by fierce opposition from both employers and the Christian parties.

From the other side, the trade unions were not eager to moderate wages. As a result of high inflation and militant activism among members, the union leadership was under great pressure to deliver wage increases. The share of national income that went to labour – the wage share – had risen to record heights in the second half of the seventies. Left-wing economists accused the unions of making any left-wing politics practically impossible by their inflationary wage demands.

In a December 1974 column titled 'Capitalist Labour Movement', the economist and social democratic politician Hans van der Doel wrote that, although the powerful industrial-sector union FNV advocated 'socialism' in its brochures, its dogged pursuit of wage increases only strengthened capitalist consumer society. As result of the inflationary environment, Van der Doel noted that the narrow trade union focus on wages and private purchasing power 'necessarily leads to a downward pressure on our country's public sector'.[45] In this way, the social wage strategy was actively undermined. In a memorable phrase, Van der Doel called it 'beefsteak socialism': a leftist politics that reduced emancipation to material gain. Ironically, the communists within the trade union movement were the most ardent supporters of that approach.[46]

After failing to achieve an agreement with the unions, Den Uyl implemented measures to keep down wages, but they proved insufficient to compensate for the eroding profits of Dutch business. The once warm relationship between the unions and the Den Uyl government quickly

43   The full-page advertisement, titled 'Waar het om gaat' [What is at stake] was published in *De Telegraaf, Trouw* and *De Volkskrant*, on 7 October 1975.

44   'Open brief van bezorgde ondernemingsleiders' [Open letter from concerned business leaders], *NRC Handelsblad*, 13 January 1976.

45   Hans van der Doel, *Lastig links: Socialistische dilemma's* (Utrecht: Spectrum, 1976), 18.

46   Hans van der Doel, *Het biefstuk-socialisme en de economie* (Utrecht: Spectrum, 1978).

cooled. The unions were not fundamentally against government imposi-
tion of wage restraint, but the loss of union influence had to be compensated.[47] When wage-earner funds and works councils were blocked, the
unions had little to offer to their members in exchange for wage restraint.

As a result, major fissures opened up in the Keynesian coalition. The
left wanted to expand the public sector and curtail private wealth, while
the right wanted the opposite. The result was a stalemate. 'Society does not
know how to choose between maintaining collective provision, on the
one hand, and maintaining private wealth on the other,' observed an
employer's brochure looking back on the 1970s.[48] Meanwhile, internationally, the critique of Keynesian economics gathered pace. The widely
felt need for an expansionary response to the oil crisis had masked a rising
scepticism towards Keynesian orthodoxy. So it came to pass that, at the
very top of the Keynesian wave in the Netherlands, the collapse set in.

The Monetarist Counter-Revolution

Internationally, a palace revolution was taking place in economic science,
in which the neoliberal economists involved in the Mont Pelerin Society
played a key role. It was the American economist Milton Friedman, along
with his kindred spirits in the Chicago school of economics, who led the
charge. In 1976, the *Financial Times* called Friedman 'undoubtedly the
most influential contemporary economist'.[49] He had taken over the mantle
from continental European neoliberals Friedrich Hayek and Wilhelm
Röpke and became the global figurehead of the neoliberal movement in
the 1970s. This was part of a larger shift within the network, as the
Americans assumed the initiative, and went hand in hand with the
increasing global dominance of American economic science.

In the late 1960s, Friedman had developed a leading critique of a
technical element of Keynesian policy: the Phillips curve.[50] This was the

---

47   Van Zweeden, 'Vakbeweging gefrustreerd door te geringe ruimte' [Trade union
movement frustrated by lack of options], *NRC Handelsblad*, 6 August 1976.

48   Simon Keyer, *De macht van de onmacht: Tien jaar om het zekerheidsdenken te
doorbreken en tot vernieuwing te komen* (Assen: Van Gorcum, 1984).

49   'The Timeliness of Milton Friedman', *Financial Times*, 15 October 1976.

50   Milton Friedman, 'The Role of Monetary Policy', *American Economic Review* 58,
no. 1 (1 March 1968): 1–17.

idea that there was an inverse relationship between inflation and unemployment. To stimulate the economy and fight unemployment, policymakers could pursue an expansionary monetary policy, at the cost of rising inflation. Conversely, inflation could be reduced at the cost of rising unemployment. For politicians the choice was clear: either protect the most vulnerable from unemployment, or protect the assets of the wealthiest citizens from being eroded by inflation. Policymakers generally took a middle course, accepting a certain level of inflation to keep unemployment relatively low.

Friedman recognized that an expansionary policy could boost employment and economic growth. But he argued that it only worked in the short term, by creating the false impression that the economy itself was growing, and not just the money supply. While people could be fooled for a while, at some point they would realize that the policy was inflationary. They then adjusted their expectations: trade unions would demand higher wages to compensate for inflation, and companies would refrain from hiring workers or making new investments. Increasingly expansionary policies were needed to achieve the same effect, resulting in an inflationary spiral. Contrary to the Phillips curve, inflation and unemployment would rise simultaneously. As early as the late 1960s, Friedman had an analysis of the stagflation crisis to hand.

He sought the solution in monetarism, a school of economic thought that attributes central importance to the money supply. According to the monetarists, the best way to fight inflation was to have fixed targets for how much money central banks put into circulation. That way, politicians could no longer finance deficits by printing money. This implied a big cut in public spending and meant that the economic crisis would be left to run its course. Unlike the Keynesians, monetarists believed in the ability of markets to self-correct. The crisis would deepen, unemployment would go up, and wages would fall. This would stamp out inflationary expectations, after which a new market equilibrium would emerge. For this reason, monetarists held, price stability rather than employment should be the overriding priority of economic policy, as this formed the basic prerequisite for a well-functioning economy. Whereas, in 1965, the image of John Maynard Keynes had still graced the cover of *Time*, by the end of 1969 it was Milton Friedman's turn.[51]

---

51   'Will There Be a Recession?', *Time*, 19 December 1969.

He proudly proclaimed a monetarist 'counter-revolution', in reaction to the Keynesian revolution of the 1930s.[52]

For politicians, monetarism was not a popular message to deliver to voters. Nevertheless, as the severity of the stagflation crisis increased, more and more took up Friedman's argument. In his 1976 Nobel Memorial Prize lecture, Friedman argued that state intervention did not solve the stagflation crisis but was in fact its main cause. Continuous attempts to control wages and prices were undermining the price mechanism of the free market. Two alternative trajectories now lay ahead: either a break with existing interventionist policies and a restoration of the market mechanism, or the 'catastrophe' of hyperinflation and 'radical political change'. He pointed to the Weimar Republic and the more recent example of Chile under the socialist Salvador Allende.[53]

The reference to Chile was striking. General Augusto Pinochet had come to power there violently in September 1973 and established a bloody military dictatorship. Friedman himself had a not insignificant role in this. Indeed, the economic policies Pinochet would roll out had been developed by Chilean economists who had been trained by Friedman and his colleagues in the Chicago school: the famous 'Chicago Boys'.[54]

Initially, Pinochet had his doubts about the free market recipes advocated by the Chicago Boys. The Chilean economy was in bad shape, and inflation had risen to an unprecedented 375 per cent. In March 1975, Milton Friedman and his Chicago colleague Arnold Harberger flew to Chile for a six-day visit, to champion the economic plan of their former students. They gave a series of lectures and spoke privately to General Pinochet. Friedman plugged the plan as 'shock therapy': to fight runaway inflation, the central bank's money supply had to be reined in.[55] Government spending was to be cut by 25 per cent in six months, wage and price policies abolished, all state-owned companies privatized, tens

52 Milton Friedman, *The Counter-Revolution in Monetary Theory: Wincott Memorial Lecture*, Occasional Paper 33 (London: Institute of Economic Affairs, 1970).

53 Milton Friedman, *Inflation and Unemployment: The New Dimension of Politics – The 1976 Alfred Nobel Memorial Lecture*, Occasional Paper 51 (London: Institute of Economic Affairs, 1976), 31.

54 See Juan Gabriel Valdés, *Pinochet's Economists: The Chicago School of Economics in Chile* (Cambridge: Cambridge University Press, 1995).

55 See Sebastian Edwards and Leonidas Montes, 'Milton Friedman in Chile: Shock Therapy, Economic Freedom, and Exchange Rates', *Journal of the History of Economic Thought* 42, no. 1 (2020): 105–32.

of thousands of civil servants fired, and capital markets deregulated. They managed to convince Pinochet of the plan. Friedman later wrote in his memoirs that 'shock therapy had a positive appeal' to the dictator.[56]

One of the Chicago Boys was appointed finance minister, and shock therapy was implemented almost to the letter. The Chilean economy contracted by 13 per cent, and purchasing power plummeted by 40 per cent, while unemployment skyrocketed. But in 1978 the Chilean economy would recover strongly, growing by as much as 36 per cent in three years. This later turned out to be the product of a speculative bubble. For that three-year period, however, Chile was the mecca of neoliberals. Pinochet would even name Chile's new 1980 constitution after Friedrich Hayek's book *The Constitution of Liberty*. This did not come out of the blue: Hayek had visited Pinochet and was supportive of the regime.[57] He defended this 'liberal dictatorship' in an opinion piece in *The Times*, writing that he 'could not find a person in much maligned Chile who did not believe that freedom was much greater under Pinochet than under Allende'.[58] Of course, he had not spoken with the tens of thousands of tortured and executed opponents of the regime.

Great controversy arose over Friedman's involvement in the Pinochet regime. Protesting students disrupted Friedman's Nobel Memorial Prize ceremony in Oslo.[59] Friedman countered by arguing that Chile was a warning to the world: what Allende had brought upon the country with his socialist policies was illustrative of what awaited the world if politicians did not change course. He had elaborated this argument in a lecture at the Catholic University of Santiago, during his 1975 visit to Pinochet's Chile. He published the lecture the following year under the title 'The Line We Dare Not Cross'.

Taking his cue from Hayek's classic *The Road to Serfdom* (in which the rise of Nazism was traced to the expansion of the German welfare state), Friedman argued that the dictatorship in Chile was 'the end result of an

---

56   Milton Friedman and Rose D. Friedman, *Two Lucky People: Memoirs* (Chicago: University of Chicago Press, 1999), 399.

57   Andrew Farrant, Edward McPhail and Sebastian Berger, 'Preventing the "Abuses" of Democracy: Hayek, the "Military Usurper" and Transitional Dictatorship in Chile?', *American Journal of Economics and Sociology* 71, no. 3 (2012): 513–38.

58   Friedrich Hayek, 'Freedom of Choice', *The Times*, 3 August 1978.

59   Bernard Weinraub, 'Friedman, in Nobel Lecture, Challenges a Tradition', *New York Times*, 14 December 1976.

expansion of the role of government in people's lives'.[60] It had begun with far-reaching state intervention under the socialist Allende, which caused entrepreneurs to fear the prospect of a leftist dictatorship. Pinochet's military coup was a response to that threat. The broader lesson to be drawn from this, Friedman told his Chilean audience, was that, at a certain level of state intervention in the economy, a tipping point is reached, causing a country to descend irrevocably into dictatorship. This threshold was somewhere between 40 and 60 per cent of national income. This theory circulated more broadly among economists at the time and became known as the 'overload thesis'.[61] In Friedman's view, Britain was also on the verge of losing its political freedom.

In the Netherlands, where economists are expected to be technocratic and studiously apolitical figures, the news of Friedman's Nobel Memorial Prize nomination was received with little sympathy. 'Especially in Europe, Friedman and co. are considered reactionaries,' remarked the liberal newspaper *NRC Handelsblad*.[62] Others simply could not understand the nomination at all; one journalist wrote: 'Immediately after the '73 coup, the US monetarist Milton Friedman came to the rescue of the junta with economic "shock therapy". Three years later, Chile has 341 per cent inflation, rapidly rising infant mortality and rampant malnutrition. And Friedman was awarded the Nobel Prize for economics last week.'[63] In more moderate form, however, the 'monetary counter-revolution' would also take hold in the Netherlands, where strikingly similar messages of doom about a dictatorial welfare state were making inroads.

Prophecies of Doom

It is exaggerated to speak of a 'monetarist counter-revolution' in the Netherlands. After all, monetarism had never gone out of fashion there.

---

60   For the original lecture, see Milton Friedman, 'The Fragility of Freedom', *BYU Studies Quarterly* 16, no. 4 (1 October 1976): 562. It was later published as Milton Friedman, 'The Line We Dare Not Cross', *Encounter*, November 1976.

61   See Anthony H. Birch, 'Overload, Ungovernability and Delegitimation: The Theories and the British Case', *British Journal of Political Science* 14, no. 2 (1984): 135–60.

62   'Geldinvloed overheerst in Friedmans theorieën' [Role of money dominates Friedman's theories], *NRC Handelsblad*, 15 October 1976.

63   'Milton Friedmans Chileense recept' [Milton Friedman's Chilean recipe], *Haagse Post*, 21 October 1976.

The Dutch Central Bank had developed its own tradition of monetarist thinking ever since the 1930s.[64] In the 1970s, central bank president Jelle Zijlstra was the main representative of this school of thought. What both Dutch and Anglo-American traditions of monetarism had in common is that they emphasized the importance of the money supply for the economy. If too much money circulated, inflation caused 'ungovernability and disruption in state and society'.[65] Both variants were therefore opposed to the Keynesian perspective, in which inflation was not an intolerable problem and the printing of money was considered an important stopgap measure in times of crisis. However, there were also important differences between the two strands. Whereas Friedman argued that 'only money matters' (inflation was solely a monetary phenomenon that could solely be combated by monetary means), Zijlstra argued that managing the money supply was only one pillar of sound economic policy, alongside fiscal and wage policies. Dutch monetarism was thus less radically opposed to government intervention. For this reason, Zijlstra described the Dutch tradition as 'moderate monetarism'.[66]

Despite these differences, Zijlstra saw an ally in Friedman and welcomed his 'counter-revolution'. The Dutch Central Bank had 'anxiously observed the neglect of the money supply' and welcomed 'the revived interest in monetary thinking', Zijlstra wrote in the 1976 annual report of the Dutch Central Bank.[67] Once the worst economic shocks of the oil crisis had passed, Zijlstra resumed his campaign for more restrictive policies. In a fire-and-brimstone sermon at the Bilderberg conference in Turkey in 1975, he warned that the world was heading towards the stage of 'completed inflation', with inflation rates above 10 per cent. If that happened, the danger of 'the greatest dictatorship' loomed.[68] Zijlstra pleaded for a shift from Keynesian demand stimulus to a supply-side policy, aimed at recovery of business profitability in the long term. In his view, this could only happen through policies that would deepen the crisis in the short term: by cutting government spending, curbing

---

64   Martin Fase, 'The Rise and Demise of Dutch Monetarism; or, the Schumpeter-Koopmans-Holtrop Connection', *History of Political Economy* 26, no. 1 (1 March 1994): 21–38.

65   Zijlstra, *Gematigd monetarisme*, 19.

66   Ibid., 27.

67   Ibid., 253.

68   Harmsma, *Jelle zal wel zien*, 337.

the money supply and deliberately letting unemployment rise, inflation could be driven out of the system and profits restored.[69]

Another key element of the shift in economic thinking was a new model from the Central Planning Bureau (CPB), the country's most influential economic think-tank and forecasting agency. Since the 1950s, the CPB's macroeconomic models had emerged as a central tool in economic policy. Not only did the CPB models make it possible to estimate the economic effects of policies, at a more basic level they determined how politicians and policymakers 'saw' the economy. 'These models are so to say in the back of the mind while preparing policy', wrote the head of the Ministry of Economic Affairs, Frans Rutten.[70] As we have seen, concerns about rising inflation, high wages and growing government spending had existed since the late 1960s – though the CPB had struggled to incorporate these concerns into its models. As a result, opponents of expansionary policies failed to get their arguments taken seriously.[71]

In response to these concerns, the CPB developed a new model, which analysed the Dutch economy in a different way. This so-called VINTAF model assumed that, due to high wage levels, companies tended to invest more in machinery, to save on labour costs.[72] In other words, high wages and high taxes encouraged businesses to replace existing technology faster, which in turn led to more unemployment. The model was able to explain the evolution of Dutch unemployment from the 1960s onwards. It shifted the focus to the supply side of the economy and identified high labour costs as the main culprit of growing unemployment. The model formed 'the preamble to the restoration of (neo-)classical thinking', a senior official at the Ministry of Economic Affairs wrote in a retrospective.[73]

It was a controversial model that was not accepted wholeheartedly by everyone. The VINTAF model 'produces peculiar results', wrote the

---

69   Ibid., 325–56. See also Wessel Visser and Rien Wijnhoven, *Baanbrekende politiek: de achterkant van de massale werkloosheid* (Kampen: Kok Agora, 1989), 86–98.

70   Rutten, *Zeven kabinetten wijzer*, 110.

71   Tom Kayzel, 'A Night Train in Broad Daylight: Changing Economic Expertise at the Dutch Central Planning Bureau 1945–1977', *Œconomia. History, Methodology, Philosophy* 9, no. 2 (1 June 2019): 337–70.

72   'VINTAF' referred to vintage function. 'Vintage' was a technical word for the 'age structure' of capital: how antiquated technology and infrastructure has become.

73   Knoester, *Economische politiek in Nederland*, 146.

Keynesian economist Jan Pen. 'An increase in government spending creates little employment. This is contrary to what some Keynesians think . . . If we allow the size of the public sector – as measured in percentage of national income – to increase, we generate unemployment non-stop.'[74] The new model formed the basis for the report *The Dutch Economy in 1980*, sent to the cabinet in the summer of 1975. It painted a much more negative picture of the future than had been assumed until then: economic growth would be lower, unemployment would continue to increase up to 300,000 in 1980, the tax burden would rise by almost 2 per cent per year and inflation would remain stubbornly high.[75]

When the report landed in the mail, there was great panic among the top brass of the Ministry of Finance. The lower economic growth meant that the 1976 budget no longer held up. Finance Minister Wim Duisenberg was on holiday on a sailing boat on the Frisian lakes, in the north of the Netherlands. An initial telephone call offered no solace: the seriousness of the situation did not immediately dawn on Duisenberg. 'I supposed, they [at the ministry] have thought up something again,' he later said.[76] The senior officials travelled by car to Friesland to personally convince him of the need for action. An overnight meeting in the cabin of the sailing boat ensued, while a storm raged ominously outside. The next morning, the conclusion was that the 1976 draft budget needed to be adjusted. Duisenberg interrupted his holiday, hurriedly returning to his ministry.

Den Uyl was not amused when Duisenberg called him at his holiday address about the sudden setback. The CPB model has sometimes been compared to a night train: when you wake up, you have reached your destination, but the voyage has taken place in utter darkness.[77] The same was true of the CPB model: although there were numbers coming out, it was impossible for outsiders to understand the route that had been taken to achieve them. The Council of Ministers had little desire to push aside the hard-won agreement on the draft budget because of a new calculation method that involved all sorts of new and unknown

---

74   Jan Pen, 'Harde computer-waarheden' [Hard computer truths], *Het Parool*, 29 June 1977.

75   José Toirkens, *Schijn en werkelijkheid van het bezuinigingsbeleid, 1975–1986* (Deventer: Kluwer, 1988), 32.

76   Ibid., 395.

77   Kayzel, 'A Night Train in Broad Daylight'.

relationships.[78] Den Uyl acknowledged that 1975 was a year of recession, with economic contraction of 1 per cent, but he saw clear cyclical causes stemming from the oil crisis. If action had to be taken, Den Uyl preferred to increase spending to restore growth. The deficit could then be borrowed against or financed by the Dutch Central Bank, by buying up government bonds.

Central bank president Zijlstra, however, refused to provide monetary financing, fearing that this would fuel inflation. Influenced partly by the international rise of monetarism, Zijlstra was changing course at the central bank. Price stability would be the top priority from now on, not fighting unemployment. This led to a fierce confrontation with Den Uyl, who compared Zijlstra to central bank president Trip, who had run the Dutch economy into the ground with austerity in the 1930s. Zijlstra sharply replied to Den Uyl that the deflation of the 1930s could not be compared with the stagflation crisis of the 1970s.[79]

A political battle ensued over the allegiance of the Ministry of Finance. Senior officials at the ministry had long felt that the social democratic Minister Wim Duisenberg did not offer enough resistance to Den Uyl's Keynesian views. 'When he began as minister, he did not yet have strong economic convictions,' one senior staff member said about his minister.[80] From both his own senior staff and the central bank, Duisenberg faced strong pressure to dig in his heels and enforce budget cuts. 'At every session he had to be hoisted back on the horse if he had to go on television, or to Cabinet. Then his staff had to get him all jazzed and girded up to get him to that point. It was a struggle, in those difficult times with Den Uyl, to urge him on,' the staff member reminisced.[81]

Duisenberg conceded and managed to push through a tighter fiscal policy in the Council of Ministers by threatening to resign. The government decided that the rise in the tax burden should be limited to 1 per cent of national income per year. Finance officials would have preferred freezing spending at existing levels, but it was nonetheless a turn to austerity. In that sense, it was a historic break. But the cuts had been

---

78   Toirkens, *Schijn en werkelijkheid van het bezuinigingsbeleid*, 36.
79   Harmsma, *Jelle zal wel zien*, 342.
80   Ibid., 340.
81   De Haas and van Lotringen, *Wim Duisenberg*, 106.

imposed by the Finance Ministry and the central bank, without a consensus on the underlying economic models and arguments.

The new forecasting model remained controversial. A group of Keynesian economists initiated a heated debate at the leading Dutch economics journal *Economic and Statistic Reports (ESB)*.[82] The Keynesian critics argued that there was certainly a correlation between high wages and unemployment; but that high wages caused unemployment was assumed a priori in the theoretical model, without CPB demonstrating it empirically.[83] Had the CPB economists not simply run the numbers until they found a model that fit their prior assumptions? How to explain the fact that countries with lower wages also had rising unemployment? Moreover, the model was only based on the industrial sector, which accounted for a small and shrinking part of Dutch employment. The new model, they argued, rather than representing a solid analysis of the development of the Dutch economy, was like sticking a wet finger in the air.

Everyone agreed that high labour costs played some role in the crisis. But this left unresolved whether wage moderation or public sector cutbacks were the best solution. Social democratic economists Hans van den Doel, Cees de Galan and (Nobel Memorial Prize winner) Jan Tinbergen argued for a new guided wage policy as the best answer to rising unemployment. In their view, the trade unions had a collective action problem: although the unions had a shared interest in wage moderation, at the sectoral and company levels there was a strong incentive to free-ride: everyone preferred to see other sectors moderate their wages. Since the trade union leadership apparently did not have the authority to enforce wage moderation at the central level, the government had to do it. By introducing a new policy of guided wages, the public sector could be spared, helping to sustain effective demand. At the same time, a public investment strategy was needed to create more high-value-added jobs.[84]

<hr>

82   Wim Driehuis and Arie van der Zwan, *De voorbereiding van het economisch beleid kritisch bezien* (Leiden: Stenfert Kroese, 1978); P. A. G. Lansbergen, *Het economiedebat: Economen contra Den Uyl en Van Agt, Intermediair bibliotheek* (Amsterdam: Intermediair, 1980).

83   Wessel Visser, 'De macht en onmacht van de CPB-modellen', in Harry van den Berg et al., eds, *Het Centraal Planbureau in politieke zaken* (Amsterdam: Wetenschappelijk Bureau Groen Links, 1993), 15–34.

84   Cees de Galan, Jan Tinbergen and Hans van den Doel, 'Pleidooi voor een geleide loonpolitiek', *ESB* 61, no. 3,044 (17 March 1976): 264–8.

The Keynesian camp published an open letter defending Den Uyl's expansionist policies in the run-up to the 1977 elections. Den Uyl's progressive reforms, they contended, were important 'to foster the social climate in which sacrifices by workers become acceptable'. They warned not to 'unilaterally blame the public sector or high wages' for the crisis and urged voters to vote for a party that would continue Den Uyl's expansionist policies. The signatories were twenty-four leading Dutch economics professors at the time, underscoring that there was no such thing as an economic consensus at the time.[85]

For the fiscally conservative camp, the new CPB model was an opportunity to stress their long-standing concerns about public spending. These conservative critics further radicalized the implications of the VINTAF model. In October 1976, the aforementioned Institute for Research on Public Spending, founded by economists Willem Drees Jr, Theo Stevers and Cees Goedhart, organized a symposium titled 'The State Entrapped'. It revolved around that year's budget memorandum. No fewer than 500 economists attended the symposium, which made newspaper headlines. Drees told his well-known story about the state that had fallen prey to pressure groups. Citizens were no longer individual consumers but had become 'group animals' living life as part of subsidized collectives (tenants, students, welfare workers) 'that can only satisfy their needs by putting pressure on the state'.[86] This was a thinly veiled reference to the leftist social movements of the 1970s. But it was the contribution of the Tilburg public finance professor, Theo Stevers, that caused the greatest controversy.

Stevers observed a vicious cycle of expanding government budgets and rising unemployment in the Netherlands.[87] He argued that Keynesian stimulus would further increase the tax burden and that this would in turn weaken the private sector, provoking more state intervention.[88] In this way, the government was taking away more and more

---

85   'Oproep hoogleraren economie' [Statement of economics professors], *Trouw*, 21 May 1977, 3.

86   Leon de Wolff et al., 'Symposium "De overheid in de klem"' [Symposium 'The state entrapped'], *NRC Handelsblad*, 1 October 1976; 'Pen heeft lof voor kabinet' [Pen praises government], *Trouw*, 2 October 1976.

87   Wolff et al., 'Symposium "De overheid in de klem"'.

88   Theo Stevers, 'Is het overheidsbeleid endogeen', *Economisch-Statistische Berichten* 61, no. 3,076 (27 October 1976): 1037–40.

economic incentives. If there was no longer an incentive to work due to generous benefits, the only way to get the unemployed back to work was through state coercion. As a result, the Netherlands was rapidly heading towards a 'centralist bureaucratic Kafka society' based on forced labour.[89] It was a historical development that had become, in Stevers's view, 'almost inevitable'.

Stevers had already proclaimed this pitch-black prophecy a week before the symposium, in a full-page analysis of the budget memorandum in a prominent newspaper. 'In principle, an economy can be coordinated in two ways. By "incentive" or by "coercion"', Stevers suggested.[90] Until now, the incentive had been the norm, but the Den Uyl government, with its wage measures and Keynesian planning, had opted for centralist coercion. The deeper problem was that the societal pressure to expand public spending was too high: 'Again and again, people are willing to trade a piece of freedom for immediate gain: willing to sell their birth-right for a bowl of lentil soup.' He warned of 'a fundamental change in our economic system with far-reaching consequences for democracy and the well-being of each of us individually'.

Columnists compared Stevers's contribution to Hayek's *The Road to Serfdom*.[91] That association was obvious, but the coincidence with Friedman's prophecy was also striking. It is unlikely that Stevers was directly influenced by Friedman's lecture. The latter received the Nobel Memorial Prize one month after Stevers's intervention and published his Chilean lecture in the November 1976 issue of the American journal *Encounter*.[92] But the parallels were unmistakable. Stevers's Manichean distinction between 'incentive' and 'coercion' was also a hallmark of Friedman's thinking: 'In principle, there are two ways of coordinating the economic activities of millions of people. The first is central control, using coercion – the technique of the military and the modern totalitarian state. The other is the voluntary cooperation of individuals – the technique of the free market,' Friedman had written in his bestseller

---

89   Wolff et al., 'Symposium "De overheid in de klem"'.

90   Theo Stevers, 'Daling werkloosheid vrome' [The pious wish of lowering unemployment], *De Volkskrant*, 22 September 1976.

91   Ton van Zweeden, 'Zwartgalligheid van Stevers lijkt Marx' wedergeboorte' [Stevers's pessimism seems like Marx reborn], *NRC Handelsblad*, 7 October 1976, 11.

92   Friedman, 'The Line We Dare Not Cross'.

Capitalism and Freedom.[93] Indeed, after reading *Encounter*, the Dutch columnist Jérôme Heldring wrote that Stevers's arguments were 'very similar to those of the classical liberal Friedman'.[94]

The prophecies of doom conjured by Friedman and Stevers were dismissed as gloomy by many commentators but nonetheless resonated widely. The Teldersstichting, the think-tank of right-wing liberals (VVD), published a controversial report on the economic order by the upcoming politician (and future European commissioner) Frits Bolkestein, in which Stevers's analysis featured prominently.[95] A combined report of the think-tanks of the three Christian democrat parties came out with a similar analysis. It described Den Uyl's policy as 'an approach from which little resistance can be expected to the rise of a totalitarian state; indeed, it induces it, however unwanted and unintended'.[96]

The overload thesis also resonated in academic debate over the crisis of the Dutch welfare state. Guided by the question 'Can democracy and the welfare state durably coexist?', the founding fathers of Dutch sociology Cees Schuyt and Jacques van Doorn had devoted an edited volume to the issue.[97] It was Van Doorn who took the firmest stand. Until then, the dominant understanding was that the economic crisis, through rising unemployment, had led to rising welfare state spending. The origins of the crisis lay in the market sector. A reverse causality was now claimed, inspired by the VINTAF discussion. It was the welfare state itself that was the source of economic stagnation: 'It is understandable that, in all this, the state is put at the centre. After all, the characteristic feature of the welfare state is the active role of the state in every area, so that the systemic crisis should first and foremost be located in the bureaucratic sphere,' wrote Van Doorn.[98]

---

93   Milton Friedman, *Capitalism and Freedom* (Chicago: University of Chicago Press, 1982), 13.

94   Jérôme Heldring, 'Socialisten voor de fatale grens' [Socialists faced with the fatal limit], *NRC Handelsblad*, 10 December 1976.

95   Frits Bolkestein, *Over de economische orde in Nederland* (The Hague: Teldersstichting, 1977).

96   Piet Steenkamp, ed., *Gespreide verantwoordelijkheid: Een christen-democratische bijdrage aan de discussie over de economische orde, Rapport van een commissie van de wetenschappelijke instituten van KVP, ARP en CHU* (The Hague: KVP/ARP/CHU, 1978), 87.

97   Jacques van Doorn and Cees Schuyt, eds, *De stagnerende verzorgingsstaat* (Meppel: Boom, 1978), 13.

98   Jacques Van Doorn, 'De verzorgingsmaatschappij in de praktijk', in ibid., 17.

An important contribution to the volume came from the political science professor Hans Daudt.[99] He had become somewhat of a cult figure due to his confrontations with the Amsterdam student movement, who protested against his classes in the early 1970s. Like Stevers, Daudt belonged to the fiscally conservative wing of the Labour Party that disdained the New Left and continued to see the frugal welfare state of the 1950s as its political ideal. Daudt had developed into a public choice thinker who introduced the overload thesis in the Labour Party journal.[100] He translated Friedman's essay 'The Line We Dare Not Cross' and organized a public symposium on the subject at the Erasmus University in Rotterdam. Daudt invited leading politicians and economists, including Den Uyl, Bolkestein and Stevers, to speak on the relevance of Friedman's dark prophecy for the Netherlands.[101] In response, the newspapers openly discussed whether the Netherlands was heading for a Kafkaesque dictatorship.[102]

When the country switched to a tepid centre-right government led by the Christian democrats, the debate on the Kafka-state soon dissipated.

99   Hans Daudt, 'De politieke toekomst van de verzorgingsstaat', in Van Doorn and Schuyt, *De stagnerende verzorgingsstaat*, 189–218.

100   Hans Daudt, 'Verzorgingsstaat, democratie en socialisme', in Jan Bank, Martin Ros and Bart Tromp, eds, *Het eerste jaarboek voor het democratisch socialisme* (Amsterdam: PvdA, 1979), 14–40.

101   Hans Daudt and Ernst van der Wolk, eds., *Bedreigde democratie? Parlementaire democratie en overheidsbemoeienis in de economie* (Assen: Van Gorcum/Intermediair, 1978).

102   Ton Cuppen, 'Nogmaals: Hoezeer bedreigt modern staat democratie?' [Again: How much does the modern state threaten democracy?], *NRC Handelsblad*, 28 January 1978, 7; Ton van Zweeden, 'Somber beeld van bemoeial staat versus economie' [Sombre image of meddling state versus economy], *NRC Handelsblad*, 11 January 1978, 7; Jan Beishuizen, 'Den Uyl: Solidariteit' [Den Uyl: Solidarity], *Het Parool*, 11 January 1978, 4; Leen Hoffman, 'Komt er een Kafkastaat' [Is the Kafkastate coming?], *Het Vrije Volk*, 31 January 1978, 4; Joop van den Berg, 'De grens die wij niet over mogen' [The line we dare not cross], *NRC Handelsblad*, 4 February 1978, 7.

3

'Ideas Are More Powerful Than Guns' (1977–81)

In spring 1977, in the final days of the Den Uyl cabinet, the Mont-Pelerin Society convened a conference at the Hilton Hotel in Amsterdam. The popular right-wing newspaper *De Telegraaf* spoke of 'a very exclusive gathering of mostly professors of economics, law and psychology, supplemented by top industry figures from around the world and influential journalists'.[1] It had been thirty years since this neoliberal think-tank had been founded in the Swiss mountain town of Mont Pèlerin, on the initiative of the Austrian economist Friedrich Hayek. According to the press release cited in Dutch newspapers, the meeting was organized in the Netherlands 'because economic freedom is currently under threat here'.[2] Recent developments in Chile gave that statement a somewhat ominous character.

Among the attendees was the now seventy-five-year-old Hayek, who had won the Nobel Memorial Prize for Economics three years earlier. Milton Friedman had to miss out due to other commitments, but sent in

---

1 Peter van der Tuin, 'Nobelprijswinnaar Friedrich von Hayek: "Laat handelsbanken eigen geld drukken"' [Nobel Prize winner Friedrich von Hayek: 'Let commercial banks print their own money'], *De Telegraaf*, 16 April 1977, 49.

2 'Economische vrijheid in Nederland bedreigd' [Economic freedom in the Netherlands under threat], *Het Vrije Volk*, 2 April 1977, 13; Jan Heitink, 'Top-economen confereren over onze vrijheid' [Leading economists discuss our freedom], *De Telegraaf*, 14 April 1977, 9; 'Vreemde ideeën kunnen ook tot nadenken stemmen' [Strange ideas make us think], *Nieuwsblad van het Noorden*, 23 April 1977, 29.

a recorded lecture, as befitted an intellectual star.[3] Also in attendance was the German neoliberal Alfred Müller-Armack, who coined the term 'social market economy' and helped inspire the post-war economic policies of West Germany. Then there were Ralph Harris and Arthur Seldon, the founders of the Institute of Economic Affairs, Britain's oldest and foremost neoliberal think-tank, which helped shape Margaret Thatcher's economic policies.[4]

At the time of its creation in 1947, the Mont Pelerin Society was an intimate gathering of forty economists and businessmen. Back then, Friedrich Hayek had just published *The Road to Serfdom*, in which he had argued that it was socialist ideas of state intervention that had inadvertently led to the rise of Nazism and that the same could happen again. The book became an unexpected bestseller. The American magazine *Reader's Digest* published an abridged version and distributed more than half a million copies to its massive readership. Hayek became an intellectual star overnight. Encouraged by this success, he brought together a range of like-minded spirits to found the Mont Pelerin Society and turn the tide of state intervention. 'Gone are the days when the few outmoded liberals walked their paths lonely, ridiculed and without response from the young,' Hayek wrote after the first MPS gatherings. 'At least personal contact among the proponents of neoliberalism has been established.'[5]

In his opening address at the first meeting of the Mont Pelerin Society, Hayek cited a famous passage by John Maynard Keynes: 'The views of economists and political philosophers, whether they are right or wrong, are more influential than we generally think. In fact, the world is governed by little else.'[6] Like the British economist, Hayek believed that

---

3   In fact, the original plan was to organize a debate alongside the Mont Pelerin Society conference between Friedman and the social democrat economist 'Jan Tinbergen or another socialist professor of economics' in front of an 'audience of socialist students'. Unfortunately, due to Friedman's absence that debate never materialized. Liberaal Archief Gent, *Archief Jacques van Offelen*, inv.nr. 1.4.2., Newsletter of the Mont Pelerin Society #11, December 1976, 8.

4   For insider histories of the institute, see Richard Cockett, *Thinking the Unthinkable: Think-Tanks and the Economic Counter-Revolution 1931–1983* (London: HarperCollins, 1995); John Blundell, *Waging the War of Ideas*, 4th edn, Occasional Papers 131 (London: Institute of Economic Affairs, 2015).

5   Friedrich Hayek, 'A Rebirth of Liberalism', *Freeman* 2 (1952): 730.

6   Cited in Friedrich A. von Hayek, *Individualism and Economic Order* (Chicago: University of Chicago Press, 1948), 108.

ideas asserted political influence only over longer periods of time. After all, most people were politically formed in their student days, but could only apply these ideas when they found themselves in positions of power, after a long career.[7] With his sketch of a long-term battle of ideas, Hayek captivated his audience.[8] His message struck a chord, including with Milton Friedman, who some years later declared: 'Ideas have little chance of making much headway against a strong tide; their opportunity comes when the tide has ceased running strong but has not yet turned.'[9]

In 1977, that moment seemed to have come. The once intimate club of forty members had grown into a widely branched network. The membership list now included some four hundred people from more than thirty countries. Milton Friedman served as president of the society. He warned in a circular in the early 1970s that the network's main problem was no longer its marginality. 'Our basic problem,' he wrote somewhat sardonically, 'stems from our success.'[10] The growth of the movement threatened to destroy the once cosy atmosphere of familiarity and camaraderie.

It was a small sacrifice, for the influence of neoliberal ideas had never been greater. Inflation and economic stagnation had led to a global crisis of legitimacy for Keynesianism. The tide was turning in economic science, and members of the Mont Pelerin Society played an important role in that development. It was not so much the outspoken free market manifestos, like *The Road to Serfdom* or *Capitalism and Freedom*, that made the difference. Crucial to the shift were a set of ascendant schools of thought in economic science: monetarism, public choice, rational expectations and supply-side economics. The role of Mont Pelerin Society members in the development of these tendencies was so pertinent that they have been called 'MPS doctrines' by leading economists.[11] In theory, these movements had an objective (or, in economic jargon,

---

7   Ibid.

8   Bernhard Walpen, 'Der plan, das planen zu beenden: Eine hegemonietheoretische studie zur Mont Pelerin Society' (PhD diss., University of Amsterdam, 2004), 73.

9   Milton Friedman, 'Neo-Liberalism and Its Prospects', *Farmand* 17 (1951): 90.

10   Angus Burgin, *The Great Persuasion: Reinventing Free Markets Since the Depression* (Cambridge, MA: Harvard University Press, 2012), 207.

11   John Williamson, 'A Short History of the Washington Consensus', *Law and Business Review of the Americas* 15 (2009): 7.

'positive') character but shared one central axiom: the belief in the supe-riority of the market mechanism.

At the same time, neoliberal think-tanks were springing up like mushrooms in the 1970s, thanks to generous financial support from organized business. In Britain, the Centre for Policy Studies was founded in 1974, followed three years later by the Adam Smith Institute. American neoliberals founded the Heritage Foundation in 1973, followed by the libertarian Cato Institute in 1974 and the Manhattan Institute in 1977. That same year, in West Germany, the neoliberal Bertelsmann-Stiftung was founded, complementing the pre-existing Ludwig-Erhard-Stiftung of 1967. All these organizations derived inspiration from the Mont Pelerin Society. The society had always been a kind of neoliberal International, but what had once been a select gentleman's club became an international hub in an increasingly large and diffuse network in which many thousands of people were active.

Think-tanks ensured the popularization of neoliberal ideas and their translation into policy, helping to shape the debate in politics and the media. Members of the MPS often formulated this ideational strategy in military terms. Arthur Seldon described the role of his Institute of Economic Affairs as that of 'artillery firing shells (ideas)' at intellectuals and journalists, while the 'face to face grappling with the enemy' would be left to the infantry of politicians and journalists.[12] Edwin Feulner of the Heritage Foundation saw it as his job to man both 'the ivory towers and the trenches' and to 'manufacture the ammunition'. He drew inspi-ration from a remark by Joseph Stalin: 'Ideas are much more powerful than guns.'[13] Both think-tanks would play a key role in the free market revolution of President Ronald Reagan and Prime Minister Margaret Thatcher.

Dutch Specificity

The Mont Pelerin Society and its affiliated think-tanks have become a privileged vantage point from which to study the global spread of

---

12   Blundell, *Waging the War of Ideas*, 6.
13   Edwin Feulner, *Waging and Winning the War of Ideas*, Heritage Lectures 84 (Washington, DC: Heritage Foundation, 1986), 4.

neoliberal ideas, which has resulted in a large and sophisticated litera-ture on the rise of neoliberalism.[14] At the same time, there are many countries where such think-tanks either do not exist or have a much more marginal role. As a result, these countries have often been over-looked. The Netherlands lacked a similar think-tank infrastructure. There was nothing remotely resembling the Institute of Economic Affairs, the libertarian Cato Institute or the Heritage Foundation. Instead, the production of policy ideas in the Netherlands has taken place largely within ministries and publicly funded think-tanks like the Central Planning Bureau (CPB) and the Scientific Council for Government Policy (WRR). This institutional infrastructure is the legacy of the religious divisions in Dutch politics. The idea was that economic policymakers in these organizations would serve as neutral arbiters, standing above the socio-religious pillars and making compro-mise possible.[15] More generally, the Dutch political landscape had always differed from its Anglo-American counterparts. The dominance of Christian democracy resulted in a distinctive dynamic. As the Christian democrats were historically split between a fiscally conserva-tive employers' wing and a progressive trade union wing, a polarizing politics à la Thatcher or Reagan was unattractive.

For these reasons, the Mont Pelerin Society conference in Amsterdam, with its combative tone, was not well received. The Committee of Recommendation of the conference did include leading Dutch figures such as the treasurer-general of the Ministry of Finance, Coen Oort, the vice-chairman of the Christian employers' association (NCW), the CEO of dredging multinational Boskalis and the CEO of asset manager Robeco, as well as the future treasurer-general of the Ministry of Finance, Pieter Korteweg.[16] But the militant rhetoric spoken in the plush halls of the Amsterdam Hilton was rather alien to Dutch political realities.

---

14   Daniel Stedman Jones, *Masters of the Universe: Hayek, Friedman, and the Birth of Neoliberal Politics* (Princeton, NJ: Princeton University Press, 2014); Quinn Slobodian, *Globalists: The End of Empire and the Birth of Neoliberalism* (Cambridge, MA: Harvard University Press, 2018); Burgin, *Great Persuasion*; Jamie Peck, *Constructions of Neoliberal Reason* (Oxford: Oxford University Press, 2010); M. Philip Mirowski and Dieter Plehwe, eds, *The Road from Mont Pelerin: The Making of the Neoliberal Thought Collective* (Cambridge, MA: Harvard University Press, 2009).

15   Arend Lijphart, *The Politics of Accommodation: Pluralism and Democracy in the Netherlands* (Berkeley: University of California Press, 1968).

16   'Economische vrijheid in Nederland bedreigd', 13.

In his pre-recorded lecture, Milton Friedman proclaimed: 'No one can spend someone else's money without first taking it from him. At the basis of the welfare state, therefore, were coercion and violence.'[17] Friedrich Hayek presented his recent book on the denationalization of money as a solution to the problem of inflation – a sort of bitcoin *avant la lettre*.[18] The reaction of the Dutch guests was dismissive. André Batenburg, the CEO of the ABN Bank, dismissed Hayek's proposal as a 'return to the Middle Ages'.[19] Leen Hoffman, the editor of economics journal *ESB*, wrote a sardonic editorial about the conference.[20] From a public relations point of view, it was not a fruitful meeting.

However, this does not mean that the neoliberal turn passed the Netherlands by. The dismissive reactions stemmed less from substantive disagreement than from a difference in political culture. The ideological polarization that is the norm in the Anglo-American political system was seen as needlessly disruptive in the Dutch context. With the polarizing rhetoric of Hayek and Friedman, one simply could not build coalitions that had the support of electoral majorities. As the American-Dutch political scientist Arend Lijphart wrote in in his classic *The Politics of Accommodation*, Dutch elites had developed a political culture focused on depoliticization. Lijphart notes that economic science played a central role in this respect:

A different method for neutralizing sensitive issues and justifying compromises to the rank and file, especially in post-war politics, has been the use of complicated economic arguments and the juggling of economic facts and figures incomprehensible to most people. The art was to present political issues that tended to stir up emotions as if they were not political and divisive at all, but issues that could be settled according to objective established criteria of economic science, arithmetic or jurisprudence.[21]

17   Van der Tuin, 'Nobelprijswinnaar Friedrich von Hayek'.

18   Friedrich Hayek, *The Denationalisation of Money*, Hobart Paper Special (London: Institute of Economic Affairs, 1976).

19   'Vreemde ideeën kunnen ook tot nadenken stemmen'.

20   Leen Hoffman, 'De Mont Pelerin Society', *ESB* 62, nos 3,098/3,099 (6 April 1977): 337.

21   Arend Lijphart, *Verzuiling, pacificatie en kentering in de Nederlandse politiek*, 2nd edn (Amsterdam: De Bussy, 1976), 122. I am citing the Dutch version, as it is slightly more extensive on 'the rules of the game'. See also Lijphart, *Politics of Accommodation*, 129.

In other words, the apolitical authority of economic science was of crucial importance in reaching compromises both between political parties and between employers and trade unions. The corporatist institutions where business and labour met, had the effect of depoliticizing the economic debate. 'The focus on consensus building led to a rationalization of discussion within the SER [Social and Economic Council] on measures of social and economic policy,' writes Sjoerd Wilts in his sociological history of Dutch economic policymaking. As a result, 'pronounced political-ideological positions weren't considered acceptable' among Dutch economists.[22] Of course, as we will see, that does not mean that they were absent; it is just that they were hidden behind a veil of technocratic language.

A second fundamental difference was that change in the United States and Britain came from outside. In both countries, the neoliberals were relative outsiders, trying to overthrow an established Keynesian policy elite. Hence, they were forced to take the institutions through a fierce battle of ideas. In the Netherlands, change came from within. Because of the long shadow cast by the market-based policy during post-war reconstruction in the Netherlands, Keynesianism had never become the dominant policy paradigm. The senior civil servants in the Ministries of Finance and Economic Affairs, who had watched the growth of public spending since the mid-1960s with increasing concern, began expanding the welfare state with great reluctance and were early to declare that the Keynesian experiment had failed. As a result, the neoliberal turn took place in a more covert and technocratic manner in the Netherlands. The internal divisions over austerity within political parties resulted in a pioneering role for economic policymakers within the ministries. An important role was played by the Ministry of Finance, where a new synthesis emerged in the 1970s between existing traditions of Dutch market-based thinking and the international doctrines promoted by the Mont Pelerin Society.

The newspaper columnist and economics professor Floor Hartog read the signs of the times, noting in 1977 that neoliberal ideas were regaining popularity, sometimes under a different name: 'Heightened

---

22   Arnold Sjoerd Wilts, 'Economie als maatschappijwetenschap: een sociologische geschiedenis van de economische wetenschap in Nederland (ca. 1930–1960)' (PhD diss., University of Amsterdam, 1997), 117.

doubts about the Keynesian prescription with its inflationary side effect are leading to increased respect for neoliberal ideas in recent years.' He pointed to the rise of monetarism and the pervasive fear that continuing inflation was paving the way to economic dictatorship. 'The latter was predicted long ago by Hayek in his famous book *The Road to Serfdom*. For years, that idea was treated with disdain by all that is Keynesian – in fact, by the entire economics establishment,' Hartog complained. 'But now we aren't so sure that Hayek is wrong.' Was it not the case that the leading economist Theo Stevers had argued roughly the same thing in the Netherlands?[23]

The Brutalist Bunker

In the autumn of 1975, the new Ministry of Finance building was inaugurated in a festive manner. The ceremony was graced by the presence of all living former finance ministers and state secretaries. The crème de la crème of the economic policy circuit was present. Former Minister Piet Lieftinck, serving executive director at the IMF, delivered an opening lecture in which he highlighted the ministry's difficult mission in a time of stagflation. The ministry had expanded prodigiously in recent decades and had outgrown the stately eighteenth-century buildings it had occupied until then. The new accommodation was an imposing building of about 100 by 150 metres, erected in the heart of the political district of The Hague. The architects had taken inspiration from brutalism, the international architectural movement known for its love of concrete. The massive panels at the corners and the concrete parapets gave the ministry the appearance of a fortress. This perception was reinforced by the psychological atmosphere at the ministry in the 1970s and 1980s. Journalists spoke of 'the brutalist bunker', a mighty 'bastion' with a 'collective sense of identity reinforced by the fear of the evil outside world'.[24] Internally, the prevailing sentiment was that the ministry was being 'defrauded' by citizens, bureaucrats and businesses alike. Looking

---

23 Floor Hartog, 'Sociale markteconomie' [Social market economy], *NRC Handelsblad*, 17 May 1977, 11.

24 'Ruding heeft overal zijn ogen en oren' [Ruding has eyes and ears everywhere], *Algemeen Dagblad*, 30 January 1988, 3.

back on that period in an interview for Dutch public television, senior official Pieter Korteweg recounted the atmosphere of a 'besieged fortress': 'Nobody understands us, everybody calls us "bookkeepers": but we are the ones that have to finance the deficits. It's not called *schuld* for nothing. You feel guilty because, by borrowing so much, you are already taking and spending income that has yet to be earned in the future.'[25]

The new building came to symbolize not only the modernization of the ministry but also the central and disciplining role it would claim in the political process. 'Anyone who is somewhat familiar with the balance of power in The Hague knows that the Ministry of Finance *is* power,' another senior official proclaimed in the 1980s.[26] In the second half of the 1970s, however, that power was still in question.

A key figure in the rise of the Ministry Finance was Coen Oort. As treasurer-general, he was the most senior official at the ministry. That such a senior bureaucrat attended the Amsterdam conference of the Mont Pelerin Society was of course striking, even if it was, as he claimed, 'in a personal capacity'.[27] Indeed, Oort's attendance did have a personal dimension: he had spent several years in the early 1950s at the Economics Department of the University of Chicago, where he attended lectures by Milton Friedman.[28] Among his colleagues, Oort was known as an economist 'who never renounced his Chicago background'.[29] His neoliberal views and his dislike of Joop den Uyl were well known. Finance Minister Wim Duisenberg once gave him a set of golf balls with Den Uyl's face printed on them. 'So you can take your frustration out on him,' Duisenberg joked.[30] Like many senior finance officials, Oort became a banker after his career in the public sector. He joined ABN's Board of

25   Pieter Korteweg, interview by the editors of the historical documentary programme *Andere Tijden*, for the episode 'Government in Crisis', broadcast on Dutch public television on 9 September 2012. In Dutch, the word *schuld* signifies both debt and guilt.

26   'Ruding heeft overal zijn ogen en oren'.

27   Van der Tuin, 'Nobelprijswinnaar Friedrich von Hayek'.

28   Cees Oort, *Decreasing Costs as a Problem of Welfare Economics* (Amsterdam: Drukkerij Holland, 1958), iv.

29   Clemens Kool, Joan Muysken and Tom van Veen, *Essays on Money, Banking and Regulation: Essays in Honour of C. J. Oort* (Dordrecht: Kluwer, 1996), x.

30   Bruno de Haas and Cees van Lotringen, *Wim Duisenberg: Van Friese volksjongen tot Mr. Euro* (Amsterdam: Business Contact, 2003), 106.

Directors in 1977 while continuing to serve the ministry as an adviser.[31] This move was symptomatic of the traditionally close ties between the Finance Ministry and the Dutch banking elite.

But Oort's participation in the MPS conference was also an illustration of the more activist stance of the ministry as a whole. Together with his successor Nout Wellink, Oort had long advocated a more austere policy and a strengthening of the ministry's position in the decision-making process.[32] As Wellink recalled: 'At the Ministry of Finance, we attached great significance to [Theo] Stevers's reflections, considered by many to be too pessimistic.'[33] The ministry agreed with Stevers that the redistributive agenda of Den Uyl had removed the incentives that gave the economy its dynamism. This created a vicious cycle of ever-growing unemployment and ever-increasing public spending.

When the first cabinet of Dries Van Agt – a centre-right coalition of Christian democrats (CDA) and right-wing liberals (VVD) took office in the autumn of 1977, the time for a shift in economic policy seemed to have arrived. Based on the new VINTAF model, senior finance officials had calculated in June 1977 that some 10 billion guilders ($4.5 billion) had to be cut by the next government to keep the budget deficit below 5 per cent. The fact that the Labour Party (PvdA) refused to accept the findings of the new VINTAF model had been a major stumbling block in attempts to form a centre-left coalition.[34] But now there was a centre-right government that promised to cut collective spending drastically through its austerity agenda Compass '81.

But the coalition proved too internally divided. The main Christian parties (the KVP, the Protestant ARP, and the CHU) had joined forces in the 1977 elections to form the Christian Democratic Appeal (CDA), a powerful centrist party. Within the new CDA, however, there was considerable controversy over the course to be followed. An influential leftist minority opposed the newly formed centre-right coalition,

31   Peter de Waard, 'Belastinghervormer Oort overleden' [Tax reformer Oort has passed away], *De Volkskrant*, 28 November 2007.

32   Jonne Harmsma, *Jelle zal wel zien: Jelle Zijlstra, een eigenzinnig leven tussen politiek en economie* (Amsterdam: Prometheus, 2018), 343.

33   Nout Wellink, 'De ontwikkelingen in de jaren zeventig en tachtig en enkele daaruit te trekken lessen', in A. Knoester, ed., *Lessen uit het verleden: 125 jaar Vereniging voor de Staathuishoudkunde* (Leiden: Stenfert-Kroese, 1987), 335.

34   Leen Hoffman, 'Struisvogelpolitiek bij kabinetsformatie' [Ostrich politics at cabinet formation], *Het Vrije Volk*, 2 August 1977, 4.

preferring a continuation of the Den Uyl cabinet. As the first Van Agt government had only a narrow majority in parliament, this left-Christian faction held a crucial lever of power.

The Christian Democratic minister of social affairs, the Keynesian economist Wil Albeda, became the face of opposition to the austerity plans. He feared that simultaneous cutbacks and wage restraint would trigger a 'negative spiral'.[35] Pressure, of course, also came from outside the government. Compass '81 was the target of a fierce wave of protests led by the public sector unions and the Dutch communist party (CPN). Wim Kok, chairman of the largest trade union (FNV), warned in a militant tone that the unions would not shy away from a 'social war'.[36] The government equivocated. It was afraid of a collapse of the coalition government, as the Labour Party was waiting in the wings. Prime Minister Van Agt watched helplessly as parliament, supported by left-wing Christian Democrats, managed to soften the cuts substantially. Compass '81 turned out to be a paper tiger.

Meanwhile, the Dutch economy was hit hard in 1979 by the second oil crisis. On top of that came the Volcker shock – the tight monetary policy that US Federal Reserve chairman Paul Volcker initiated to fight inflation. In one fell swoop, Volcker raised interest rates to a nominal 20 per cent and drastically curtailed the money supply. This draconian policy would indeed reduce inflation sharply, but at the cost of a deep economic recession, also internationally.[37] As a result of these two shocks, record numbers of Dutch companies went bust, and unemployment rose to levels not seen since the 1930s. While the unemployment rate was still 250,000 in 1977, by 1981 it had almost doubled.[38] At the same time, the high interest rates caused Dutch housing prices to lose a quarter of their value in two years. Meanwhile, the budget deficit had risen from about 3 per cent of national income in 1977 to a whopping 8 per cent in 1981.[39] This was reason enough for Christian Democratic

---

35   Duco Hellema, *Nederland en de jaren zeventig* (Amsterdam: Boom, 2012), 236.

36   Ibid., 239.

37   Jan Luiten van Zanden, *The Economic History of the Netherlands 1914–1995: A Small Open Economy in the 'Long' Twentieth Century* (London: Routledge, 1998), 167–8.

38   Wessel Visser and Rien Wijnhoven, *Baanbrekende politiek: de achterkant van de massale werkloosheid* (Kampen: Kok Agora, 1989), 54.

39   Anthonie Knoester, *Economische politiek in Nederland* (Leiden: Stenfert Kroese, 1989), 153.

Finance Minister Frans Andriessen to try to push through an additional austerity package in 1980. He defiantly proclaimed that the government should not give way in the 'fierce battle between the pressure groups for the biggest chunks from the state's coffers'.[40] After failing to mobilize sufficient support, Andriessen angrily resigned – an unprecedented trauma for the Finance Ministry.[41] The 'brutalist bastion' had been overrun by pressure groups. It was time to restore order.

Public Choice and the Stagflation Crisis

A famous line by Milton Friedman states that 'only a crisis – actual or perceived – produces real change'. The actions taken 'depend on the ideas that are lying around'.[42] For the Finance Ministry, public-choice theory was an important intellectual key to the crisis of the 1970s. The ministry itself had played a major role in developing this theory in the Netherlands, working closely with a series of economics departments in the Netherlands. The baton was now passed to a new generation, who derived inspiration from the international ascent of neoliberal ideas.

An important figure here was the Frisian economist Lense Koopmans. He had graduated in 1968 with a PhD thesis titled 'Decisions on the State Budget'.[43] Koopmans discussed the work of proto-public choice thinkers such as Kenneth Arrow and Anthony Downs and tested their theories, using interviews with senior finance officials, especially the treasurer-general Willem Drees Jr. The young graduate then experienced a rapid rise. He was offered a job at the Ministry of Finance under Drees. There he worked on the textbook *Public Finance*, which in short order became the standard work for Dutch students of public finance. Through forty years and over

---

40   'Minister Andriessen: "Niet wijken in gevecht om de staatsruif"' [Minister Andriessen: 'No budging in conflict over public coffers'], *NRC Handelsblad*, 28 February 1979, 1.

41   Gerrit Zalm, *De romantische boekhouder* (Amsterdam: Balans, 2009), 39.

42   Milton Friedman, *Capitalism and Freedom* (Chicago: University of Chicago Press, 1982), 7.

43   Lenze Koopmans, *De beslissingen over de rijksbegroting* (PhD diss., University of Groningen, 1968).

fourteen revisions, Koopmans's book was used to train economists for work in the public sector.[44]

In 1973, at the tender age of twenty-eight, Koopmans was appointed professor of public finance at Erasmus University Rotterdam. In his inaugural speech, 'Controlling Public Spending', Koopmans launched the dry but alarmist thesis that public finances had become 'ungovernable'.[45] He drew on the work of Drees and Stevers, which he combined with the ideas of American public-choice thinkers James Buchanan and William Niskanen – both members of the Mont Pelerin Society and closely involved with neoliberal think-tanks in the United States and Britain.[46] In his 1971 book *Bureaucracy and Representative Government*, Niskanen had launched the thesis that the rational self-interest of civil servants encouraged them to lobby for their department to maximize its budget.[47] According to Koopmans, this theory, combined with the existing ideas of Drees and Stevers, could explain the 'overproduction of public services' in the Netherlands since the 1960s.[48]

According to Koopmans, controlling public spending required a fundamental reform of government. First, he wanted to introduce financial incentives in the public sector. This involved implementing a 'quasi-profit system'. Civil servants would be 'awarded certain cash prizes' if they stayed within their allocated budgets.[49] For this, however, it was necessary to develop 'output measures'. Otherwise, officials could simply collect the rewards for delivering less quality within a given budget. According to Koopmans, the science of public finance should start by focusing on defining and quantifying output in the public sector. In the 1990s, this application of pseudo-market techniques in the public sector

---

44   Lenze Koopmans, *Overheidsfinanciën* (Haarlem: De Erven Bohn, 1971). The latest (fourteenth) edition is from 2015. See Flip de Kam, L. Koopmans and A. H. E. M. Wellink, *Overheidsfinanciën*, 14th edn (Groningen: Noordhoff, 2015).

45   Lenze Koopmans, *Beheersing van de overheidsuitgaven* (Deventer: Kluwer, 1973), 5.

46   Melinda Cooper, *Counterrevolution: Extravagance and Austerity in Public Finance* (Princeton, NJ: Princeton University Press, 2024); Jacob Jensen, *The Marketizers: Public Choice and the Origins of the Neoliberal Order*, Goldsmiths Press/PERC Papers (London: Goldsmiths, 2022).

47   William Arthur Niskanen, *Bureaucracy and Representative Government* (Chicago: Aldine, Atherton, 1971); William A. Niskanen, *Bureaucracy: Servant or Master? Lessons from America* (London: Institute of Economic Affairs, 1973).

48   Koopmans, *Beheersing van de overheidsuitgaven*, 10.

49   Ibid., 14.

came to be known as New Public Management.[50] Koopmans further advocated 'cutting off the path of interest groups' to political decision-making.[51] The ministries and sectoral specialists from political parties had become too loyal to their own sector and the interest groups operating within it. To rein in the ministries, Koopmans suggested centralizing the decision-making process and pinning down the budget during the government formation. Only after the decision on the budget would ministers be appointed. To rein in parliament, Koopmans suggested abolishing sectoral specialists in political parties altogether and deciding by lot which policy area MPs would focus on.

He soon had the opportunity to put some of his ideas into practice. In 1975, on the initiative of Finance Minister Wim Duisenberg (PvdA), Koopmans was appointed deputy director-general of the state budget, where Duisenberg wanted him to balance out the influence of the Keynesian policymakers in his department.[52] Koopmans had his work cut out for him. His task was to suggest 'austerity measures to other departments, from the perspective of the Ministry of Finance'.[53] Koopmans's lightning career illustrates the early rise and institutionalization of a neoliberal critique of bureaucracy within the Dutch government.

Like all major economic crises, the stagflation crisis of the 1970s was a complex phenomenon – a perfect storm involving a wide range of factors. It began with the end of the Bretton Woods system and the ensuing monetary instability, then came the inflationary shock of the oil crisis and the global weakening of demand. Of course, high wage levels that put pressure on profits and investment also played a role. In the background, there was an ongoing process of de-industrialization and automation, resulting in increased unemployment and rising social spending.[54]

Public-choice theorists, however, were much more selective in their focus. They identified the core of the problem as the faulty architecture

---

50   Tjerk Budding and Tom Groot, 'De ontwikkeling van New Public Management in Nederland', *MAB* 82, no. 4 (2008): 152–60.

51   Koopmans, *Beheersing van de overheidsuitgaven*, 17.

52   De Haas and van Lotringen, *Wim Duisenberg*, 89.

53   Toirkens, *Schijn en werkelijkheid*, 40.

54   Erik Jones, *Economic Adjustment and Political Transformation in Small States* (Oxford: Oxford University Press, 2008), 135–69; Van Zanden, *Economic History of the Netherlands*, 161.

of the democratic system itself, which had an inherent tendency towards overspending. Now, it was one thing to argue that Keynesian policies were not having the desired effect. But it was something else entirely to claim that it was not even the intention of politicians and Keynesian policymakers to resolve the crisis effectively. According to public-choice analysis, politicians and officials spent more money than there was because it was simply in their own short-term interests to maximize their votes and please their pressure groups. The ambitious appeals for economic planning that had characterized the 1970s thus gave way to a much more cynical perspective on government.

'The rosy picture of government is changing,' Theo Stevers wrote, with the 'emergence of the New Political Economy (also known as Public Choice Theory).' Stevers referred to the work of James Buchanan, who had by now succeeded Friedman as president of the Mont Pelerin Society. This analysis, Stevers wrote approvingly, 'leads to a much more nuanced picture of government, though also less pretty'. It involved

> a civil service that is compartmentalized and focused on territorial expansion, or in any case is vehemently opposed to reduction, voters who pursue short-sighted self-interest and have little understanding of how the market works. And when the state intervenes in the economic process, that provokes unforeseen negative developments. It's a government driving out demons with Beelzebub so that seven new devils return.[55]

This far-reaching analysis had not yet been substantiated by research. As Koopmans himself wrote in his inaugural lecture, it involved 'behavioural assumptions [that] have not yet been empirically tested'.[56] The sinister image of government was, above all, a consequence of neoclassical assumptions about the utility-maximizing *Homo economicus*, assumed to exist not only on the marketplace but also in the political and bureaucratic sphere. Despite the theoretical nature of this critique, public-choice theory exerted a powerful influence on political practice.

55   Theo Stevers, 'Waar staat de staat?', in Theo Stevers, ed., *Waar staat de staat? Een conferentie van het convent van christelijk-sociale organisaties* (The Hague: Boekencentrum B.V., 1984), 18.

56   Koopmans, *Beheersing van de overheidsuitgaven*, 17.

In 1981, Lense Koopmans contributed to a report for the think-tank of the right-wing liberal party (VVD), with the same title as his inaugural address: *Controlling Public Spending*.[57] The report could be read as an intervention by the Ministry of Finance itself: the upcoming treasurer-general, Pieter Korteweg, edited the report, and Lense Koopmans, together with former treasurer-general Coen Oort and former director of the budget Dick Meys, wrote the chapter 'Revising Decision-Making Procedures'.[58] (Both Oort and Meys had, by this point in time, continued their careers in the boards of major Dutch banks.) Based on public-choice theory, the authors made a number of proposals to strengthen the position of the Ministry of Finance decisively. There had to be a strict budget norm, developed by the Study Group Fiscal Space, a powerful bureaucratic committee led by the Ministry of Finance. This committee had existed since 1973 and was originally quite moderate in its opinions. But in the 1980s and 1990s it turned to public-choice theory and monetarism. The chairman of the Study Group promoted William Niskanen's controversial theories. 'Budget-maximization is the highest goal for bureaucrats,' he stated in a high-profile interview in 1983.[59]

The report further proposed to 'cut back the public deficit at the fastest possible pace', even though it could be expected that this would have 'negative macroeconomic repercussions in the short term'. Keynesian policies were firmly rejected: 'Any attempt to ease this necessary pain will only exacerbate the problem.'[60] For cutbacks, the report proposed to draw on the broad review launched in 1981. This new programme, also called 'the austerity bible' in the corridors of The Hague, consisted of a series of senior finance department working groups thinking up austerity proposals.[61] It was coordinated by the then twenty-eight-year-old economist Gerrit Zalm, a senior finance official. In their report, Koopmans, Meys and Oort advised making this programme a 'permanent activity' and suggested excluding 'officials from spending departments' from taking

57 Pieter Korteweg, ed., *Beheersing van de overheidsuitgaven* (The Hague: Teldersstichting, 1981).

58 Lenze Koopmans, Dick Meys and Cees Oort, 'Herziening van besluitvorming-sprocedures', in Korteweg, *Beheersing van de overheidsuitgaven*, 15–26.

59 Henk Brons, 'Dr. Bart le Blanc. Bezuinigingsideoloog' [Dr Bart le Blanc: Austerity idealogue], *Het Vrije Volk*, 30 July 1983, 4.

60 Koopmans, Meys and Oort, 'Herziening van besluitvormingsprocedures', 22.

61 Zalm, *De romantische boekhouder*, 43.

part. The authors of the report would not get their way on all points. But in the 1980s the Ministry of Finance would nevertheless live up to its reputation as a 'brutalist bastion'.

Meanwhile, Lense Koopmans had made a move into the business world, where he stood out for his fondness for driving Porsches and his carefully blow-dried hairdo. In 1978 he had become CFO of the construction conglomerate OGEM. Less than four years later, the company went spectacularly bankrupt. Koopmans and the board had fiddled the accounts while paying themselves spectacular salaries and evading Dutch taxes through a letterbox company in Cyprus. The Dutch press portrayed Koopmans as the Gordon Gecko of the Netherlands, after the financier in Oliver Stone's film *Wall Street*, whose motto 'greed is good' became a watchword of the 1980s.[62]

The 'Friedmaniacs' on the March

Alongside public-choice theory, a second neoliberal current made a name for itself in the 1970s: Anglo-American monetarism. Monetarists believed that the inflation of the 1970s was caused by governments allowing too much money to circulate in the economy. As we saw in the previous chapter, there was already an established tradition of 'moderate monetarism' in the Netherlands, propagated mainly by the Dutch Central Bank. During the 1970s, however, Friedman's more militant monetarism also started to gain ground among Dutch economists. Friedman's Dutch disciples were initially known as a somewhat marginal and fanatical bunch – referred to in the press as 'Friedmaniacs' – but soon claimed a central role in the economic debate. A key figure was Pieter Korteweg, one of the few Dutch speakers at the Amsterdam congress of the Mont Pelerin Society. Korteweg had studied economics in Rotterdam and had obtained a PhD in 1971 for a thesis in the tradition of Dutch monetarism.[63]

This was, however, a time of increasing internationalization. Korteweg encountered the ideas of Karl Brunner and Allan Meltzer. Together with

---

62 'Zwart schaap Lense Koopmans weer in genade aangenomen' [Black sheep Lense Koopmans returned to grace], *Trouw*, 20 February 2002.

63 Pieter Korteweg, *De monetaire sector, het aanbod van geld en de instrumenten van de monetaire politiek* (Leiden: Stenfert Kroese, 1971).

Milton Friedman, they were the figureheads of the Anglo-American monetarist movement and all prominent members of the Mont Pelerin Society. The Swiss-American Karl Brunner was among the early founders of the MPS and served as a personal adviser to Margaret Thatcher. Allan Meltzer was highly influential in the United States: he worked for a long time at the American Enterprise Institute and advised Ronald Reagan. In an obituary of Allan Meltzer, the *Washington Post* wrote that there was 'an unspoken division of labor' between Friedman and Meltzer. 'Friedman, who wrote a *Newsweek* column and had several popular books, was Mr. Outside. He concentrated on convincing the public that government, through the Fed, had caused high inflation. Meltzer was Mr. Inside, focusing on his fellow economists.'[64] At Meltzer's invitation, Korteweg spent a year as a visiting professor at Carnegie Mellon University in the United States. After returning home, he sought to bring the monetarist counter-revolution to the Netherlands.

Korteweg was a man of clear convictions, who had the habit of boldly presenting controversial economic theories as self-evident laws of nature. Behind Keynesianism, he said, was a mistaken perspective on life itself. 'The idea that an economy does not naturally restore to equilibrium' was dead wrong: 'There is nothing in nature that is out of control. There are forces restoring natural equilibrium everywhere.'[65] Korteweg headed the Department of Monetary Economics at Erasmus University Rotterdam in the 1970s. Together with his PhD student Eduard Bomhoff, he built the department into a small but well-funded and strident stronghold of neoliberal ideas. The department acted as a think-tank of sorts: it published the series *Rotterdam Monetary Studies*, which translated and summarized contributions by influential monetarist and public-choice thinkers such as Karl Brunner, James Buchanan, Allan Melzer and Mancur Olson.[66] The department also organized a range of influential conferences and prestigious debates, such as between

---

64   Robert Samuelson, 'Economist Allan Meltzer, 1928–2017', *Washington Post*, 16 May 2017.

65   Pieter Korteweg, interview by the author, Bosch en Duin, 7 January 2020.

66   See, for example, Karl Brunner, *Monetaire politiek in de V.S.* (Rotterdam: Stichting Rotterdamse Monetaire Studies, 1982); Allan H. Meltzer, *De onzekere wereldeconomie* (Rotterdam: Stichting Rotterdamse Monetaire Studies, 1984); Mancur Olson, *Pressiegroepen en economische groei* (Rotterdam: Stichting Rotterdamse Monetaire Studies, 1984); James McGill Buchanan, *Politiek schuldbesef* (Rotterdam: Stichting Rotterdamse Monetaire Studies, 1984).

Karl Brunner and Joop den Uyl (1982), between James Buchanan and sociologist Abram de Swaan (1984) and between William Niskanen and the Dutch senior civil servant Roel in 't Veld (1986).

Following in the footsteps of Brunner and Meltzer, who lambasted the Federal Reserve for causing runaway inflation, Korteweg took the Dutch Central Bank to task. In his 1973 inaugural address, *Controlling the Money Supply*, Korteweg rode a monetarist hobbyhorse: he proposed the introduction of a fixed monetary rule to combat inflation. According to monetarists, the inflation of the 1970s was caused by governments and central banks that pumped too much money into the economy. If central banks publicly committed themselves to curbing the money supply, inflation could be reduced. In practice, this meant that borrowing money would become more expensive. In the short term, it would amount to a deflationary policy and a deepening of the crisis. In the longer run, however, Korteweg believed the market would find a new equilibrium, once wages had fallen.[67]

Writing in the leading Dutch economics journal *ESB*, Korteweg criticized central bank president Jelle Zijlstra's annual reports and argued for tighter monetary policy. A long-running discussion unfolded with economists from the Dutch Central Bank (DNB), CPB and the Ministry of Finance.[68] It was a debate with far-reaching political implications, but it was conducted in such technical, esoteric language that it could be followed only by a small group of experts. When DNB in the late 1970s – following the German Bundesbank's lead – took a tougher line, implementing credit restrictions, Korteweg seemed to have won a major victory. But it did not go nearly far enough for him.[69]

Korteweg and Bomhoff also introduced a related school of economic thinking, which built on monetarism. The main representative of this current was the Chicago school economist Robert Lucas, who had radicalized Friedman's critique of Keynesianism. Whereas Friedman argued that it took some time for firms, trade unions and consumers to adapt their expectations in response to expansionary policies, Lucas argued that this happened immediately. Economic actors had 'rational

---

67   Pieter Korteweg, *Over de beheersbaarheid van de geldhoeveelheid in Nederland* (Haarlem: Bohn, 1973).

68   For a retrospective on this debate, see Martin Fase, 'The Dutch Monetary Debate and the Role of Monetarism', *ESB* 101, no. 4,726 (21 January 2016): 44–8.

69   Ibid., 47.

expectations' and understood the economic system as much as economists themselves. In times of crisis, the government could increase spending, but people could reasonably foresee that the bill would have to be paid later, through higher taxes or higher inflation. Therefore, trade unions responded with higher wage claims, and businesses and consumers would cut back and save rather than spend. As a result, countercyclical spending policies had little to no effect. Indeed, Lucas argued that expansionary monetary and fiscal policies 'have the capacity only to disrupt'.[70]

Part of the 'rational expectations revolution' was a fundamental critique of Keynesian modelling. In a famous 1976 paper that would go down in history as the 'Lucas critique', Lucas questioned the existing Keynesian macro models.[71] Since they were based on historical data obtained from a previous economic context, they could not say much about how actors would respond to policies in a new context. The solution, Lucas suggested, was to combine macroeconomic models with insights from microeconomics. Whereas macroeconomics traditionally focuses on the large causal relations and aggregates, such as purchasing power and gross national product, microeconomics is concerned with modelling the behaviour of individual market actors, who act according to rational self-interest. Lucas and colleagues developed new, mathematically highly ingenious macro-models, launching a new scientific paradigm: new-classical macroeconomics.[72] As the name suggests, this meant a return to the old assumptions of neoclassical economics that had previously been cast aside by the Keynesian revolution.

Drawing on their monetarist and new-classical inspirations, Korteweg and Bomhoff developed their own econometric model of the Dutch economy. Before, they had accused the CPB of not paying attention to

70   Cited in Rune Møller Stahl, 'From Depoliticisation to Dedemocratisation: Revisiting the Neoliberal Turn in Macroeconomics', *New Political Economy* 26, no. 3 (4 May 2021): 411.

71   Robert E. Lucas Jr, 'Econometric Policy Evaluation: A Critique', in *Carnegie-Rochester Conference Series on Public Policy*, vol. 1 (North-Holland, 1976), 19–46.

72   'New-classical economics' is the name given to an economic school of thought that sought to base macroeconomics entirely on neoclassical microeconomics, especially rational expectations. Jacqueline Best, 'The Quiet Failures of Early Neoliberalism: From Rational Expectations to Keynesianism in Reverse', *Review of International Studies* 46, no. 5 (December 2020): 594–612; Preston J. Miller, ed., *The Rational Expectations Revolution: Readings from the Front Line* (Cambridge, MA: MIT Press, 1994).

monetary considerations and structurally underestimating inflation.[73] According to Korteweg and Bomhoff's own model, the inflation rate predicted by the CPB was structurally 2 per cent too low.[74] Bomhoff claimed the reason was political. The bureau had a monopoly, and this made it 'difficult for the CPB not to give in when there is pressure from the government'.[75] Korteweg and Bomhoff offered their services, they had made a competing rational expectations model, developed in dialogue with Brunner and Meltzer.[76] The model showed that economic growth could be restored to its full glory by 'drastically reducing' the tax burden and social spending.[77] At the 1977 annual meeting of the Dutch Royal Society for Economics, Korteweg presented his model as superior to that of the CPB.[78]

These technical debates were accompanied by a critique of the large role of the state in the economy. Internationally, monetarists such as Friedman, Brunner and Meltzer had popularized the 'crowding-out' theory.[79] In direct opposition to Keynesianism, monetarists argued that government stimulus policies resulted in a decline of economic activity. The argument ran as follows: When the government borrows extra money to pay for its spending, it competes directly with the private sector for its financing needs. With its budget deficits, the government

73   See 'Planbureau dient politieke doeleinden' [Planning bureau serves political ends], *NRC Handelsblad*, 14 September 1976, 13; Mayte Beekman, 'An Ordered Economy or Free Market? The Public Dissemination of Monetarist Ideas in the Netherlands' (master's thesis, Utrecht University, 2020).

74   'Prof. dr. P. Korteweg: "Ook onze prognose komt niet onder schattingen CPB uit"' [Prof. Dr P. Korteweg: 'Our prognosis is higher than the estimation of the CPB'], *NRC Handelsblad*, 10 November 1976, 1. The prediction turned out to be incorrect. Inflation in 1977 fell to 7 per cent, as the CPB had estimated, and did not rise to 9 per cent as the model of Korteweg and Bomhoff predicted.

75   'Planbureau dient politieke doeleinden'.

76   Pieter Korteweg, 'The Economics of Inflation and Output Fluctuations in the Netherlands, 1954–1975: A Test of Some Implications of the Dominant Impulse-Cum-Rational Expectations Hypothesis', *Carnegie-Rochester Conference Series on Public Policy* 8 (1978): 17–79.

77   Pieter Korteweg, *Herstel van economische groei* (Rotterdam: Stichting Rotterdamse Monetaire Studies, 1982), 26.

78   Pieter Korteweg, 'De stagflatie in de jaren zeventig: feiten en verklaringen', in Dirk Schouten, ed., *Preadviezen van de Vereniging voor Staathuishoudkunde* (Leiden: Stenfert Kroese, 1978), 31–108.

79   See Karl Brunner and Allan Meltzer, 'Government, the Private Sector, and "Crowding Out"', *Banker*, July 1976, 765–9.

drives up interest rates and squeezes business. The crowding-out theory had great political appeal for the right: you could blame the welfare state for high interest rates and argue that deep spending cuts resulted in a prompt economic recovery. 'A guilder not spent by the government will be spent elsewhere by someone else,' Korteweg promised.[80]

Korteweg introduced the crowding-out theory in the Netherlands in *ESB* in 1975, and soon Dutch economists were queuing up to confirm or disprove its relevance.[81] In subsequent years, the controversial theory was used by DNB president Jelle Zijlstra and the Ministry of Finance to bolster their case for reducing the budget deficit.[82] Critics of the theory argued that high interest rates were a result of international developments, over which the budget deficit of a small country like the Netherlands held little sway. Moreover, the Netherlands still had a savings surplus, and there were no signs that Dutch business was experiencing a lack of funding. By the mid-1980s, large budget deficits and high levels of private investment in the US and Japan would further disprove crowding-out. Yet economist Jan Pen observed that the crowding-out theory became a 'key talking point in the Hague' in the first half of the 1980s.[83]

In this way, the ideas of Milton Friedman and the monetarists made inroads among Dutch economists and policymakers, but Friedman's name remained little known among the wider public. This changed in January 1981, when Friedman's PBS documentary series *Free to Choose* was broadcast in its entirety on Dutch public television by the small

---

80   'OESO-landen vestigen hoop op bezuinigen' [OECD countries place hope in austerity], *Het Parool*, 11 May 1982, 6.

81   The first mention of 'crowding out' in *ESB* is by Pieter Korteweg, in one of his reviews of the Dutch Central Bank's annual reports: Pieter Korteweg, 'Jaarverslag 1974 van De Nederlandsche Bank', *ESB* 60, no. 3,004 (4 June 1975): 532–6. In the following decade, more than thirty articles on 'crowding out' appeared in the journal, including pieces by monetarists such as Bomhoff, Knoester and Buitelaar and Keynesians such as De Galan, Driehuis and Pen, as well as by Rabobank chief Herman Wijffels and soon-to-be Minister of Economic Affairs Koos Andriessen.

82   The theory was used by central bank president Zijlstra in a notorious protest letter to the government in 1980 and would go on to feature prominently in the Budget Memorandum, written under Korteweg's leadership. 'Boodschap Zijlstra: we moeten tering naar nering zetten' [Message Zijlstra: We must cut our coat according to our cloth], *NRC Handelsblad*, 14 March 1980, 1.

83   Jan Pen, 'De ideologie achter de Miljoenennota 1986', *ESB* 70, no. 3,527 (16 October 1985): 1039.

right-wing network TROS.[84] The series introduced neoliberal ideas in an accessible manner and turned out to be an unexpected hit. Ronald Reagan and Margaret Thatcher had both just come to power, and there was much interest in the ideologue behind their free market revolution. 'It struck such a chord that schools and companies were requesting videotapes of this broadcast,' wrote the right-wing newspaper *De Telegraaf* enthusiastically.[85] Other newspapers devoted extensive coverage to what was now called 'the Friedman phenomenon'.[86] 'There is an unshakeable, almost sacred belief in the free market', and TROS was 'currently lying in worship before its prophet', wrote the centre-left broadsheet *de Volkskrant* in a full-page analysis.[87] The response was predominantly negative, but commentators could not deny that Friedman was 'by now in vogue'.[88]

Friedman's newfound fame reflected back on Korteweg and Bomhoff. After the success of Friedman's documentary, an extra programme was added in which Bomhoff was invited to defend Friedman's ideas.[89] Seated in a sober studio with a cheerful flower arrangement in the middle, Bomhoff crossed swords for an hour with Cees de Galan, a prominent Keynesian economist and social democrat. Meanwhile, Pieter Korteweg was introduced as 'the Dutch Friedman' in an interview with a Dutch weekly. It was a title he accepted with great pride: 'Of course Friedman is right,' Korteweg said.[90] He explained that markets

84   The series was a response to the earlier successful documentary series of arch-enemy John Kenneth Galbraith. See Angus Burgin, 'Age of Certainty: Galbraith, Friedman, and the Public Life of Economic Ideas', in Tiago Mata and Steven G. Medema, eds, *The Economist as Public Intellectual* (Durham, NC: Duke University Press, 2013), 191–219.

85   'Veel films op de buis dit weekeinde' [Many films on TV this weekend], *De Telegraaf*, 23 January 1981, 2.

86   Arend Vermaat, 'Het verschijnsel Milton Friedman' [The phenomenon Milton Friedman], *Trouw*, 14 May 1981, 13; Jan Beishuizen, 'Simplistische kijk van een monetarist' [Simplistic view of a monetarist], *Het Parool*, 13 February 1981, 14.

87   Harry Lockefeer, 'De tros en de vrije jongens van Milton Friedman' [The TROS and Milton Friedman's free spirits], *De Volkskrant*, 17 January 1981, 3.

88   Ger Vaders, 'Friedman en de heroverweging' [Friedman and retrenchment], *Nieuwsblad van het Noorden*, 12 February 1981, 4.

89   'Aan ons de keus (Slot)' [*Free to Choose* (conclusion)], TROS, 15 May 1981.

90   Gerard Driehuis and Dirk Kuin, 'Professor Pieter Korteweg en de verrechtsing. "De mensen zijn niet bang voor Friedman, ze zijn bang voor zichzelf"' [Professor Pieter Korteweg and the shift to the right: 'People are not afraid of Friedman, they are afraid of themselves'], *De Tijd*, 6 March 1981, 24–6.

naturally reached equilibrium and that government intervention only disrupted the economy. That same year, at the initiative of senior finance officials, he was appointed treasurer-general and became the highest official in the ministry.[91] In his own words, he saw it as his task to 'unleash the market and fence in the collective sector'.[92] According to a prominent economic journalist, the finance ministry had in the 1980s become a stronghold of 'ardent supporters of monetarism'.[93]

The Struggle over Fiscal Policy

Korteweg came as a godsend. Under the new finance minister, Fons van der Stee (CDA) – the successor to Frans Andriessen (of the same party), who had resigned in 1980 – the ministry actively campaigned to convince the public of the need for a harsher austerity policy. 'Getting the parliament behind you requires a special approach,' Van der Stee had concluded after his predecessor's downfall. 'The parliament reacts only to public opinion. And public opinion reacts to the press. So you have to work the media.' Van der Stee decided to send his senior officials to do that job: 'Boys, go sell my story. They have to take every opportunity they get, to get our message out there. Interviews, speeches, opinion pages – couldn't give a damn, take the stage.'[94] Thus, in the early 1980s, Pieter Korteweg and Bart le Blanc featured in an impressive series of interviews and newspaper reports, in which they took a polemical stance on the need for austerity.[95]

---

91   De Haas and Van Lotringen, *Wim Duisenberg*, 106.

92   Korteweg, interview by the author.

93   José Toirkens, 'Een mijnenveld voor socialisten' [A minefield for socialists], *NRC Handelsblad*, 8 November 1989, 21.

94   'Fons van der Stee: als je als minister van financiën even de deur uitloopt, ben je al vijf miljoen kwijt' [Fons van der Stee: If the finance minister so much as walks out of the door, you already lose five million], *De Tijd*, 4 March 1988.

95   A small selection of the dozens of newspaper articles: 'Begrotingsproblemen: verloedering stoppen' [Budget deficit: Stop deterioration], *NRC Handelsblad*, 18 July 1981, 1; 'Groei overheid gaat nu ten koste van de lonen' [Public sector growth now at the expense of wages], *NRC Handelsblad*, 24 March 1982, 15; 'Thesaurier-generaal prof. Korteweg: Nederlands beleid op het spoor van IMF' [Treasurer-General Prof. Korteweg: Dutch policy on IMF track], *De Telegraaf*, 15 May 1982, 47; 'Top Financiën: alleen dan lagere rente. Beroep op besparingen van overheid moet verder terug' [Finance official: Only then lower interest rates. Reliance on government money must fall further],

Around the 1981 parliamentary elections, a fierce political battle had erupted over the economic policy to be pursued. In contrast to the dominant historical image of a Dutch policy consensus, there were in fact two antagonistic camps. 'Roughly speaking, there are two schools in combating the economic crisis,' observed CDA party chairman Ruud Lubbers in a guest lecture at Twente University:

The proponents of fiscal stimulus, neo-Keynesians, want to expand the deficit. The public sector will keep demand from falling . . . The proponents of fiscal retrenchment, often neoliberals, today don the clothes of monetarists: reduce government spending, adapt the money supply to stagnation, enforce higher savings and lower spending through a higher interest rate if needed, and restructure the economy.[96]

The first approach was especially popular on the left and among trade unions, the second on the right and among employers. The challenge for CDA Prime Minister Van Agt was that this fault line ran straight through the CDA itself.[97]

In a seminal speech in the illustrious Amsterdam music venue Paradiso, Labour leader Den Uyl had tried to frame the 1981 elections as a referendum on neoliberalism. Den Uyl spoke for two and a half hours, in what later turned out to be the swansong of Keynesian social democracy. He impressed upon the public that Dutch society stood at a crossroads. The choice was either to continue walking the democratic road, or to choose the path represented by the 'new right': Thatcher and Reagan and the 'free market ideology' of Hayek and Friedman. According

---

Leeuwarder Courant, 27 May 1982, 27; 'Prof. Korteweg van Financiën: Staatstekort moet naar nul' [Prof. Korteweg from the Ministry of Finance: Budget deficit must go to zero], *De Volkskrant*, 21 August 1982, 2; 'De patiënt heeft nu echt zeer hoge koorts' [The patient now really has a very high fever], *NRC Handelsblad*, 21 September 1982, 1.

96   Ruud Lubbers, 'Weg met de geest van Jan Salie', guest lecture, Hogeschool Twente, 22 March 1982 – published in Ruud Lubbers, *Samen onderweg: Over democratie, christendom en samenleving, economie en internationale vraagstukken*, ed. Arendo Joustra and Erik Van Venetië (Utrecht: Het Spectrum, 1991), 212.

97   Jelle Zijlstra and Frans Andriessen belonged to the first camp, Wil Albeda and Bert de Vries to the second. Lubbers was, as always, somewhere in between. See Hans Borstlap, 'De economische crisis en het "Plan-Schouten"', *Christen Democratische Verkenningen*, 9 September 1982, 400–15.

to Den Uyl, these ideas were also flourishing in the Netherlands. After the democratization movement of the 1970s, there was now an attempt to turn back the clock, to depoliticize economic policy and 'return the steering wheel to a small group of powerful people.'[98]

When the 1981 elections were held, the centre-right failed to win a parliamentary majority. Van Agt was forced, utterly against his will, to form a government with Den Uyl. The resulting second Van Agt cabinet was, from the very start, embroiled in continuous in-fighting over economic policy.[99] Fons van der Stee (CDA) had been reappointed as finance minister and again deployed his senior officials to maximum effect. The finance officials had weekly crisis meetings with the prime minister and were actively used by Van Agt to fight the PvdA. One well-known journalist called it 'the toaster tactic': 'With a toasting iron, whatever is inside runs a good chance of either burning or melting away. Both possibilities were permissible because the candidate to sit in the iron was Den Uyl's Labour Party.' One half of the iron was represented by the prime minister, who was constantly creating polemics; the other half of the iron was the government budget and the continuous interventions of the Ministry of Finance in that area. Both halves were thoroughly heated up.[100]

Van Agt and Den Uyl had reached an unstable compromise in the coalition agreement: the government would follow a twin-track policy, giving equal priority to reducing the budget deficit and preserving employment. The Labour Party wanted to offset budget cuts with an employment plan to create 200,000 jobs. When the government took office, however, the finance minister announced major financial setbacks and demanded additional cuts, invoking the crowding-out theory.[101] A new compromise had not yet been forged, and the finance ministry again came with new shortfalls. Meanwhile, the employment plan designed by economist Jo Ritzen (PvdA) was actively sabotaged by

98   Joop den Uyl, *Tegen de stroom in* (Amsterdam: Trommel, 1981), 23.

99   Hans Rodenburg, 'De finale strijd om de collectieve sector', in Carla van Baalen and Anne Bos, eds, *Grote idealen, smalle marges: Een parlementaire geschiedenis van de lange jaren zeventig (1971–1982)*, vol. 10, *Parlementaire geschiedenis van Nederland na 1945* (Amsterdam: Boom, 2022), 520–40.

100   Marc Chavannes, 'De formatie van het CDA' [The forming of the CDA], *NRC Handelsblad*, 5 September 1981, 1.

101   Rodenburg, 'De finale strijd om de collectieve sector', 523.

senior finance officials.[102] 'We wrecked that,' Pieter Korteweg admitted proudly.[103] After yet another financial setback, the ministers of the Labour Party concluded that the Ministry of Finance was strategically leaking setbacks to the press to create a continuous crisis atmosphere, putting the Labour Party on the defensive.[104] 'You from Finance, you are swindling us!' PvdA Minister Marcel van Dam let slip in the Council of Ministers.[105] He expressed the widely held suspicion that the Ministry of Finance was deliberately torpedoing the coalition. In October 1981, the Labour Party ministers resigned, before the government policy statement had even been drafted. When economists Cees de Galan and Victor Halberstadt were appointed to broker a peace and mend the coalition, they asked a senior finance official plainly: 'How politicized is the bureaucratic elite of the finance ministry?'[106] While their attempt at reconciliation succeeded in the short term, it could not prevent the coalition government from collapsing six months later.

With the meltdown of the PvdA, however, the battle was not yet over. In the subsequent third Van Agt minority cabinet (CDA and D66), the conflict between monetarists and Keynesians dragged on. Tilburg economist Dick Schouten, chairman of the Committee of Economic Experts of the corporatist Social and Economic Council, seemed to offer a glimmer of hope. He had developed the Schouten plan, a moderate-Keynesian austerity agenda centred on a four-year wage freeze. In return, the government would cut payroll taxes.[107] The advantage of this plan was that it would reduce labour costs while maintaining effective demand. The downside, however, was that the budget deficit would increase further in the short term. Keynesian economists considered this permissible, but for monetarists it was unthinkable. The Schouten plan had the support of a majority of the Dutch parliament. According to the CPB the plan scored

---

102   Max van Weezel, 'Hoe de ambtenaren van Van der Stee en Terlouw het banen-plan onderuithaalden' [How the officials of Van der Stee and Terlouw knocked down the employment plan], *Vrij Nederland*, 20 February 1982.

103   Korteweg, interview by the author.

104   Toirkens, *Schijn en werkelijkheid*, 410; Johan van Merriënboer, Peter Bootsma and Peter van Griensven, *Van Agt biografie: Tour de force* (Amsterdam: Boom, 2008), 432.

105   Bart le Blanc, *Schrijven met een vork*, commemorative booklet for anniversary of senior finance officials (self-published, 2009), 5.

106   Ibid., 31.

107   Borstlap, 'De economische crisis en het "Plan-Schouten"'.

better on employment than the existing austerity plans. Den Uyl even described the plan as an alternative to neoliberalism, 'the one-sided emphasis on supply-side economics and monetary strangleholds'.[108]

The Finance Ministry immediately launched a fierce media campaign against Schouten's proposal. Even before Finance Minister Van der Stee had a chance to respond, Pieter Korteweg had already dismissed the plan as an 'alluring ruse' and 'golden veneer'.[109] 'Senior Finance Official Slams Schouten Proposal', announced *De Telegraaf* on its front page.[110] According to Korteweg, the competitive advantage bought with cheaper wages would soon evaporate due to the appreciation of the Dutch guilder. In the short term, only 'reducing the deficit' could prevent 'further breakdown of production capacity and employment'. This reasoning was exactly the opposite to that of the Keynesians. Eduard Bomhoff joined his former supervisor on the opinion pages, where he launched a frontal attack: 'There is no such thing as self-raising flour in economics. What Dr Oetker can do, Schouten cannot.'[111] Bart le Blanc also stepped in. In a high-profile interview, he described reducing the government deficit as the first priority: 'The government's continued reliance on the capital market naturally affects interest rates and crowds out other investors.'[112] With the help of his senior officials, Prime Minister Van Agt managed to sideline the Schouten plan, going against the will of his own party.

This unprecedented media blitz by senior civil servants prompted the speaker of the Dutch parliament, Dick Dolman (PvdA), to admonish

---

108   Joop den Uyl, *Small marges, grote gevolgen* (The Hague: 1982), 7–8.

109   'Van der Stee wijst plan-Schouten af' [Van der Stee rejects Schouten plan], *Leeuwarder Courant*, 24 June 1982, 3; 'Nieuwe begroting vertoont nu al gat van tien miljard' [New budget shows hole of ten billion], *De Volkskrant*, 25 June 1982, 1; 'Korteweg: 10 miljard extra bezuinigen' [Korteweg: 10 billion additional cuts], *NRC Handelsblad*, 24 June 1982, 1.

110   'Topman Financiën kraakt voorstel Schouten af' [Senior finance official runs Schouten plan into the ground], *De Telegraaf*, 25 June 1982; 'Van der Stee maakt korte metten met plan-Schouten' [Van der Stee makes short work of Schouten plan], *Trouw*, 25 June 1982, 1. See also 'Nog meer loonmatiging heeft weinig zin' [More wage moderation has little use], *De Volkskrant*, 14 August 1982, 2.

111   'Prof. Bomhoff mist stimulans voor export in plan econoom Schouten: "Sociale uitgaven moeten fors omlaag"' [Prof. Bomhoff misses stimulus for export in the Schouten economic plan: 'Social expenditures need to go down substantially'], *De Volkskrant*, 26 June 1982, 9.

112   'De patiënt heeft nu zeer hoge koorts'.

Van Agt to 'restore constitutional relations as soon as possible' and not to leave governing to his senior officials. 'The newspapers are filled to the brim with political statements by officials,' he complained, in response to Le Blanc's interview.[113] Journalists wrote that Finance Minister Van der Stee was 'controlled' by his senior officials. 'Casually, he reproduces the views of his officials,' another newspaper noted.[114] With the 1983 Budget Memorandum, the third Van Agt cabinet was preparing a historic austerity operation that would both retrench the public sector and cut wages. Commentators cynically joked that Van der Stee had developed a twin-track policy of his own: 'On the one hand, cut spending to reduce the deficit and on the other, cut spending to boost employment.'[115] In November 1982, this budget would be adopted almost unchanged by the incoming government.[116]

The intellectual high point of the monetarism debate was yet to come. The following year, Eduard Bomhoff and his Rotterdam department brought the monetarist Karl Brunner to the Netherlands. Opposition leader Joop den Uyl had been invited to debate him.[117] The debating venue itself illustrated the changing *Zeitgeist*. Rather than the usual drab university lecture hall, the organizers had hired the chic Rotterdam Hilton Hotel, thanks to the generous support of US oil company Chevron. The guests were all asked to dress in suits and ties and consumed a three-course meal while listening to the speakers.

Karl Brunner – introduced as Margaret Thatcher's personal adviser – claimed in his lecture that the stagflation crisis had its roots in the expansion of the welfare state in the 1960s. The unintended consequence of this generosity was the uncontrolled creation of money and the

113   Harry van Wijnen, 'Ambtenaren maken de dienst uit' [Officials call the shots], *Het Parool*, 25 September 1982, 9.

114   'Minister in houdgreep van zijn ambtenaren' [Minister controlled by his officials], *Het Vrije Volk*, 21 October 1982, 7.

115   Ton van Zweeden, 'Van der Stee's tweesporenbeleid' [Van der Stee's two-track policy], *NRC Handelsblad*, 19 June 1982, 7.

116   Rodenburg, 'De finale strijd om de collectieve sector', 537.

117   'Den Uyl: vrijemarkteconomie leidt tot verdere ontwrichting' [Den Uyl: Free market economy leads to further breakdown], *NRC Handelsblad*, 30 November 1982, 10; 'Economen "in de ring"' [Economists 'in the ring'], *Het Vrije Volk*, 30 November 1982, 9; 'Debat tussen economen' [Debate between economists], *De Telegraaf*, 1 December 1982, 4; 'Het debat Karl Brunner–Joop den Uyl' [The Karl Brunner–Joop den Uyl debate], *Intermediair*, 30 December 1982.

discouragement of private initiative. Curtailing the welfare state and reducing the regulatory burden on business would lead to recovery. Den Uyl replied that deregulating the economy would lead only to further disruption. After all, the real bottleneck for business was a lack of demand for its products, and this was precisely what required more government intervention and international coordination.

In his newspaper column of that week, social democratic intellectual Bart Tromp wrote that the content of the debate should no longer surprise anyone. The arguments of monetarists and Keynesians were by now familiar. What astonished Tromp was 'the ideological shift expressed by this event itself': 'Fifteen years ago, social democracy had to defend itself against the neo-Marxism of a new student generation; currently [it must defend] against the neoliberalism that is spreading like wildfire among bankers, economists, senior civil servants and entrepreneurs.'[118]

118   Bart Tromp, 'Van Delft naar Rotterdam' [From Delft to Rotterdam], *Het Parool*, 4 December 1982, 4.

4

Businesslike Politics (1982–89)

On Monday 22 November 1982, a new era was ushered in. Prime Minister Ruud Lubbers (CDA) read out the government statement of the incoming centre-right cabinet of CDA and VVD. He spoke in sober tones of an 'economic winter that has set in'.[1] The number of unemployed had now passed the half-million mark, and the budget deficit was over 8 per cent. Lubbers announced an unprecedented 7 billion guilders ($3 billion) a year in spending cuts – an amount that would eventually rise to 10 billion a year. At the same time, the government insisted on wage moderation, marking an important turning point in economic policy. Under the banner 'more market, less government', the state would step back to reduce the burden on business. Lubbers promised that 'various forms of privatization, including letting citizens do more things now done by the government, will be promoted as much as possible.'[2] The government cut public sector wages and unemployment benefits by a whopping 3 per cent and began removing 'rigid regulations' to give business more leeway.

In his government policy statement, Lubbers took a clear stand in the ongoing debate between Keynesians and monetarists. He rejected the idea that the government should maintain effective demand and

---

1 Parliamentary records, HTK 1982–1983, government policy declaration, 22 November 1982, 637.

2 Ibid., 636.

employment in times of crisis, considering it no longer effective. As the monetarist Anton Knoester wrote in his history of Dutch economic policy, this was the first cabinet that 'across the board, has done away with the Keynesian ideas that have for so long helped determine the practice of economic policy'.[3] The government decided to abandon employment policies altogether, even though unemployment had reached a post-war record of 10 per cent of the working-age population in 1983. The priority was restoring profitability, on the assumption that this would revive investment and employment in the longer term.

As Knoester rightly noted, the new cabinet's austerity policy was explicitly inspired by the controversial crowding-out theory of the US monetarists: the idea that budget deficits were crowding out private investments.[4] 'Reducing the budget deficit,' Lubbers told the Dutch parliament that Monday, 'is not an end in itself, but a means to reinvigorate our economy. After all, with the deficits gone, real interest rates will be able to come down.'[5] This made it 'easier to achieve the required return on investment', which would 'boost business activity and thus employment'. This was the opposite of what the Keynesians and the CPB held to be true: namely, that austerity without compensatory policies led to a lack of demand and additional unemployment.[6] Anyone listening carefully to Lubbers's presentation of the government statement on that November Monday in 1982 could hear behind his woolly words the firm voice of monetarist and treasurer-general Pieter Korteweg.

With this policy shift, the first Lubbers cabinet joined the free market revolution started by Margaret Thatcher and Ronald Reagan in previous years. Internationally, Lubbers was seen as a kindred spirit. When he visited President Reagan in 1984, *Time* magazine portrayed him glowingly as Ruud 'Shock' – supposedly tougher than the Iron Lady. The article cited a witticism from Margaret Thatcher, who had been on a state visit to the Netherlands earlier that year: 'Mr Lubbers, are you really

---

3 Anthonie Knoester, *Economische politiek in Nederland* (Leiden: Stenfert Kroese, 1989), 159.

4 Ibid., 162.

5 Government policy declaration, 22 November 1982, 635.

6 'Grote werkloosheid bij beleid à la Van der Stee' [High unemployment under policies], *Trouw*, 22 September 1982, 1; 'Macro-economische verkenningen: Planbureau bespeurt geen enkel lichtpunt' [Macroeconomic outlook: Planning bureau detects no bright spot], *NRC Handelsblad*, 21 September 1982, 14.

intending to cut the salaries of your public employees by more than 3%? That's a disaster. I am supposed to be the toughest in Europe. You are going to ruin my reputation as the Iron Lady.'[7]

In the Netherlands, though, Lubbers never attained that tough reputation. In fact, it would have been more appropriate for *Time* to call him Ruud 'Smog', due to his reputation for opaque language. Commentators pointed to Lubbers's 'sphinx-like character' and remarked on his consensual 'magic formulas', so 'Jesuitically unclear' that 'all participants left with the impression that they had been proved right'.[8] All in all, Lubbers lacked the ideological drive of Reagan and Thatcher. There was nothing resembling Thatcher's ambition to change 'the heart and soul of the nation', no Dutch equivalent of Reagan's promise of an American renaissance: 'Let's Make America Great Again'.[9] The fiery anti-government rhetoric that could be heard on the other side of the Atlantic – 'Government is not the answer to our problem, government is the problem,' Reagan said in his inaugural address – was wholly absent from Lubbers's government statement.[10] Instead, he soberly claimed to represent a new era of 'no-nonsense' politics, after years of heated quarrels and stalemates.[11] The new prime minister unfolded no grand vision or inspired rhetoric, just a dry enumeration of proposed austerity measures.[12] 'What isn't there isn't there, and what is there is there,' was his dry explanation of his government's budget philosophy.

The Christian Democrats had good reason to present their policy as apolitical. Because of their position in the political centre, the Christian Democrats had little to gain from open confrontation. Lubbers had to keep the progressive wing of his party on board, as well as the Christian trade union CNV, the Christian civil society organizations and the left-leaning part of his electorate. As a result, the Dutch policy shift lacked the ideological rhetoric that emerged in the US and the UK. Asked about the philosophy behind the cuts, Housing Minister Pieter

---

7 'The Netherlands: Ruud Shock', *Time*, 23 January 1984.

8 Pim Fortuyn, *Aan het volk van Nederland: De contractmaatschappij, een politiek-economische zedenschets* (Amsterdam: Contact, 1992), 111.

9 Ronald Butt, 'Interview with Margaret Thatcher', *Sunday Times*, 3 May 1981.

10 Ronald Reagan, 'Inaugural Address', 20 January 1981.

11 Oscar Garschagen and Redmar Kooistra, 'Een no-nonsense-kabinet laat ook zijn lege zakken zien' [A no-nonsense government shows its empty pockets], *De Volkskrant*, 15 January 1983, 49.

12 Government policy declaration, 22 November 1982.

Winsemius (VVD) referred to the crowding-out theory and replied tell-ingly: 'There is an agreement within the government not to elaborate too much on that.'[13] Sometimes it is argued that austerity 'lacked a scientific theory', a senior official of the Ministry of Economic Affairs later said. 'While that was not the case, it was deemed wiser to not make it too explicit.'[14] The head of the government's communication depart-ment described this ideological restraint as a deliberate strategy:

> If you take away 3 per cent of people's wages, it is better to refrain from grand narratives. Then you will certainly fall flat on your face. You can proselytize on television with a blackboard on your side, but that doesn't work. All the viewers can count for themselves. Lubbers understands this. This is a frugal policy, and it is better to present it in a businesslike and depoliticized manner. It will seem somewhat corporate, but you shouldn't loudly proclaim that it is your holy mission to fire so many teachers and care workers. The guideline is: be reserved, a bit boring if need be, don't react too quickly and leave your opponents with their dignity.[15]

The language of the new government was received in the press as a fundamental change in style, after the heated debates of the 1970s. 'Something like a small miracle happened last week,' wrote a prominent journalist. Parliament had debated the government statement for four days, and there was 'no [ideological] rhetoric, the tone was strictly busi-nesslike'. The debate 'would probably go down in history as one of the dullest in recent years,' he readily admitted. But, more importantly, 'for the first time in years, decisions can be made'. The journalist hailed this dry and sober style as the 'new businesslike politics'.[16]

The term referred to the classic book by American-Dutch political scientist Arend Lijphart: *The Politics of Accommodation*. As noted

13   Max van Weezel and Joop van Tijn, *Inzake het kabinet-Lubbers* (Amsterdam: Sijthoff, 1986), 59.

14   Ad Geelhoed, 'Making a Difference: De beleidsagenda en AEP', *Tijdschrift Voor Politieke Economie* 24, no. 1 (2002): 60–72.

15   Cited in Van Weezel and Van Tijn, *Inzake het kabinet-Lubbers*, 245.

16   Willem Breedveld, 'Naar een nieuwe zakelijkheid?' [A new businesslike style?], *Trouw*, 27 November 1982, 5. See also 'VNO-voorzitter Van Veen is blij met nieuwe zakelijkheid' [Chairman is happy with new businesslike style], *De Volkskrant*, 20 May 1983, 18; 'De verbijstering van de jaren tachtig' [The bewilderment of the 1980s], *NRC Handelsblad*, 13 April 1984, 13.

before, Lijphart had argued that Dutch politicians had developed an elite culture of compromise to govern the country and keep it from falling apart. According to Lijphart, 'businesslike politics' was the single most important rule of this political culture.[17] It meant that politics was above all about achieving results, not about winning an ideological contest. In the 1960s and 1970s, the time of politicization and democratization, the politics of accommodation seemed to have run its course. The first Lubbers cabinet, however, was widely seen as a return to the politics of old.[18]

Hans Daalder, the doyen of Dutch political science, saw it as a paradoxical development. In his eyes, the aim of the Lubbers cabinets to 'roll back the state' had an obvious ideological character. It was inspired by a 'neoliberal or, if you will, neoconservative ideal that has also made great strides elsewhere in the Western world'.[19] At the same time, however, Daalder observed that Lubbers was ushering in a revival of the old Dutch tradition of 'depoliticizing political choices'. The Dutch neoliberal turn was sold to the public as an apolitical and technocratic fix, using language such as 'no-nonsense' and 'finishing the job'. 'It is as if some of the old rules of the game that Lijphart once identified in Dutch politics have returned, albeit in a different guise. It is "businesslike politics" again, now packaged as "no-nonsense" government,' Daalder concluded.[20]

The era of 'businesslike politics' that Lubbers ushered in had another, more literal meaning. It denoted the return of business to the heart of Dutch political life, after a decade marked by leftist and trade union mobilization. Lubbers had risen to prominence as director of his family-owned steel company and served on the board of the Christian employers' federation (NCW). His ministerial team was largely recruited from the Dutch business elite. Onno Ruding (CDA), the finance minister, was a senior banker at AMRO bank and executive director at IMF; Minister

17   Arend Lijphart, *The Politics of Accommodation: Pluralism and Democracy in the Netherlands* (Berkeley: University of California Press, 1968), 123.

18   Rudi Andeweg and Galen A. Irwin, *Governance and Politics of the Netherlands* (Basingstoke: Palgrave Macmillan, 2009), 41.

19   Hans Daalder, *Politiek en historie: Opstellen over Nederlandse politiek en vergelijkende politieke wetenschap*, ed. Joop van den Berg (Amsterdam: Bert Bakker, 1990), 249–50.

20   Hans Daalder, 'De Nederlandse politiek in 1984 en de nieuwe flinkheid', in *Van oude en nieuwe regenten: Politiek in Nederland* (Amsterdam: Bert Bakker, 1995), 98.

of Transport Neelie Smit-Kroes (VVD) was commissioner of the merchant bank Mees & Hope; Pieter Winsemius (VVD), the minister of housing, spatial planning and the environment, came from consultancy firm McKinsey; and the minister of economic affairs, Gijs van Aardenne (VVD), was commissioner at the Holland Sea Search oil company.[21]

In a more figurative sense, too, business became the dominant metaphor for thinking about politics. Lubbers was called 'a manager in politics'; he and his ministers presented themselves publicly as hard-headed managers who had to steer a company through a major crisis. They did not engage in politics: they ran the 'Netherlands Inc.' ('BV Nederland') – a metaphor that construed the entire country as one giant corporation. Like an ailing company that had to be restructured, it was said that the state had to go 'back to core business' and divest from all peripheral activities.[22] The Dutch Minister of Transport (and later European Commissioner) Neelie Kroes saw no difference between working in the business sector and in politics. 'The nature of our work shouldn't be different. Every business leader has as much contact with society as we do. They have to keep their business going, just like we have to keep the Netherlands Inc. running.' Lubbers later explained that he conceived of this no-nonsense management style as a 'break with the Den Uyl period'. Instead of abstract theories on equality or quality of life, there was management:

> I meddled in things, I managed processes. I was a manager in politics. At the time, 'manager' implied, and this was often said, 'That man has no political ideals, he is just a manager.' But I wanted the Netherlands to change – dynamism, individualization, modernization. It was a journalistic typology, of course, but I also considered it a badge of honour, because at least you managed something, you got things done.[23]

All of this formed part of a larger international trend. Ronald Reagan was known for his 'CEO approach to the Oval Office', while Margaret

21   Van Weezel and Van Tijn, *Inzake het kabinet-Lubbers*, 8.

22   Frans Rutten, 'Voortgang met de nieuwe zakelijkheid', *ESB* 72, no. 3,592 (1 January 1987): 4–10.

23   Ronald Kroeze and Sjoerd Keulen, 'Managerpolitiek. Waarom historici oog voor management moeten hebben', *BMGN – Low Countries Historical Review* 127, no. 2 (25 June 2012): 104.

Thatcher was called 'the manager'. This convergence between politics and business management took place against a background of increased global competition. It was argued that the fate of nations was entangled with the fate of its major enterprises, while, at the same time, the investment climate provided by national states was seen as a major condition of business success. The forerunner of the World Economic Forum in Davos, at that time called the European Management Forum, began publishing its Global Competitiveness Report in 1979. It measured, compared and ranked nations in terms of their business climates. As the sociologist William Davies writes, 'A new vision of political authority was invented, in which the nation was comparable to a corporation, of which the political leader was the CEO and the citizens were employees.'[24] As a result, public policy and institutions now came to be seen as a business resource. But it was not just that business colonized politics; business itself was changing. Global demand for industrial products had peaked, and corporations were looking for ways to cut costs and innovate. There was a boom in management literature, which dominated the bestseller lists in the 1980s. In their seminal 1982 management book *In Search of Excellence*, the McKinsey consultants Thomas Peters and Robert Waterman had argued that companies should focus on their core competencies.[25] This went hand in hand with new business practices such as 'downsizing' and 'outsourcing'. Laying off thousands of workers and delegating peripheral tasks to other companies allowed corporations to cut costs. The idea was that managers could introduce the same processes in government.

Pivotal in this conceptual merger of politics and business was the Ministry of Economic Affairs. It was traditionally known as the 'business ministry' and acted as the voice of the private sector in Dutch politics.[26] The ministry was not merely an instrument for the

---

24   William Davies, *The Limits of Neoliberalism: Authority, Sovereignty and the Logic of Competition* (London: Sage, 2016), 97.

25   John Kay, 'A Brief History of Business Strategy', in John Kay, ed., *Foundations of Corporate Success: How Business Strategies Add Value* (Oxford: Oxford University Press, 1995), 337–63.

26   Jonne Harmsma, 'Dominante boys die alles regelen', *Binnenlands Bestuur* 42, no. 10 (28 May 2021): 20–3; Robert Hoppe, *Economische zaken schrijft een nota: Een onderzoek naar beleidsontwikkeling en besluitvorming bij non-incrementeel beleid* (Amsterdam: VU Uitgeverij, 1983); Hans de Bruijn, *Economische Zaken: Profiel van een ministerie*, Departementale studies, vol. 1 (The Hague: VUGA, 1989).

government to adjust the course of Dutch business; it also had the opposite aim: to correct the course of government in the interests of Dutch business. In the 1980s, the ministry was quite successful in this latter aim. It was inspired by a current of economic thought that rose to prominence in the late 1970s along with monetarism and public-choice theory: supply-side economics. Supply-siders argued that strengthening the private sector by lowering taxes, deregulation, liberalization and flexibilization was the key to economic recovery. In the Netherlands, this idea was not new. The export-led strategy of post-war reconstruction in the 1950s had been a supply-side policy. Inspired by Reaganomics abroad and the policy legacy of the 1950s at home, the Ministry of Economic Affairs would lead the way in moving from Keynesian demand management to a neoliberal supply-side policy.

Not Wassenaar but Wagner

In existing accounts of the policy shift of the 1980s, the Wassenaar Accord occupies a central place. In this famous bipartite agreement of 24 November 1982, Dutch employers and trade unions agreed to a moderation of wages in exchange for a reduction in working hours. The dominant narrative portrays this moment as the beginning of a new political-economic consensus that enabled the market-oriented reforms of the 1980s.[27] 'A remarkable aspect of the rather radical change in government policy is that it was shared by all major parties involved,' writes leading economic historian Jan Luiten van Zanden. 'A new consensus emerged in Dutch politics in the early 1980s.'[28] In a leading

---

27   Jelle Visser and Anton Hemerijck, '*A Dutch Miracle': Job Growth, Welfare Reform and Corporatism in the Netherlands, Changing Welfare States* (Amsterdam: Amsterdam University Press, 1997); Frank Hendriks, *Polder Politics: The Re-Invention of Consensus Democracy in the Netherlands* (Routledge, 2017); P. de Rooy, *A Tiny Spot on the Earth: The Political Culture of the Netherlands in the Nineteenth and Twentieth Century* (Amsterdam: Amsterdam University Press, 2015); Friso Wielenga and Lynne Richards, *A History of the Netherlands: From the Sixteenth Century to the Present Day*, (London: Bloomsbury Academic, 2024).

28   Jan Luiten van Zanden, *The Economic History of the Netherlands 1914–1995: A Small Open Economy in the 'Long' Twentieth Century* (London: Routledge, 1998), 169–70.

history textbook, Herman de Liagre Böhl writes of the 'undeniable success of Lubbers' causing 'a certain de-ideologization': 'The mainstream parties were actually in agreement on the type of policy needed.'[29] As noted before, this rather celebratory view of history has become part of the national self-image, known internationally as 'the polder model'. It offers a highly distorted image of political reality in the 1980s.[30] At this point in time, there was no consensus to speak of. Nor did the Wassenaar Accord play a large role in laying the groundwork for the market-based reforms of the 1980s. Its importance has been exaggerated. The accord merely confirmed a turnaround that had already been initiated elsewhere, by the Ministry of Economic Affairs.

A key figure in this development was the ministry's most powerful official, secretary-general Frans Rutten. He was known as 'the sphinx of Economic Affairs' because of his somewhat shy appearance – an impression reinforced by his soft southern accent. Nevertheless, he was credited by friend and foe alike with great influence over the rise of free market ideas in the Netherlands. A newspaper profile in the mid-1980s that praised Rutten as a 'modern prophet' gives an idea of the prestige he enjoyed:

> He lectures the university, the government, the nation. He is assisted by the economic thinkers he personally recruited for the Department of General Economic Policy. They celebrate him . . . His New Year's article in *ESB* is read by everyone that matters. On the national news, he explains himself in more detail: predictions, warnings and recommendations. An economic oracle whose pronouncements are realized in policy . . . For Rutten, economics is not only the science of

29   Herman De Liagre Böhl, 'Consensus en polarisatie: Spanningen in de verzorgingsstaat, 1945–1990', in Remieg Aerts, Piet de Rooy, Henk te Velde and Herman de Liagre Böhl, eds, *Land van Kleine Gebaren. Een Politieke Geschiedenis van Nederland 1780–1990* (Amsterdam: Boom, 2013), 331.

30   See Merijn Oudenampsen, 'Between Conflict and Consensus: The Dutch Depoliticized Paradigm Shift of the 1980s', *Comparative European Politics* 18, no. 5 (2020): 771–92; Merijn Oudenampsen and Bram Mellink, 'Bureaucrats First: The Leading Role of Policymakers in the Dutch Economic Paradigm Shift of the 1980s', *TSEG – The Low Countries Journal of Social and Economic History* 18, no. 1 (2021): 19–52. Uwe Becker, ' "Miracle" by Consensus? Consensualism and Dominance in Dutch Employment Development', *Economic and Industrial Democracy* 22, no. 4 (2001): 453–83.

mathematical models but also the delicacy of the finger on the national pulse.[31]

Many authorities (churches, teachers, parents) may have lost authority since the tumultuous 1960s, but the Dutch reverence for its economists still had a certain religious quality to it. Rutten was trained as an econometrician at Tilburg Catholic University under the moderate Keynesian Dick Schouten. As Rutten himself stressed, he had never been a Keynesian; he had obtained his PhD with a neoclassical dissertation titled 'Price Formation in Industry'.[32] He worked for a brief period as economics professor at the Erasmus University in Rotterdam, where he supervised the monetarist Pieter Korteweg, among others. In 1973 Rutten was appointed secretary-general at the Ministry of Economic Affairs, on the recommendation of the right-wing liberal minister of economic affairs, Harrie Langman (VVD).[33] Rutten would retain that position for an unprecedented seventeen years. Following established tradition, Rutten wrote the so-called 'New Year's article', published every January in the economics journal *ESB*. In these influential articles, he outlined the country's economic situation and offered advice on economic policy. In his early years, Rutten showed himself a pragmatist who defended the Keynesian conjunctural policies of the Den Uyl government as a form of damage control. At the end of the 1970s, however, Rutten became increasingly outspoken in his views. In 1978 he renounced his belief in 'activist' cyclical spending.[34] In short order, he developed into an ardent 'supply-sider' who, in his own words, 'tried with some colleagues to replace Keynes with Friedman'.[35]

In the 1987 New Year's article, 'The New Businesslike Politics', Rutten explained the long-term vision behind Lubbers's policies. Transposing the popular motto of business management to the state, Rutten wrote that the

31   Paul Friese and Maarten Huyge, 'De sfinx van EZ' [The sphinx of economic affairs], *NRC Handelsblad*, 7 June 1986, 25.

32   Frans Rutten, *Prijsvorming in de industrie* (Leiden: Stenfert Kroesse, 1965).

33   Harrie Langman, 'Ik geloof in lange golven', in Jarig van Sinderen, ed., *Het sociaal-economisch beleid in de tweede helft van de twintigste eeuw* (Groningen: Wolters-Noordhoff, 1990), 4.

34   Frans Rutten, 'Bijsturen van de economie', *ESB* 63, no. 3,136 (1978): 4–7.

35   Frans Rutten, 'Politiek en economie', *Onderneming en overheid*, no. 14 (1993): 103; Rogier Boulogne, 'Twaalf jaar Rutten op EZ: Van Keynesiaan tot supply-sider', *ESB* 70, no. 3,488 (9 January 1985): 49–51.

government had to 'concentrate on core business (such as justice, education, roads, defence) and should limit the less essential tasks (all kinds of subsidies and other interventions in the market economy)'.[36] According to Rutten, rational expectations theory, public-choice and supply-side economists had shown that government intervention had all sorts of negative side effects, which removed the incentive to produce. Leaving more to private initiative and local government allowed market incentives to be built into the public sector, especially in healthcare, education and housing. The government needed to move away from 'cerebral', counter-cyclical policies and focus on a few simple rules of thumb about permissible deficits and the tax burden.[37] Rutten said he derived this vision from Robert Lucas and Milton Friedman. In the long run, the government had to move away from so-called 'quasi-public goods (social security, healthcare, education)' altogether, instead turning these areas into markets through the use of individual vouchers – a well-known hobbyhorse of Friedman's.[38]

Rutten had a central position in the policymaking process. He chaired the Central Economic Committee (CEC), colloquially called the 'cockpit' of economic policymaking. In this committee, senior officials from the key ministries prepared the decisions taken by the Council of Ministers. Rutten also headed the Ministry of Economic Affairs' Department for General Economic Policy (AEP), where economic strategy was devised. Using his connections at Erasmus University Rotterdam, Rutten recruited young, talented economists with sympathies for neoliberal ideas. These young officials were soon referred to in the corridors as the 'Rutten Boys' – the Dutch equivalent of the illustrious Chicago Boys.

Among these so-called Rutten Boys was Anton Knoester. He headed AEP's economic think-tank and had completed his PhD on monetarist modelling under Rutten and Korteweg.[39] Another key member was Jarig van Sinderen, who focused on supply-side economics and made the case for Reaganomics in the Netherlands.[40] Perhaps the best-known

---

36   Rutten, 'Voortgang met de nieuwe zakelijkheid', 6.

37   Frans Rutten, *Zeven kabinetten wijzer: de nieuwe zakelijkheid bij het economische beleid* (Groningen: Wolters-Noordhoff, 1993), 99.

38   Frans Rutten, *Verval, herstel en groei: lessen voor het economisch beleid gelet op het leergeld van twintig jaar* (Utrecht: Lemma, 1995), 35–7.

39   Anton Knoester, *Over geld en economische politiek* (Leiden: Stenfert Kroese, 1980).

40   Jarig van Sinderen and Ab van Ravenstein, 'Meer markt en minder overheid: De

AEP member was Gerrit Zalm, who had come over from the Ministry of Finance, where he had originally arrived as a denim-wearing, long-haired, left-wing social democrat who could roll a cigarette on his thigh with one hand.[41] Once inside, he was quickly transformed into a free market advocate. In the decades that followed, he served as director of the CPB, minister of finance, and then party leader for the VVD and eventually director of the ABN-AMRO bank. This was a relatively small group of people, but, because of their strategic position in the policy-making process, AEP managed to exert great influence. 'Under Rutten, AEP sharpened the knives for the supply-side revolution,' AEP economists later wrote in a retrospective.[42]

Supply-Side Economics

In the Dutch rise of 'supply-side economics', two different developments converged. On the one hand, there was the international breakthrough of supply-side economics under Reagan in the United States. As the economic adviser to Reagan and member of the Mont Pelerin Society Martin Feldstein wrote, supply-side economics was not so much a single, well-defined theory.[43] It was a somewhat vague container-term that encompassed the whole spectrum of neoliberal ideas that emerged in the 1970s. In a strict sense, it referred to a policy shift from a Keynesian focus on the demand side of the economy towards a focus on improving the investment climate. More specifically, this meant restoring business profitability through tax cuts, deregulation, liberalization and privatization.

Supply-side economics was a major pillar of Ronald Reagan's election

---

visies van nieuw-klassieken en aanbodeconomen', *ESB* 72, no. 3,590 (1987): 68–72; Jarig van Sinderen, *Belastingheffing, economische groei en belastingopbrengst: Een evaluatie van aanbodeconomie* (Groningen: Wolters-Noordhoff, 1990); Jarig van Sinderen, *Aanbodeconomie acht jaar later: De theorie en de praktijk van Reaganomics* (Rotterdam: Stichting Rotterdamse Monetaire Studies, 1989).

41   Bruno de Haas and Cees van Lotringen, *Wim Duisenberg: Van Friese volksjongen tot Mr Euro* (Amsterdam: Business Contact, 2003), 110.

42   Stefan Raes et al., 'Het maken van economisch beleid: De rol van AEP in de afgelopen vijftig jaar', *Tijdschrift Voor Politieke Economie* 24, no. 1 (2002): 23.

43   Martin Feldstein, 'Supply Side Economics: Old Truths and New Claims', *American Economic Review* 76, no. 2 (1986): 26–30.

campaign. After his victory, it became an international trend that could not be ignored. One of the more controversial assumptions of supply-side economics was the idea that tax cuts could eventually pay for themselves through the economic stimulus they generated. This premise was central to the so-called 'Laffer curve', after the economist Arthur Laffer, who had famously explained this theory by drawing a graph on a napkin in 1974 for Republican politicians Dick Cheney and Donald Rumsfeld.[44] The curve inspired a new direction for the Republican Party, which culminated in a series of famous tax cuts.

The 'supply-side revolution' soon made waves in the Netherlands. The economics journal *ESB* devoted a special issue to the subject in the summer of 1982, which was followed by the annual meeting of the Royal Dutch Economic Association (KVS).[45] Dutch economists wrote about 'the irresistible rise of supply-side economics' and promptly declared Keynes 'dead'.[46] It was clear that the mood was now changing rapidly. The United States had always been seen in the Netherlands as a harbinger of future developments, and this case was no different. For the Ministry of Economic Affairs, the American supply-side revolution was an important source of inspiration. As AEP's Jarig van Sinderen said in a later interview: 'There was a huge crisis, with a budget deficit of 8, 9 per cent . . . At the AEP, people were thinking about different policies. The staff had looked towards the United States, where President Reagan wanted to revive the economy with his Reaganomics prescriptions: cut taxes and let the market do its work.'[47] Cees Oudshoorn, AEP member and later managing director of the employer's federation VNO-NCW, recalled 'a fierce battle between the Keynesians, who wanted to use the wage instrument to combat the economic crisis with public spending, and the supply-side economists who, under the influence of Reagan's politics, saw more salvation in tax cuts, budget cuts, promoting

---

44   Arthur B. Laffer and Jan P. Seymour, *The Economics of the Tax Revolt: A Reader* (New York: Harcourt Brace Jovanovich, 1979); Melinda Cooper, *Counterrevolution: Extravagance and Austerity in Public Finance* (Princeton, NJ: Princeton University Press, 2024).

45   Jaap van Duijn, 'Ontstaan en opkomst van "supply-side economics"', *ESB* 67, no. 3,362 (1982): 672–8.

46   J. J. van Duijn, ed., *De economie van het aanbod: preadviezen 1982, Prae-adviezen van de Vereniging voor de Staathuishoudkunde 1982* (Leiden: Stenfert Kroese, 1982).

47   Hans Obbink, 'Beleidseconomen zijn het tegenwoordig veel te veel eens', *SER-bulletin* 2 (2003): 2.

investments and moderating wages'. With his influential articles for the *ESB* journal, 'Rutten made Reaganomics fashionable in the Netherlands', Oudshoorn recalled.[48]

On the other hand, the shift to supply-side thinking was also a domestic development. There was renewed attention for the Dutch supply-side policy of the 1950s. An important influence in the reappraisal of the post-war period was provided by the 1980 report *The Place and Future of Dutch Industry* (PTNI), written by the leading economist and social democrat Arie van der Zwan.[49] Due to high wages, elevated oil prices and peaking interest rates, Dutch industry was in a deep crisis, and Van der Zwan sounded the alarm. He called for a new economic strategy to reindustrialize the country, similar to that of upcoming 'Asian Tigers' South Korea and Taiwan. There was no time for corporatist deliberation with the trade unions. What was needed was a 'responsible elite' of businessmen and civil servants who could take decisive action. With this report, the former adviser and confidant of Den Uyl seemed to have switched allegiance to the Dutch employers.

According to Van der Zwan, Dutch industry could only be saved by a new, state-led industrial policy. His report drew on the supply-side policies of Dutch post-war reconstruction. Van der Zwan was above all impressed with the way that the Ministry of Economic Affairs had managed to create broad societal support for its policy. He linked the success of the post-war policy to the authoritative and depoliticizing approach of the post-war Minister of Economic Affairs Jan van den Brink.[50] Based on the experience of the 1950s, Van der Zwan proposed the establishment of a powerful technocratic committee of experts who could chart a new course, outside the existing political and corporatist channels.

The report led to a revival of interest in the post-war supply-side policy. Historians and sociologists launched much-discussed

---

48 Elsje Jorritsma and Michèle de Waard, 'De sg is weer staatsdienaar, geen mooie zangvogel' [The secretary-general is again servant of the state, not a colourful figure], *NRC Handelsblad*, 5 January 2009, 2.

49 Wetenschappelijke Raad voor het Regeringsbeleid, *Plaats en toekomst van de Nederlandse industrie, Rapporten aan de regering 18* (The Hague: Staatsuitgeverij, 1980); Munise Varisli, 'Grenzen aan de groei? Sociaal-economische debatten in de jaren 1971–1983' (master's thesis, University of Amsterdam, 2018).

50 Arie van der Zwan, 'Sociaal-economische vraagstukken', *Socialisme en Democratie* 38, no. 11 (1981): 526.

historical studies, while the retired Jan van den Brink published his memoirs.[51] As president of the Board of Directors of the AMRO bank in the 1970s, Van den Brink had been a prominent member of the Dutch banking elite and a signatory of the famous protest letter against the policies of Den Uyl. But it was Van der Zwan who really captured the nation's attention, launching a high-profile 'crusade against rigidity' upon the publication of his report.[52] As part of his campaign, he organized a conference on the relevance of the supply-side policies of the 1950s at Erasmus University Rotterdam. Journalists wrote of the 'wonder doctors of the 1950s' who shared their secret recipes with a new generation of policymakers.[53] The former ministers and senior officials from the 1950s stressed the importance of a clear plan that could build support.

Meanwhile, Arie van der Zwan drifted further to the right: he wanted to suspend the disability allowance and replace it with an emergency law, reduce benefits, widen income disparities, introduce performance-related pay and increase subsidies for business.[54] In his view, these measures were necessary to force a change in the lacklustre mentality of the Dutch population. 'The measures we advocate should create a kind of shock effect – and then the change in mentality will come naturally,' Van der Zwan told journalists. 'Major structural changes are not brought about by democratic processes but by a push.'[55] The ultimate goal was to

51   See Herman de Liagre Böhl, Jan Nekkers and Laurens Slot, *Nederland industrialiseert!: politieke en ideologiese strijd rondom het naoorlogse industrialisatiebeleid 1945–1955*, Sunschrift 165 (Nijmegen: Socialistiese Uitgeverij Nijmegen, 1981); Jan van den Brink, *Zoeken naar een 'heilstaat': opbouw, neergang en perspectief van de Nederlandse welvaartsstaat* (Amsterdam: Elsevier, 1984); Pim Fortuyn, *Sociaal-economische politiek in Nederland 1945–1949* (Groningen: Rijksuniversiteit Groningen, 1980).

52   'Van der Zwans kruistocht tegen verstarring' [Van der Zwans crusader against rigidity], *NRC Handelsblad*, 19 June 1980, 12.

53   'Wonderdokters van toen: vertrouwen en consensus zijn nu erg nodig' [Miracle doctors of the past: Confidence and consensus are highly needed], *NRC Handelsblad*, 15 May 1982, 15.

54   Arie van der Zwan and Wim Driehuis, 'De Nederlandse economie in de jaren 1980–1985 (I)', *ESB* 66, no. 3,304 (6 May 1981): 448–54; Arie van der Zwan and Wim Driehuis, 'De Nederlandse economie in de jaren 1980–1985 (II)', *ESB* 66, no. 3,305 (13 May 1981): 480–4; Arie van der Zwan and Wim Driehuis, 'De Nederlandse economie in de jaren 1980–1985 (III)', *ESB* 66, no. 3,306 (20 May 1981): 508–15.

55   'Vraagtekens bij reddingsplan van Driehuis en Van der Zwan' [Question marks about the solution of Driehuis and Van der Zwan], *NRC Handelsblad*, 13 June 1981, 3.

change hearts and minds: 'It will become a more competitive society, and that is exactly the intention.'[56]

His fellow economists on the left were dismayed by this sudden conversion. 'I would prefer not to,' the Keynesian economist Jan Pen responded understatedly, 'it sounds just a bit too much like Friedman to me.'[57]

The Netherlands Inc.

At the Ministry of Economic Affairs, the PTNI report was seen as a great opportunity. Van der Zwan's social democratic background gave his plea an unsuspicious, apolitical character.[58] As chairman of the CEC, Frans Rutten was in charge of preparing the official government position on the report. The centralist approach advocated by Van der Zwan was rejected by the CEC senior officials, but the idea of a depoliticizing expert committee was received with enthusiasm.[59] These were still the final days of the first Van Agt cabinet (1977–81). Political divisions over economic policy were stark, especially within the CDA; outsourcing the initiative to an extra-parliamentary committee offered a way out. The momentum Van der Zwan had generated for a new industrial policy was handily put to use by Frans Rutten. Minister of Economics Affairs Gijs van Aardenne ordered his department to create an independent expert committee charged with developing a new industrial policy, building on the PTNI report.

It was called the Wagner Committee, after its president Gerrit Wagner, outgoing CEO of oil giant Royal Dutch Shell. The most important meetings took place in Wagner's private home. Frans Rutten helped select the committee's members, and his department also ran the secretariat. The Wagner Committee was therefore widely seen as a brainchild of the Ministry of Economic Affairs and Rutten. 'Rutten has a great ability to play on many chessboards simultaneously, in the network of bureaucratic,

---

56   'The Competitive Society of Arie van der Zwan', *Intermagazine*, 28 October 1982.

57   'Economen: levendig volkje' [Economists: A lively people], *Het Parool*, 22 May 1981, 8.

58   Varisli, 'Grenzen aan de groei?', 42.

59   Ibid., 43.

political and societal contacts,' trade union leader Wim Kok later concluded. 'I found that Rutten's influence on its sociopolitical and economic recommendations, although he himself was not part of the Wagner Commiteee, was quite strong.'[60] Harrie Langman, the former minister of economic affairs and prominent banker, was of a similar opinion: 'At the time of the Wagner Committee and its reports, the Ministry of Economic Affairs and secretary general Rutten were perhaps at the apex of their power.'[61]

Arie van der Zwan was asked to join and to rework his earlier PTNI recommendations into a more market-oriented approach. Other prominent members, all providing advice in a 'personal capacity', were Anton Dreesmann (chairman of the executive board of department store Vroom & Dreesmann), Eduard Pannenborg (vice-chairman of the executive board of electronics company Philips), Wim Bogers (chairman of the executive board of chemical company DSM), Wiero Beek (chairman of the executive board of Unilever Research Laboratory) and the aforementioned Harrie Langman (member of the executive board of ABN bank). The committee played host to a who's who of the Dutch business elite. Again, this formed part of a wider international trend. Both Reagan and Thatcher used powerful committees chaired by CEOs to develop policies on privatization, state retrenchment and economic competitiveness. The idea was that business managers had superior expertise in achieving efficiency and economic success.[62]

Trade union representation, on the other hand, was fraught with controversy. Frans Rutten had found Piet Vos, a more market-oriented economist of the industrial-sector union FNV, willing to participate in a personal capacity. Within the wider trade union movement, this was not positively received. The complaint was that Vos 'subscribed to employers' positions in the Wagner Committee.'[63] The controversy over trade union representation continued in the follow-up reports in

---

60   'Moet de metaaldraaier soms bejaardenhelper worden?' [Should the metalworker become a helper for the elderly?], *Het Parool*, 12 September 1985, 15.

61   Langman, 'Ik geloof in lange golven', 4.

62   Ronald Kroeze and Sjoerd Keulen, 'The Managers' Moment in Western Politics', *Management and Organizational History* 9, no. 4 (16 December 2014): 397; Davies, *Limits of Neoliberalism*, 97–125.

63   'De vakbeweging fuseert, maar wacht nog steeds op "de klare, schone dag dat het volk zijn boeien breekt"' [The trade unions are merging but still wait for 'the clear, bright day that the people will break their chains'], *De Volkskrant*, 5 September 1981.

1982 and 1983. Trade unionists 'recognized too little of the unions' views in the committee's final report'.[64] The row transpired against the background of a growing rift between the unions of the private and public sectors. Due to dramatic job losses, the industrial-sector union Industriebond FNV had moved much closer to the employers' point of view. The days when the Industriebond FNV preached socialism in its brochures were gone forever. Drastic public sector cuts and far-reaching liberalization of the labour market were no longer taboo for the Industriebond, Piet Vos stated in the press.[65] The public sector unions and FNV leader Wim Kok took a very different position.[66] By engaging the more market-oriented wing of the trade union movement, the Wagner Committee successfully drove a wedge into the once powerful trade union movement.

The Wagner Committee did not limit itself to industrial policy. Or, to put it another way, the committee saw almost all government policy as industrial policy. To make Dutch industry competitive again, it recommended reducing the tax burden, abolishing automatic inflation adjustment in wages, moderating wages and decentralizing wage policy, cutting social security and reducing the budget deficit to bring down interest rates.[67] In a follow-up report, the committee proposed cutting the link between public sector and private sector salaries and delinking benefit levels from the minimum wage. Taken together, all this entailed a major break with existing labour market policy. The old commitment to full employment was abandoned. 'We did not prioritize employment. We do not believe you should pursue industrial policy as a solution for employment,' said committee member Harrie Langman.[68]

More generally, the committee proposed a fundamental change in the government's role. The Wagner Committee originated the term

---

64   'Terlouw handelde zeer onfris' [Terlouw acted very unethically], *Het Vrije Volk*, 14 January 1982, 7.

65   'Moet Piet Vos spits afbijten?' [Should Piet Vos go ahead?], *Het Vrije Volk*, 13 November 1982, 4.

66   'Wim Kok over uitspraken Industriebond econoom: ontkoppelen botst met fnv-beleid' [Wim Kok on statements by industrial union economist: Decoupling clashes with FNV policy], *De Volkskrant*, 13 November 1982, 7.

67   Adviescommissie inzake het industriebeleid, *Een nieuw industrieel elan* (The Hague: Ministry of Economic Affairs, 1981).

68   Henrik van Dellen, *Een nieuw elan: de marktsector in de jaren tachtig* (Deventer: Kluwer, 1984), 247.

'Netherlands Inc.' – the metaphor in which the entire country was conceived as one big company.[69] The central idea wasn't that government should be rolled back, although that was certainly part of the agenda, but rather that all state intervention should be made subservient to improving Dutch competitiveness. Gerrit Zalm later spoke of a 'forward movement' of economic policy 'in areas previously still considered to be in the purely political domain':

> Not only the overall size of the public sector but also all sorts of specific policy domains were now considered part of economic policy. The organization of social security, the rent subsidy system, environmental policy, the healthcare system, the tax system, etc.; these are terrains that in the past were largely left to the specialist departments with a budgetary control from the Ministry of Finance. Today, those policy areas are not only judged on their own merits and budgetary norms but explicitly on their economic impact.[70]

This was a transposition of ends and means. Whereas the Dutch economy had previously been seen as a sector that provided support for government policy, it was now seen as the function of public policy to support the economy. The Wagner Committee played an important role in this fundamental shift in thinking. It advised the government to start making economic cost–benefit analyses of all new laws and government policies – a signature policy of the Reagan administration. To this end, it proposed that the position of the Ministry of Economic Affairs and the CEC needed to be strengthened. This was somewhat self-serving advice, since the Wagner Committee was, after all, run by the ministry. Rutten would later write that he had seized on this advice and 'taken great care to develop interdepartmental policy committees', led by the Ministry of Economic Affairs, to introduce economic incentives in sectors such as education, healthcare and public housing.[71]

---

69 'Het élan van Mr. G. A. Wagner' [The élan of Mr G. A. Wagner], *NRC Handelsblad*, 9 January 1981, 21.

70 Gerrit Zalm, *Mythen, paradoxen en taboes in de economische politiek*, inaugural lecture (Amsterdam: Free University Amsterdam, 1990), 1–2.

71 Frans Rutten, 'Markt en macht in de komende drie decennia', in Arie Ros and Jarig van Sinderen, eds, *Drie decennia tussen markt en macht*, Papers and Proceedings 001 (Rotterdam: Ocfeb, 2000), 35.

The Wagner Committee's second report came at a crucial time, in June 1982, just after the implosion of the second Van Agt cabinet. On the right and in employer circles, the Wagner report was received enthusiastically.[72] On the left and within the trade unions, it was rejected as 'one-sided'.[73] As we saw in the previous chapter, there was a running battle over economic policy. A parliamentary majority seemed to support the moderate-Keynesian Schouten plan. The Wagner reports gave Prime Minister Van Agt the opportunity to bend developments to his will ahead of the new elections in September 1982. Before the second report had even been published, Van Agt had already embraced its conclusions in no uncertain terms: 'The basis for the new cabinet formation has been provided. One can almost take for granted that what this report says must happen. The parties should prepare for that, so they can join in on time.'[74]

By canonizing the report in this way, Van Agt caused resentment, not least within his own party, which had voted by a narrow majority for the Schouten plan. Some party members wondered why an external report served as a point of departure rather than the Christian Democrats' own party programme. They complained of being presented with a fait accompli. But Van Agt dismissed the criticism and told the party council that the Wagner report 'should be received as if it were a gift, with a positive disposition'.[75] He succeeded in strong-arming his party to prepare the crucial budget for 1983 based on the recommendations of the Wagner Committee. At Van Agt's behest, Frans Rutten, together with senior finance officials Pieter Korteweg and Bart le Blanc, further elaborated on the Wagner Committee's recommendations in a confidential report, *The Bitter Pill*. Van Agt received it shortly before the elections, with the idea of using it to form his cabinet. The senior officials

72   'CDA vervreemdt van historische functie' [CDA alienated from historical function], *Het Parool*, 10 July 1982, 19.

73   'Verdeelde reacties op nieuw rapport-Wagner' [Divided reactions to new Wagner report], *Trouw*, 1 July 1982, 1; 'Vakbeweging kenmerkt rapport als eenzijdig' [Trade union characterizes report as one-sided], *De Volkskrant*, 1 July 1982, 7.

74   'Van Agt noemt nieuw rapport Wagner basis voor kabinet' [Van Agt says new report is basis for government], *NRC Handelsblad*, 26 June 1982, 3; ' "Hierop wacht het land". Van Agt omarmt Wagner 2' ['The country is waiting for this': Van Agt embraces Wagner 2], *Het Vrije Volk*, 26 June 1982, 7.

75   'Van Agt ziet rode kaart voor PvdA komen' [Van Agt sees red card for PvdA], *NRC Handelsblad*, 5 July 1982, 3.

introduced the report in stern terms as a 'serious attempt at a frank answer to the question of what should be required of all members of a new cabinet and of a new parliament for at least the next four years'.[76]

The elections proved successful for the Christian Democrats. The door to a centre-right coalition was open. Van Agt, however, was burned out. He resigned immediately after the elections and appointed Ruud Lubbers as his successor. It is unclear whether Lubbers had knowledge of the secret report. But historian Peter van Griensven has shown that many of the recommendations from *The Bitter Pill* reappeared in the final coalition agreement of the first Lubbers cabinet. Some passages were even copied verbatim.[77] This was not all that surprising, as Rutten, Le Blanc and Korteweg were also involved in drafting the crucial financial section of the coalition agreement – a highly unusual arrangement. In this way, senior officials played an unprecedented role in bringing about the economic policy shift of the 1980s. It was as if the classic relationship between politicians and bureaucrats had been reversed. 'Our philosophy is as follows: the civil servants have come up with solutions, and then it is our turn,' CDA Minister of Welfare, Public Health and Culture Elco Brinkman told journalists.[78] When Frans Rutten later reflected on his legacy, he was not modest about his role:

> When I became secretary-general at Economic Affairs, a colleague at Finance said, 'Frans, all you need is a secretary to type for you and then you and I will make the financial-economic policy of the Netherlands together; we don't need anyone else for that.' That was overconfidence, but that's how it went at first. In the early 1980s, the Dutch economy was in a deep decline. The [corporatist] Social and Economic Council was no longer functioning, the trade union movement was obstructing, and politicians would not come to their senses. On the initiative of two senior officials from the Ministry of Finance and Economic Affairs, an informal club was formed with people from the business community and civil servants. That group plotted a new economic course. When the first Lubbers cabinet took office at the

---

76   Peter van Griensven, 'De zure appel in tijden van economische crisis', *Jaarboek Parlementaire Geschiedenis* 11 (2009): 59–71.

77   Ibid., 65.

78   Van Weezel and Van Tijn, *Inzake het kabinet-Lubbers*, 161.

end of 1982, the matter had already been thought out. It's one of the brightest feats of economic policy in this century.[79]

This was, of course, an exaggeration. Rutten was only so powerful because it served the purposes of politicians to grant him that power. Passing the initiative to senior officials was a good blame-avoidance strategy for unpopular reforms.[80] Still, even Rutten's opponents credited him with an outsized role. As the Keynesian economist Jan Pen observed, the power of 'the civil service came into its own' at the Ministry of Economic Affairs 'during the time of Rutten'. According to Pen, 'they cared little for the ministers who happened to be there. The struggle became more and more ideological, as Rutten wanted more market and less government.'[81] Wil Albeda, Christian Democratic minister of social affairs in the first Van Agt cabinet, reacted stoically to Ruttens's self-congratulation: 'That seems a bit too much honour. A group like this could draw on the neoliberal arsenal as conceived in the United States.' Without the 'sea change in the ideological thinking of economists', the turnaround of the 1980s would not have happened.[82]

The Dutch neoliberal turn thus took shape under the political leadership of Dries van Agt, and it was his successor Ruud Lubbers who inherited the policy shift. In the years before, Lubbers had still been in the moderate Keynesian camp and had reservations about the Wagner Committee's proposals.[83] Lubbers was a pragmatist, however – a man without clear political preferences. According to colleagues, he was less

---

79   'Simonis is net zo oppervlakkig als ik vroeger was' [Simonis is just as superficial as I used to be], *Trouw*, 3 July 1999, 19.

80   See Paul Pierson, *Dismantling the Welfare State? Reagan, Thatcher and the Politics of Retrenchment* (Cambridge: Cambridge University Press, 1994).

81   Jan Pen, 'Economische Zaken moet blijven' [Economic Affairs has to stay], *Het Parool*, 15 May 1999.

82   Wil Albeda, 'De droom van een humaan kapitalisme', *Maandschrift Economie* 63, no. 6 (1999): 420.

83   Peter van Griensven, 'Eendracht, daadkracht, no-nonsense. De formatie van het kabinet-Lubbers I', in Carla van Baalen and Alexander van Kessel, eds, *Kabinetsformaties 1977–2012* (Amsterdam: Boom, 2016), 131; Dik Verkuil, *Een positieve grondhouding: de geschiedenis van het CDA* (The Hague: SDU Uitgeverij, Koninginnegracht, 1992), 233. See also 'CDA neemt afstand van Miljoenennota' [CDA distances itself from budget memorandum], *De Volkskrant*, 22 September 1982, 1; 'CDA: sociaal beleid komt slecht uit de verf' [CDA: Social policy comes out badly], *NRC Handelsblad*, 21 September 1982, 15.

interested in 'the final outcome of a solution' than in finding a solution that worked politically.[84] As party leader and prime minister, he now made a different assessment. 'He opted for a neoliberal politics in 1982,' Wil Albeda concluded.[85]

A Time of Dissensus

It was the Wagner Committee much more than the Wassenaar Accord that constituted the real turning point in the 1980s. Of course, that the most important policy shift in Dutch post-war history was prepared in the home of the former CEO of the Shell oil company paints a picture of Dutch politics rather different from that associated with 'the polder model'. As economic historian Jeroen Touwen rightly argues, it was the Wagner reports and not the Wassenaar Accord that 'provided the ideological basis for the switch from state intervention to the market mechanism'.[86]

The Wassenaar Accord covered a much smaller part of economic policy and followed logically from the Wagner Committee's plea to decentralize and moderate wages. Gerrit Wagner had even visited negotiators Wim Kok, of the trade union FNV, and Chris van Veen, of the employer's organization VNO, with four of his committee members ten days before the Wassenaar Accord was finalized: 'Very informally, we said how we viewed the matter and in which direction we were thinking ... Later I read in the newspaper that they had reached an agreement.'[87] Since both the new Lubbers government and the employers had decided on this path, the trade union movement had few options left. Lubbers had threatened the social partners with a state-imposed

---

84 Pieter Gerrit Kroeger and Jaap Stam, *De rogge staat er dun bij: macht en verval van het CDA, 1974–1998* (Amsterdam: Balans, 1998), 129.

85 Wil Albeda, 'Lubbers als econoom', in Ruud Lubbers, *Manager in de Politiek*, ed. Arendo Joustra and Erik van Venetië (Amsterdam: Anthos, 1989), 179.

86 Jeroen Touwen, 'How Does a Coordinated Market Economy Evolve? Effects of Policy Learning in the Netherlands in the 1980s', *Labor History* 49, no. 4 (2008): 454. See also Jeroen Touwen, *Coordination in Transition: The Netherlands and the World Economy, 1950–2010* (Leiden: Brill, 2014); Frans Rutten, who writes of Wassenaar as the 'affirmation' of an 'earlier intervention of the Wagner Committee' (Rutten, *Zeven kabinetten wijzer*, 99).

87 Van Dellen, *Een nieuw elan*, 230.

wage measure, while signalling that his preferred solution was for trade unions and employers to moderate wages in a decentralized fashion. The trade union stood, as Wim Kok later said, 'with its back against the wall'. The trade unions were sceptical that wage moderation would generate jobs. 'It was a risky bet on the future, in which risks were certainly not shared in equal fashion: the trade union movement had to take on more risk.'[88] The idea was that, in exchange for wage moderation, trade unions would receive a reduction in working hours, leading to more jobs overall. But this end of the deal never really materialized. The trade unions decided to cut their losses and concluded the Wassenaar Accord in November 1982, a mere two days after Lubbers's presentation of the government policy statement in the Dutch parliament.

Contrary to the conventional polder mythology, neither the Wagner Committee nor the Wassenaar Accord inaugurated a new consensus on economic policy. While there was agreement on wage moderation in the market sector, fierce controversy persisted over the proposed cuts in the public sector and to social security. Large trade union demonstrations would define the face of the first half of the 1980s. The text of the Wassenaar Accord explicitly referred to this controversy. It stated that the accord had been concluded 'with each party holding on to their views and feelings regarding the new government's policy aims.'[89] One year later, FNV leader Wim Kok wrote in the journal of the Labour Party:

> It hardly needs saying that the current government policy is in almost all respects at odds with the approach advocated by the FNV. Achievements of the welfare state, like inflation-adjusted benefits, the minimum wage and dismissal procedures have to suffer in this neoliberal approach. In general, neoliberalism leads to a rather unsubtle pursuit of 'deregulation' and 'public sector cutbacks' . . . Reducing the budget deficit has been declared the highest policy priority. The consequences, socially and economically, have been disastrous. In 1983, the government deliberately unleashed a deflationary process with gigantic spending cuts and tax increases, which has so far only

88 Piet de Rooy and Henk te Velde, *Met Kok: Over veranderend Nederland* (Amsterdam: Wereldbibliotheek, 2005), 27.

89 Stichting van de Arbeid, *Centrale aanbevelingen inzake aspecten van het werkgelegenheidsbeleid* (The Hague: Stichting van de Arbeid, 1982), 2–3.

led to an accelerated implosion of employment in the private sector and in the (semi-)public sector.[90]

Wim Kok grew to become an iconic figure. He was born into a socialist carpenter's family in a small village in a polder close to Rotterdam. After early years of hard work, frugality and poverty, his intelligence and perseverance allowed him to climb the ladder to become first a trade union leader, then the successor of Den Uyl as Labour Party leader, and ultimately prime minister in the so-called Purple Cabinets (1994–2002) – the Dutch equivalent of the Third Way of Bill Clinton and Tony Blair.

After his death in 2018, Kok was hailed by right-wing liberal Prime Minister Mark Rutte (VVD) as the 'architect and contractor' of the polder model.[91] From the other side of the globe, former US President Bill Clinton released a statement calling Kok a visionary who had come up with 'innovative policies to meet the challenges of globalization' and praised him for having 'managed to create the consensus' to implement those policies.[92] And in a newspaper obituary, historian Piet de Rooy argued that Kok 'went against the grain' of the leftist trade unions, brought 'a sense of reality' back on the left and 'found a solution to the problem of mass unemployment' with the Wassenaar Accord.[93] It all formed part of the consensual narrative constructed around Kok and the Wassenaar Accord.

Ironically, Kok was one of the fiercest critics at the time of the neoliberal reforms that would later be attributed to the Wassenaar Accord and his own personal efforts. The real Wim Kok dubbed Ruud Lubbers a 'dictator' for imposing public sector wage cuts and in 1983 led the largest and longest civil service strike in Dutch history. He continued to espouse Keynesian views for most of the 1980s. Kok took a stance against 'the ideology of state retrenchment' and pleaded for an expansionary policy, instead of 'far too severe cuts in social services and public

---

90   Wim Kok, 'Volledige werkgelegenheid: Uitdagingen voor de jaren tachtig', *Socialisme en Democratie* 45, no. 7/8 (1983): 5.

91   'Wim Kok herdacht als zowel "architect als aannemer" van het poldermodel' [Wim Kok remembered as 'architect and builder' of the polder model], *De Volkskrant*, 20 October 2018.

92   'Statement from President Clinton on the Passing of Former Prime Minister of the Netherlands, Wim Kok', Clinton Foundation, 22 October 2018.

93   Piet de Rooy, 'Met Kok verdween het vertrouwen' [With Kok, trust disappeared], *NRC Handelsblad*, 26 October 2018.

spending'.[94] Analysis of FNV policy documents in the 1980s shows a clear preference for job creation through a shorter working week and internationally coordinated expansionary policies, rather than austerity and wage moderation.[95] Even after the Wassenaar Accord, Wim Kok was largely an oppositional figure: a people's tribune speaking to angry crowds protesting the 1980s austerity measures.

The trade unions were not the only voice of opposition to the new economic policies. The Labour Party was also opposed to the new, 'no-nonsense' government. According to Labour Party leader Joop Den Uyl, the economic crisis 'was used to launch an offensive against the welfare state and the influence acquired by the trade union movement'.[96] 'Monetarists, neoclassicals and supply-chain economists have conquered the battlefield,' he noted with regret.[97]

Even within the CDA, opinions were divided. In the 1980s, the party had a neoliberal wing, led by former banker, IMF director and Finance Minister Onno Ruding. But there was also a moderate Keynesian wing, led in parliament by Bert de Vries. The two kept up a 'fiery internal correspondence' on economic policy. Ruding was into monetarism and public-choice theory and wanted to pursue smaller government as a matter of principle.[98] De Vries only favoured austerity to restore balance to the existing policy paradigm. During the course of the 1980s, De Vries became increasingly 'antagonized by those who did not seem to know when to stop cutting'.[99] As prime minister, Ruud Lubbers deftly navigated between these two wings of his party, trying to maintain a middle ground. 'Whereas Onno and [new Central Bank president] Wim Duisenberg will probably pull on one end of the rope, it is useful to me if you take the other end,' he instructed one of his ministers on one

---

94   Wim Kok, 'Een maakbare samenleving. Enkele overwegingen', *Tijdschrift Voor Politieke Economie* 9, no. 2 (1985): 24–34.

95   Becker, ' "Miracle" by Consensus?'

96   Joop Den Uyl, *Smalle marges, grote gevolgen* (Amsterdam: Partij van de Arbeid, 1982), 8.

97   Joop Den Uyl, 'De nieuwe orthodoxie en het gezond verstand', in A. van der Zwan and Andries Batenburg, eds, *Nederland in zaken: investeren, winst en werkgelegenheid* (Utrecht: Veen, 1985), 311.

98   Merijn Oudenampsen and Bram Mellink, 'The Roots of Dutch Frugality: The Role of Public Choice Theory in Dutch Budgetary Policy', *Journal of European Public Policy* 29, no. 8 (3 August 2022): 1206–24.

99   Kroeger and Stam, *De rogge staat er dun bij*, 200.

occasion.[100] Because of this internal disagreement, there was no clear vision of what the long-term aspiration of the Lubbers cabinets was. This was a hallmark of Christian democracy, with its historic internal class-divisions. Lubbers was a master at paving over such internal contradictions through his famously woolly language, soon dubbed 'Lubberian' in the media. It was, according to one columnist, 'a way of speaking, being silent, concealing, masking or sometimes lying a little'.[101]

Economists were predominantly critical of the austerity policies. OECD secretary-general Emiel van Lennep and IMF president Johan Witteveen warned in advance that 'too much austerity harms the economy'.[102] Particularly painful for the first Lubbers cabinet was the fact that the economic forecasts of the CPB were exceedingly negative about the cuts. Based on the 1983 Budget Memorandum, CPB director Cees van der Beld estimated that the effects of increasing world trade and resurgent exports would be completely neutralized by the spending cuts and the absence of any policy to create jobs.[103] Similar gloomy tidings came from the CPB in 1984 about the long-term effects of austerity policies. It wrote of 'an increasing amount of underspending, which is connected with a reluctant business sector', and warned of increasing unemployment.[104]

While in the 1970s it was the Keynesians and social democrats who had rejected the results of the CPB's forecasting models, it was now the turn of the other camp. After presenting the CPB forecasts in 1984, Minister of Economic Affairs Gijs van Aardenne (VVD) simply stated that the figures were 'too gloomy'.[105] The CEC had even prepared a cover letter for parliament with its own, much more favourable calculations.[106]

---

100   Ibid., 196.

101   Jan Blokker, 'Lubberiaans' [Lubberians], *De Volkskrant*, 9 November 1991, 63.

102   'OESO-topman waarschuwt tegen bezuinigingen' [OECD director warns against cutbacks], *Trouw*, 9 October 1982, 13; 'Van Lennep van de OESO: "Te veel bezuinigen schaadt economie"' [Van Lennep of the OECD: 'Too much austerity harms the economy'], *De Volkskrant*, 9 October 1982, 2.

103   'Grote werkloosheid bij beleid à la Van der Stee'; 'Macro-economische verkenningen: Planbureau bespeurt geen enkel lichtpunt'.

104   José Toirkens, 'De drie sporen van het kabinet Lubbers' [The three tracks of the Lubbers government], *NRC Handelsblad*, 6 March 1984, 12.

105   'Centraal Planbureau te somber' [Central Planning Bureau too gloomy], *De Telegraaf*, 24 March 1984, 7; 'Van Aardenne: cijfers Planbureau te somber' [Van Aardenne: Planning bureau numbers too negative], *NRC Handelsblad*, 24 March 1984.

106   See Frans Rutten, 'Het gebruik van voorspellingen bij het macro-economisch beleid', *ESB* 71, no. 3,583 (26 November 1986): 1166.

Lubbers also disputed the CPB's estimates in a public speech.[107] The CPB models had lost status. According to Pieter Korteweg, he and Rutten had agreed to ignore the director of the CPB, who also had a seat on the Central Economic Committee: 'We said to the Planning Bureau: you can say what you want, we won't pay any more attention to it. We just said that. So, Cees van der Beld, who was sitting there at the time – yes, he was just sitting there – at a certain point, he didn't count anymore. It wasn't forever, only for a while. We had to swallow the bitter pill.'[108]

The falling out formed part of a heated debate on the use of economic models. Neoliberals like Rutten, Zalm, Korteweg and Bomhoff denounced the Keynesian assumptions that, in their eyes, were still embedded in CPB models.[109] They argued that the CPB had to adopt the insights of the monetarists, supply-siders and rational expectations. These currents of economic thought worked with smaller and simpler models. Bomhoff stated that the CPB's large econometric models would be a laughingstock in the United States: 'simulations with these models' were no longer admitted as sound evidence in 'serious scientific circles'.[110] Responding to this criticism, Nobel Memorial Prize winner Jan Tinbergen, the intellectual godfather of the CPB forecasting models, had called for a 'new synthesis' between Keynes and Friedman. 'The present emergency,' Tinbergen wrote in December 1982, 'makes it a duty for economists to stop confrontations between monetarists, supply-siders, anti-regulation economists and Keynesians . . . If we as economists continue to pit ourselves against each other, we forsake the duty of scholars. What are politicians and citizens to do if we do not reach a more or less unified verdict?'[111]

It was a striking statement, characteristic of the paradoxical nature of economic modelling in the Netherlands. After all, in no social science

---

107   Kroeger en Stam, *De rogge staat er dun bij*, 195.

108   Pieter Korteweg, interview by the author, Bosch en Duin, 7 January 2020.

109   Rutten, 'Het gebruik van voorspellingen bij het macro-economisch beleid'; Frans Rutten, 'De betekenis van macro-econometrische modellen in de beleidsvoorbereiding', in H. den Hartog and J. Weitenberg, eds, *Toegepaste economie grenzen en mogelijkheden* (The Hague: CPB, 1984), 79–101.

110   Eduard Bomhoff, 'De prijs van de staatsschuld en het aanbod van kapitaal', in *De economie van het aanbod, Preadviezen van de Vereniging voor de Staathuishoudkunde* (Leiden: Stenfert Kroese, 1983), 101.

111   Jan Tinbergen, 'De noodzaak van een synthese', *ESB* 67, no. 3,383 (1 December 1982): 1284.

discipline is it a 'duty of scholars' to reach a consensus. Tinbergen seemed to be confusing a scientific with a political obligation. How could economics fulfil its traditional role as an apolitical arbiter and instrument of depoliticization if economists were constantly at odds with each other? Tinbergen saw an important role for the CPB – 'our biggest model factory' – in constructing a depoliticized synthesis between Keynesianism and neoliberalism. Rutten, in response, made it clear that he 'still did not believe in a great new synthesis between the various schools'.[112]

Although the austerity policies of the 1980s were successful in restoring business profitability, unemployment remained stubbornly high in the 1980s, at around 700,000 people in the second half of the decade.[113] Restored business profitability did not appear to translate automatically into higher employment. This allowed both camps in the debate to claim to have been proved right. The same logic applied to international developments in the UK and the US. Thatcher's policies were initially unsuccessful, and monetarist experiments to control the money supply were soon abandoned. Leading economists spoke of 'the failure of monetarism'.[114] While Reagan's economic policy was successful; it was not an easy reference point for other reasons. Reaganomics was an eclectic policy mix: on the one hand, it deployed the familiar neoliberal recipe of retrenching the public sector, pursuing a tight monetary policy and deregulating the economy; but, on the other, Reagan stimulated the economy in an almost Keynesian fashion, through tax cuts and large investments in defence, financed by huge budget deficits. The US economic rebound that followed was good news for the Dutch export sector and gave the first Lubbers administration some economic breathing space. At the same time, it played into the hands of proponents of Keynesian stimulus spending.

After a visit to the United States in 1984, a slightly annoyed Onno Ruding fielded questions from journalists on why the Netherlands could not follow the Americans in their spending spree. He claimed that he had heard from reliable sources that the Americans would change track and rather follow the Dutch policy, bringing down the American budget

---

112   Rutten, 'Voortgang met de nieuwe zakelijkheid', 10.
113   Knoester, *Economische politiek in Nederland*, 166.
114   Nicholas Kaldor, 'How Monetarism Failed', *Challenge* 28, no. 2 (1985): 4–13.

deficit. Not Reaganomics but 'Rudinomics' was going to become the international norm from now on.[115] That was overly confident. In the Netherlands, too, the Ministry of Finance was receiving less and less of a hearing for its belief in austerity. According to reports in the press, this philosophy had now taken on religious features:

> There is a story circulating about senior officials at the department, who have to report in battle order to the treasurer-general every morning. 'What is our purpose on earth?', their superior asks in a peremptory tone. 'To reduce the budget deficit,' the officials reply in unison. After that morning roll call, the group goes to work in good spirits.[116]

Critics accused the Ministry of Finance of 'deficit fetishism', or insensitivity to the adverse economic impact of austerity.[117] Confronted with this criticism by a leading newspaper, Ruding first threatened to end the interview and then simply denied that austerity could harm the economy: 'That's the thinking of the 1970s. That has given us a lot of trouble and ultimately led only to more unemployment.'[118] On the initiative of Treasurer-General Pieter Korteweg, the Ministry of Finance had removed any references to conjunctural policy, decline in demand and underspending from the Budget Memoranda of the 1980s.[119] These Keynesian notions, it was thought, would weaken the position of the ministry in enforcing budget discipline. Lubbers publicly called Ruding to order in 1985: 'You are going to bite your own tail with too severe austerity.'[120] The financial reins would be somewhat loosened again in the second half of the 1980s, and Lubbers cautiously moved the CDA back towards the centre and the Labour Party.

---

115   'Dag Reaganomics, hier komt Rudinomics' [Goodbye, Reaganomics, here comes Rudinomics], *NRC Handelsblad*, 10 March 1984, 11.

116   'Strategische positie Ruding sterk na royaal gebaar' [Ruding's strategic position strong after generous gesture], *De Volkskrant*, 18 August 1987.

117   Henk Brons, 'Dr. Bart le Blanc. Bezuinigingsideoloog' [Dr Bart le Blanc: Austerity ideologue], *Het Vrije Volk*, 30 July 1983.

118   'Ruding over 1988: het meest sociale beleid is mijn beleid' [Ruding on 1988: The most social policy is my policy], *NRC Handelsblad*, 30 May 1987, 13.

119   Knoester, *Economische politiek in Nederland*, 159.

120   'Lubbers vindt dat Ruding overdrijft' [Lubbers finds that Ruding exaggerates], *Trouw*, 11 May 1985, 1.

In 1987 Wim Kok, who had succeeded Joop den Uyl as leader of the Labour Party, wrote a remarkable contribution to a volume of the Royal Dutch Economic Association (KVS). It was a fierce critique of Frans Rutten's New Year's article on the new businesslike politics.[121] Through the widespread dismissal of politicians as 'vote-maximizing market actors' who constantly run up deficits out of fear of pressure groups, the idea had arisen that the economy was best not left to politicians. 'The Dutch solution', Kok noted, was to put 'more or less apolitical entrepreneurs at the helm'.[122]

In the 1980s and 1990s, the success of the Wagner Committee had inspired the creation of similar reform committees, led by various CEOs. As the historians Ronald Kroeze and Sjoerd Keulen have noted, at least thirty-one committees headed by a CEO or a former CEO were set up in the two decades after Wagner. The CEO of electronics giant Philips, Wise Dekker, led a committee that proposed to privatize Dutch health-care; former senior finance official and now ABN banker Coen Oort led a committee on tax reform; CEO Herman Wijffels, of the agricultural bank Rabobank, chaired a committee on the privatization of the national railways; and Arie van der Zwan, who had been appointed as an executive at department store Vroom & Dreesmann, led a committee on the privatization of student loans, together with former finance official Bart le Blanc, now at Van Lanschot investment bank. Former finance official Pieter Korteweg, who became an investment banker at Robeco, was even tasked with writing the VVD party programme. Kok drily remarked that business elites had interests, too. He described the new businesslike style as representative of

a development in which the free play of [market] forces wins out over the pursuit of social consensus. In that development, a government that goes beyond its 'duties as night watchman' is a 'spoilsport'. That spoiling then consists of the 'artificial' pursuit of, say, full employment or a less unequal income distribution. This approach to government is at odds with my view, in which a democratic government is not a

---

121   Wim Kok, 'Het bestuurlijke in de economie: Een kritiek op de nieuwe zakelijkheid', in Antonie Knoester, ed., *Lessen uit het verleden: 125 jaar vereniging voor Staathuishoudkunde* (Leiden: Stenfert Kroese, 1987), 369.

122   Ibid.

disruptive outsider, but – however imperfect – the expression of the wishes of the people with a special emphasis on solidarity (protector of the poor). Of course, such a view is subjective and normative. But so are the principles of the person who wraps himself in the seemingly objective garb of the new businesslike politics.[123]

Frans Rutten returned to this polemic six years later, in 1993, after Wim Kok had become finance minister in the third Lubbers cabinet – a centre-left coalition of Christian Democrats and the Labour Party. 'The objections at the time have not been translated into action by the current finance minister,' Rutten wrote triumphantly. 'On the contrary. The elements of the "new businesslike politics" define not only the macro-economic policies of the first and second Lubbers cabinets but also those of the third. Minister Kok's good work on the EMU treaty is going to anchor that more firmly than ever.'[124]

123   Ibid., 374.
124   Rutten, *Zeven kabinetten wijzer*, 87.

5

The Yearning for a Dutch Thatcher (1989–94)

'The time of no-nonsense is behind us,' Wim Kok defiantly declared before a room of 500 political science students in the eastern city of Nijmegen.[1] It was 6 June 1989, exactly three months before the elections. The world was at a crossroads: the Berlin Wall had not yet fallen, but the omens were there. In Poland, Hungary and the Soviet Union, the Communist regimes had begun to liberalize. At the same time, student protests in Beijing's Tiananmen Square were being bloodily crushed. Against the background of these grand historical developments, Kok set out the new course for the Labour Party.

Wim Kok had prepared his speech carefully. It was the result of several years of debate and reorientation within the party.[2] In the press, the 'Nijmegen Speech' was received as historic.[3] Kok performed a

1   Wim Kok, 'De tijd van no-nonsense ligt achter ons' [The time of no nonsense is passed], *NRC Handelsblad*, 7 June 1989, 9; Wim Kok, 'Het conservatisme van de jaren tachtig is voorbij' [The conservatism of the 1980s is over], *De Volkskrant*, 7 June 1989, 15.

2   'Kok verklaart tijd van grote visioen ten einde' [Kok declares time of grand visions at an end], *De Volkskrant*, 7 June 1989, 1.

3   Jan Joost Lindner, 'Lubbers de goochelaar en Kok de reformist' [Lubbers the conjurer and Kok the reformist], *De Volkskrant*, 10 June 1989, 19; Hans Buddingh, 'Voorwaarts en de markt niet vergeten' [Forwards and don't forget the market], *NRC Handelsblad*, 22 June 1989, 27; Marcel ten Hooven en Koos Schwartz, 'Wim Kok, met die man valt te werken' [Wim Kok, a man you can work with], *Trouw*, 4 November 1989, 23.

delicate balancing act. He began by describing a neoliberal critique of the welfare state and social democracy, developed by 'supporters of monetarism' and economists 'who emphasized the supply side of the economy'.[4] These neoliberal ideas had 'found their way within CDA and VVD and found expression in the policies of the Lubbers cabinets'.[5]

On the one hand, the Labour Party leader harshly attacked these policies. Anyone taking stock after ten years of neoliberalism, he noted, 'cannot but conclude that the pendulum has swung too far'.[6] The austerity policies had led to an increase in social inequality and long-term unemployment, leaving large groups of citizens by the wayside. It was no coincidence that this 'economic policy was accompanied by an authoritarian style of government'. The Lubbers cabinets in the 1980s had kept the door firmly shut to the Labour Party, trade unions and civil society interest groups. Kok was certainly not the only one to see it that way. Political scientist Hans Daalder had called political culture in the 1980s 'the new toughness'. He observed that 'the government sometimes seems bent on affronting societal interest groups and consultation structures and even on breaking with them'.[7] Wim Kok considered this unilateral style of government untenable in the long run: 'In the Netherlands, with its rich cultural tapestry of independent associations and movements ... everyone loses if you govern by decree'.[8]

On the other hand, he stressed that the Labour Party took the neoliberal critique seriously and 'hadn't conveniently ignored it'.[9] Under Kok's leadership, the Dutch Labour Party published a series of reports that

---

4   In his lecture, Kok described Lubbers's policy as 'neoconservative', a somewhat unfortunate term for neoliberalism that had come into vogue in the Anglophone world to refer to the renewal of conservative politics under Thatcher and Reagan. Dutch Labour Party politicians soon adopted it. In his May 1981 Paradiso lecture, Den Uyl referred to the 'neoconservative thinking' of Hayek and Friedman. See Joop den Uyl, 'De ontmoediging en Nieuw Rechts' [The political disenchantment and the new right], *Het Parool*, 5 May 1981, 4.

5   Kok, 'De tijd van no-nonsense ligt achter ons'.

6   Kok, 'Het conservatisme van de jaren tachtig is voorbij'.

7   Hans Daalder, *Politiek en historie: Opstellen over Nederlandse politiek en vergelijkende politieke wetenschap*, ed. Joop van den Berg (Amsterdam: Bert Bakker, 1990), 97.

8   Kok, 'Het conservatisme van de jaren tachtig is voorbij'.

9   Ibid.

advocated a pragmatic middle ground between the Keynesianism of the 1970s and the neoliberal policies of the 1980s.[10] In his lecture, Kok reached out to the Christian Democrats, stating that, under his leadership, the Labour Party had 'developed a keen eye [for] over-regulation by the government, for the need to monitor the budget deficit strictly and to bring down the national debt, for the reciprocity of duties and rights in social security'. In short, Kok advocated a new socioeconomic compromise that he later called 'a Third Way'.[11]

Under Joop den Uyl, the Labour Party had followed a strategy of polarization. The idea was to politicize the socioeconomic cleavage, driving a wedge through the Christian Democrats to achieve a left-wing majority. This majoritarian strategy was now abandoned by Wim Kok. Time and again, the new leader underlined his party's willingness to compromise: 'Social democracy contributes to social change but does not embody the Alternative . . . What I have in mind is a style of political action that seeks consensus and connection'. Kok's speech marked a departure from the leftist politics of Den Uyl, but he also criticized the CDA, which he accused of having neglected its traditional role as guardian of Dutch consensus politics.

The 'Nijmegen Lecture' was well received by the Christian Democrats.[12] Prime Minister Ruud Lubbers had experienced a similar development. The press noted a gradual change in the style of Lubbers's actions at the end of the 1980s: 'Lately, a new term has emerged: consensus.'[13] In previous cabinets, the emphasis had been on hardheaded restructuring, without too much consultation. Now that the economy had recovered somewhat, Lubbers wanted a broader mandate

---

10   More specifically, these were the reports 'Politiek à la carte' (Internal organization), 'Schuivende panelen' (Ideology and policy) and 'Bewogen beweging' (Party-political strategy).

11   He did so in his lecture at the special congress on the disability benefit crisis. Wim Kok, 'Emancipatie in solidariteit', lecture at the PvdA party congress, 28 September 1991. It was published in abridged form as Wim Kok, 'Partij die wil vernieuwen, moet aan vernieuwing deelnemen' [The party that wants to renew must participate in the renewal], *Trouw*, 30 September 1991, 4.

12   See Bert de Vries, 'Kok bepleit zelfde koers die hij CDA jarenlang verweten heeft' [Kok advocates same course he long criticized], *NRC Handelsblad*, 8 June 1989, 3.

13   Erik van Venetië, 'Consensus moet vadertje Lubbers aan derde ambtstermijn helpen' [Consensus must help Lubbers win third term], *De Volkskrant*, 29 October 1988, 9. See also Willem Breedveld, 'Miljoenennota' [Budget memorandum], *Trouw*, 21 September 1988.

for reform. Perhaps even more important was the fact that the relationship between the CDA and the VVD had soured. In the 1986 elections, the VVD had lost nine seats to the CDA, leaving the party half the size of its senior coalition partner. The right-wing liberals were struggling internally with a leadership crisis and felt increasingly belittled by the CDA.[14] All in all, it was not surprising that Lubbers set a course towards a coalition with the Labour Party at the end of the 1980s. Wim Kok's somewhat tame technocratic style also played a role in this. After a reliable but dull performance as opposition leader, he now had the chance to show 'the other side of his dullness' in government, as two journalists wrote.[15]

The Swedish Model

Although the government presented the reforms of the 1980s as a resounding success, in reality their results were mixed. By the end of the 1980s, the dominant sentiment was that the neoliberal reforms of the past decade had achieved limited success. It is true that wage levels had been moderated, Dutch business was competitive again and the growth of public spending had been halted. But, at the same time, the Dutch economy had fallen seriously behind. In its *Economic Outlook* of December 1998, the OECD placed the Netherlands among the worst-performing economies in the 1980s. Unemployment remained stubbornly high (12.5 per cent against the OECD average of 7.5 per cent), Dutch economic growth lagged structurally 1 per cent behind the OECD average, while public debt had doubled from 40 per cent of GDP in 1977 to 80 per cent in 1988.[16] As the 1992 Budget Memorandum of the Ministry of Finance noted, the Netherlands had experienced the slowest growth in per capita GDP of all European countries in the 1980s and was increasingly falling behind.[17]

---

14   Pieter Gerrit Kroeger and Jaap Stam, *De rogge staat er dun bij: macht en verval van het CDA, 1974–1998* (Amsterdam: Balans, 1998), 233; Gerrit Voerman and Patrick van Schie, *Zestig jaar VVD* (Amsterdam: Boom, 2008), 57–9.

15   Ten Hooven and Schwartz, 'Wim Kok, met die man valt te werken'.

16   OECD, *Economic Outlook* (Paris: OECD, 1988), 122, 166.

17   Ministry of Finance, *Miljoenennota 1992* (The Hague: Ministry of Finance, 1991); Eduard Bomhoff, *Een Haagse lente?* (Schoonhoven: Academic Service, 1994);

In the Dutch press, economists of various stripes criticized the reforms in no uncertain terms.[18] Hugo Keuzenkamp and Rick van der Ploeg spoke of a 'failed restructuring': short-sighted spending cuts had left the Netherlands worse off than surrounding countries.[19] Due to the financial straitjacket that Christian Democrat Finance Minister Onno Ruding imposed, the government had failed to invest in public infrastructure or in training and education programmes. This had created an army of long-term unemployed who were estranged from the labour market and thus no longer exerted any downward pressure on wages. The neoliberal idea that the market would find a new equilibrium on its own – 'the fever is a balancing force, you have to allow it', as senior finance official Pieter Korteweg said – turned out not to be true in practice.[20] As unemployment grew, an increasing share of public spending was lost to benefits, while public investment reached an all-time low. In other words, the austerity policy had been penny-wise, pound-foolish. A similar criticism was voiced by Wim Kok, who blamed the government for letting unemployment run its course on dogmatic grounds: it made you want to 'go through the roof'.[21]

Jeroen J. M. Kremers, *Inspelen op Europa: Uitdagingen voor het financieel-economische beleid van Nederland* (Schoonhoven: Academic Service, 1993).

18   For criticism from economists in the press, see José Toirkens, 'Geen visie op bevorderen werkgelegenheid' [No vision on fostering employment], *NRC Handelsblad*, 15 September 1987; Flip de Kam, 'De toverformules van secretaris-generaal Rutten' [Secretary-General Rutten's magic formulas], *NRC Handelsblad*, 19 September 1987, 9; ' "De Hollandse aanpak is een puinhoop" ' ['The Dutch approach is a mess'], *De Volkskrant*, 13 February 1988, 9; Coen Teulings, 'Topambtenaar Rutten bepleit voortzetting van harde lijn' [Senior official Rutten advocates continuation of hard line], *De Waarheid*, 14 January 1989, 4; ' "Saneringsbeleid van Lubbers heeft gefaald" ' [Lubbers's austerity policy has failed], *De Volkskrant*, 23 August 1989, 3.

19   See Hugo Keuzenkamp and Rick van der Ploeg, 'Seven Lost Years? The Failed Restructuring', *Intermediair* 25, no. 34 (1989): 5–11; Hugo A. Keuzenkamp and Frederick van der Ploeg, *Saving, Investment, Government Finance and the Current Account: The Dutch Experience*, CEPR–Bank of Greece Conference, 'Macroeconomics and the External Constraint: The European Experience', Athens (1990).

20   Pieter Korteweg, interview by the author, Bosch en Duin, 7 January 2020. A more nuanced critique of the usefulness of public investment was offered by AEP economist Gerrit Zalm in the policy paper *De mythe van de overheidsinvesteringen* (The Hague: Ministry of Economic Affairs, 1985). He argued that public investment was in direct competition with tax relief and that the latter option was more attractive because it reduced the distorting effect of high taxes on the labour market.

21   Breedveld, 'Miljoenennota'. For the left-wing debate on the absent labour market policies of the Lubbers cabinets, see Paul de Beer, 'Onwil of onvermogen?',

On the same day in December 1988 on which the OECD released its dismal figures, the Swedish professor Göran Therborn gave a lecture at a Dutch conference on employment policy. Therborn knew the Netherlands well. From 1981 to 1987, he had been a visiting professor of political science in Nijmegen, where he had worked on his book *Why Some Peoples Are More Unemployed than Others*.[22] Using data compiled by the OECD, he showed that countries differed widely in terms of their success in fighting unemployment. The Netherlands, with 14 per cent unemployment in the mid-1980s, represented one extreme, while Sweden, with only 3.5 per cent, represented the other. He argued that the role of the state and social partners was crucial. In Therborn's view, the government and Dutch business had been far too passive and had never developed the institutional capacity for an active employment policy. Compared to neighbouring countries Belgium and the UK, the Netherlands had spent three times less on furthering employment. The Netherlands had fixated on bringing down wage costs and public spending – but that had done nothing to solve the unemployment problem. Therborn warned in his lecture that, if nothing changed, 'there would arise ghetto-cultures of poverty and unemployment' in the Netherlands, as could already be seen among ethnic minorities and single mothers dependent on welfare.[23]

His lecture touched a nerve. At the conference, a senior Ministry of Social Affairs official in charge of the Dutch job centres surprised the audience by agreeing with Therborn: 'Looking back, perhaps we've made the wrong decisions.'[24] This concession formed part of a broader reorientation. Prime Minister Lubbers had begun to doubt his no-nonsense policies in public. At the beginning of his second cabinet in 1986, Lubbers had placed the reduction of unemployment at the centre of his agenda. Three years later, he had to admit defeat: 'We have

---

Socialisme en Democratie 46, no's 7/8 (1986): 260–3. For Kok's more extensive criticism of the no-nonsense policies, see Wim Kok, '60%: Nieuwe normen en gedachten', *ESB* 73, no. 3,680 (20 January 1988).

22   Göran Therborn, *Why Some Peoples Are More Unemployed than Others* (London: Verso, 1986).

23   Göran Therborn, 'Nederland en de falende arbeidsmarkt', in Pieter Broertjes, ed., *Getto's in Holland: Visies op armoede en werkloosheid* (Amsterdam: Van Gennep, 1989), 33.

24   Broertjes, *Getto's in Holland*, 12.

misjudged, me in the first place, the cause and character of the problem of unemployment.'[25]

Ever since the mid-1980s, Dutch policymakers had begun looking to Sweden for clues on how to combat unemployment. The Swedish model was seen as a viable 'third way' between Anglo-American neoliberalism and the failed French neo-Keynesianism under François Mitterrand. There was far less long-term unemployment in Sweden in the 1980s – partly because the unemployed were actively retrained and assisted in finding new jobs, and partly because the government created jobs in the public sector. Many more women also participated in the labour force. As a result, the Swedish welfare state rested on a much broader base of tax-paying citizens. From this perspective, the problem in the Netherlands was not the welfare state as such but its 'passive' and 'conservative' character. In 1987, as part of an official state visit, an entire coach of Dutch trade unionists and employers visited Swedish job centres to see it for themselves.[26] Therborn's lecture – soon published in a widely read book with responses from politicians and policymakers – coincided with a shift in strategy.

The Netherlands had traditionally been reluctant to pursue active labour market policies, preferring to leave initiative to the private sector. And, thanks partly to the long-established dominance of confessional parties, women's labour participation was exceptionally low. The Swedish example offered the Labour Party an excellent opportunity to acknowledge the crisis of the welfare state and offer a distinctive, social democratic solution. Active labour market policy and women's emancipation in the workplace would keep the welfare state affordable.[27] The CDA, despite its attachment to the traditional breadwinner model, seemed to be open to this approach. As the Labour Party later wrote in its 1994 election manifesto,

---

25   Ibid., 15.

26   Mark Kranenburg, '"Lutherse overwaardering voor betaalde arbeid": Zweedse model geen panacee' ['Lutheran overvaluation of paid work': Swedish model no panacea], *NRC Handelsblad*, 23 May 1987.

27   In the Labour Party, these ideas were elaborated by the Wolfson Committee report. Wolfson Committee, *Niemand aan de kant. Om de toekomst van de verzorgingsstaat* (Amsterdam: PvdA, 1992). The Swedish model also assumed a Keynesian conjunctural policy, but this was not adopted by the Labour Party.

For very different reasons and based on very different experiences, around 1989, Christian Democrats and social democrats came to the conclusion that neoliberalism had gone too far in the 1980s. A new balance was needed between austerity on the one hand and social integration on the other. Both parties were impressed by the Swedish model and sought solutions in an active labour market policy.[28]

In the early 1990s, the new centre-left government presented the 'active welfare state' as an alternative to the no-nonsense policies of the 1980s. Even though workfare and the active welfare state are often associated with neoliberalism, these ideas were originally copied from Sweden, the ideal type of the social democratic welfare state.[29] The coalition agreement of the third Lubbers cabinet therefore marked a major course correction.[30] It referred to a shift from a 'private supply-side strategy' to a 'public supply-side strategy'.[31] The key to economic recovery would be provided not by tax relief for business but by public investment. Under the banner of 'social renewal', the government would tackle problems at the bottom of society, both in the labour market and in poorer neighbourhoods. At the same time, the cabinet wanted to let benefits and public sector wages rise with wages in the private sector. In total, the government was planning on spending an extra 10 billion guilders. Moreover, the trade unions and the corporatist Social and Economic Council would again be involved in the development of socioeconomic policy. After twenty years of disagreement and polarization, corporatism seemed to be back in action.[32]

In 1989 and 1990, the economy was booming, with 4 per cent growth.

28   PvdA, 'Wat mensen bindt: Partij van de arbeid verkiezingsprogramma 1994–1998' (The Hague: PvdA, 1994).

29   See 'Het Zweedse model' [The Swedish model], *NRC Handelsblad*, 11 June 1991, 16.

30   Coalition agreement third Lubbers cabinet, 1989–1990, Kamerstuk 21.132, 8.

31   Breedveld, 'Miljoenennota'.

32   Broer Akkerboom, 'Tijd is gunstig voor opstellen sociaal akkoord' [Time is favourable for drafting social pact], *Het Parool*, 12 August 1989, 21. The article contained an illuminating passage on how the Wassenaar Agreement was still seen at the time: 'The important agreement in the Labour Foundation of 24 November 1982 was not the start of a period of renewed cooperation. Real consensus was lacking. With the agreement, employers and trade unions reached the conclusion that they were in deep disagreement on many issues. They agreed only in the opinion that excessive wage increases should be prevented from tempting the government to issue a wage diktat.'

When the third Lubbers cabinet took office, however, it became clear its budget had been based on overly optimistic economic expectations. Also, various skeletons had come out of the closet. Onno Ruding had failed to inform Kok of a deficit of 2.5 billion guilders.[33] To make matters worse, world trade suffered a major collapse in the following year. Meanwhile, negotiations on European Monetary Union led to the application of strict provisions on the budget deficit and public debt levels, making painful intervention inevitable. In the revised plans of February 1991, informally called the 'second coalition agreement', the cabinet announced cuts totalling 17.5 billion guilders. Little remained of the 'public supply-side strategy'. The cabinet would now make pro-cyclical cuts in the same way as its predecessors, even though there was financial room for a different approach.[34] Wim Kok had also made the unfortunate choice of becoming finance minister, which meant that he himself was going to deliver the bad news and could not politicize the outcome. While governing, the third Lubbers cabinet changed colour. It became a drab vehicle for continuation of the austerity policies pursued earlier, rather than the intended left-wing correction. At the same time, Sweden had entered into a deep economic crisis, and talk of the Swedish model dissipated.

Nevertheless, Ruud Lubbers's choice to form a centre-left government was seen as a big disappointment in the neoliberal camp. The new corporatist consensus politics pursued by the cabinet also met with much resistance. The sluggishness of the consultation model meant that the Netherlands would never be able to catch up and realize a more market-oriented economic order, the critics argued. In response to the crisis-plagued cabinet, a neoliberal plea for more radical reforms emerged, above all within VVD and CDA. What had been only half achieved could still be fully accomplished.

---

33   'Ruding was op de hoogte van belastingtegenvallers' [Ruding was aware of tax setbacks], *De Volkskrant*, 21 November 1989, 3; 'WIR-spook en Ruding blijven minister Kok verrassen' [WIR skeleton and Ruding continue to surprise minister Kok], *De Volkskrant*, 20 December 1990, 2.

34   Economist Dik Wolfson, influential SER member and prominent advisor of Kok, characterized the return to austerity as 'bleeding the patient until we're again at the right path for the budget deficit and tax burden', relying on 'the voodoo of the new-classical supply-side economics'. Dik Wolfson, 'Kunde', *ESB* 77, no. 3,889 (9 December 1992): 1183.

The Sluggish State

'If only we had a Margaret Thatcher in Dutch politics.'[35] With this lamentation, Eduard Bomhoff concluded a much-discussed newspaper column in November 1990. Thatcher was due to step down that week, and Bomhoff was taking stock. He made no secret of his admiration for the Iron Lady, noting that Prime Minister Lubbers paled in comparison. Thatcher had the courage to impose a clear ideological agenda on her party and on society and was not afraid to make enemies in the process. Her 'greatest success', Bomhoff believed, was 'the victory over the trade unions'. Thatcher had refused on principle to attend even one meeting of the British corporatist National Economic Development Council. Lubbers, on the other hand, confused the pursuit of corporatism and consensus with having an agenda.

Bomhoff was certainly not an isolated critic. The leading journalist Marc Chavannes was quick to agree with him. Thatcher's lessons had been ignored in the Netherlands, Chavannes wrote, 'because we conveniently imagine her to be a mal-coiffed lady in a country full of strange types who seem to have walked out of a TV series'.[36] But a Thatcherite élan in the Netherlands was not so crazy after all. 'How do we get rid of late-corporatist structures that are manifestations of a dysfunctional corporatist model that threatens the prosperity and well-being of the Dutch people?' he asked. Chavannes devoted an influential series of articles and a book to 'the sluggish state': 'the never-ending consultations with all social and asocial partners' that obstructed market-oriented reforms.[37] This criticism resonated widely.[38]

Another prominent figure to ride the wave of free market ideas was the former Marxist sociologist Pim Fortuyn. In 1991 he accepted an endowed professorship at Erasmus University Rotterdam and launched his new career as a right-wing columnist with his inaugural lecture, 'Without Civil

35   Eduard Bomhoff, 'Thatcher en Lubbers' [Thatcher and Lubbers], *NRC Handelsblad*, 26 November 1990, 9.

36   Marc Chavannes, 'Nannie in Nederland' [Nanny in the Netherlands], *NRC Handelsblad*, 28 November 1990, 9.

37   Marc Chavannes, 'De stroperige staat' [The sluggish state], *NRC Handelsblad*, 23 February 1992, 29; Marc Chavannes, *De Stroperige Staat: Kanttekeningen Bij de Liefste Democratie Op Aarde* (Amsterdam: Atlas Contact, 1994).

38   Willem Breedveld, 'Kabinet dreigt aan stroperigheid ten onder te gaan' [Government threatens to fall victim to sluggishness], *Trouw*, 9 June 1990, 4.

Servants.'[39] It became the first of a series of pamphlets in which Fortuyn opened a frontal attack on bureaucracy and consensus culture in the Netherlands. Like Bomhoff, Fortuyn complained that Lubbers had missed a wonderful opportunity. The prime minister had defied the public sector unions with his 'government of vital men of action'. He had only failed to deliver the final blow. 'Needless to say, we would have been a lot further ahead by now if the first Lubbers cabinet had opted for the method of amputation rather than the administration of a temporary medicine.'[40] Fortuyn pleaded for a 'Dutch iron lady' to tackle the unions, wanted to sack half of all civil servants and proposed banning permanent contracts.[41] In his view, the third Lubbers cabinet was so incredibly boring that it could not inspire anyone, not even in a negative sense.

Bomhoff's lament was echoed by Frits Bolkestein, who had become the VVD's new leader in 1990. In a Festschrift for Lubbers, he reproached him for not following through with his no-nonsense policy. According to Bolkestein, Lubbers had been politically educated under Den Uyl and had 'never developed into a convinced supply-sider'.[42] Lubbers had never squarely supported his finance minister, Onno Ruding. As a result, the legacy of the 1970s still had not been buried – which was not all Lubbers's fault. Also, the VVD had offered 'too little resistance to the dilution of the austerity policies in the late 1980s'. Bolkestein wanted to get rid of 'the mouldy structures' of corporatism, so that the country could finally move forward.[43] A similar dissatisfaction with slow consensual decision-making was present among the right-wing of the CDA, led by Elco Brinkman. 'Politics should not make pretty promises but proceed to cut through knots,' Brinkman said, in an implicit criticism of Lubbers.[44] Looking back at the 1980s, many right-wing politicians felt that too little had come of the neoliberal reforms.

A first major theme was privatization. Although the finance minister, Onno Ruding, had started energetically in the 1980s, the privatization

39   Pim Fortuyn, *Zonder ambtenaren: De ondernemende overheid* (Amsterdam: Van Veen, 1991).

40   Pim Fortuyn, *Aan het volk van Nederland: De contractmaatschappij, een politiek-economische zedenschets* (Amsterdam: Contact, 1992), 111.

41   Pim Fortuyn, *Het zakenkabinet Fortuyn* (Utrecht: Bruna, 1994), 113.

42   Frits Bolkestein, *Het heft in handen* (Amsterdam: Prometheus, 1995), 218.

43   Ibid., 219–20.

44   Elco Brinkman, 'Knopen Doorhakken', in CDA, ed., *Jaarboek 1993–1994* (The Hague: CDA, 1993), 11–13.

process went less rapidly than expected. Since there were relatively few companies in the Netherlands in public ownership to start with, privatization focused above all on public services. 'All services that do not necessarily have to be performed by the government are candidates for privatization,' the government declaration of the second Lubbers cabinet stated boldly in 1986. Ruding installed a high-level bureaucratic working group that developed plans to leave non-essential public services to the market. Among the largest operations were the privatization of the post and telephone service and of the publicly owned Postbank. They were first made autonomous in the 1980s before being privatized in the 1990s. The Ministry of Finance had a stated preference for privatizing public services completely, but this often met with resistance from the responsible ministries and the trade unions.[45]

There was no lack of grand plans. In 1987, for instance, a committee led by Philips executive Wisse Dekker had drawn up a plan to marketize the healthcare sector.[46] Enneüs Heerma, the CDA state secretary for housing, came up with a memorandum in 1989 proposing the far-reaching privatization of social housing.[47] And, in 1992, a committee led by Rabobank chief Herman Wijffels advised on the privatization of the Dutch Railways.[48] In all of these cases, however, privatization proceeded much more slowly than expected.

In the autumn of 1989, the new minister of economic affairs, the Christian Democrat Koos Andriessen – outgoing chairman of the Christian employer's association – wanted to raise the stakes. In the week before the formal start of the third Lubbers cabinet, he gave a lecture titled 'Privatisation, Only the Beginning' at the Vrije Universiteit Amsterdam. Andriessen noted that the agenda of privatization had until then only addressed 'the tip of the iceberg'. The real goal of privatization 'should be to reconstruct the public sector in such a way as to allow it to

---

45   Jouke deVries and Kutsal Yesilkagit, 'Core Executives and Party Policies: Privatisation in the Netherlands', *West European Politics* 22, no. 1 (1 January 1999): 115–37.

46   Wise Dekker and Commissie Structuur en Financiering Gezondheidszorg, *Bereidheid tot verandering* (The Hague: DOP, 1987).

47   Ministry of Housing and Spatial Planning, *Volkshuisvesting in de jaren negentig: van bouwen naar wonen* (The Hague: SDU, 1989).

48   Herman Wijffels, Roel in 't Veld and Jan de Soet, *Sporen voor straks: advies over de toekomstige relatie tussen overheid en Nederlandse Spoorwegen* (The Hague: Ministry of Transport and Water Management, 1992).

become as efficient as the private sector'. Andriessen proposed a 'really big reorganization of the central government', based on the latest insights from the business world. Since the early 1980s, outsourcing had emerged as a new business strategy. Multinationals began to outsource parts of their production process to locations with cheaper labour, while focusing on their core business at home. This allowed companies to reduce the size of their head offices by up to 40 per cent. Andriessen proposed that the Dutch state should organize itself as a modern business, outsourcing and privatizing all non-essential tasks.[49]

Senior public officials were a major driver behind this idea and developed it further.[50] In 1993 the Wiegel committee presented a plan that took up these suggestions. It proposed to cut back the ministries to 'core departments', while privatizing and decentralizing all non-essential tasks to the private sector or local government. The committee also recommended the creation of a new management layer of senior officials who could rotate between ministries to prevent bureaucratic compartmentalization. Like interim managers in business, the most senior civil servants would no longer need subject-specific knowledge. If the committee's plan had been fully implemented, it would have meant a radical change in the organization of the state: only 15,000 out the 150,000 civil servants were to remain at the national level.[51] For reference, today the Dutch national government still employs around 120,000 civil servants.

The fact that the Labour Party was part of the governing coalition and that Wim Kok had become finance minister proved to be a moderating factor. 'The holy fire for privatization that was present in the previous government does not burn within me,' Kok stated in the Dutch parliament in 1990.[52] In the 1980s, under the Christian Democrat Onno Ruding, privatization formed part of a clear ideological agenda to reduce the size of the state. The Labour Party was less enthusiastic. Kok

49   'Hoe de bestuurlijke knoop te ontwarren' [How to untangle the administrative knot], *De Volkskrant*, 22 June 1991, 65.

50   Ministry of the Interior, *De organisatie en werkwijze van de rijksdienst: Rapportage van de secretarissen-generaal* (The Hague: Ministry of the Interior, 1993).

51   'Commissie-Wiegel: aantal ambtenaren terug naar 15.000' [Wiegel committee: Number of civil servants back to 15,000], *NRC Handelsblad*, 24 June 1993.

52   Cited in Marnix Krop, *Wim Kok: Een leven op eigen Kracht*, part 1, *Voor zijn mensen 1938–1994* (Amsterdam: Prometheus, 2019), 292.

abolished the bureaucratic working group on privatization in 1992. He 'did not want to promote or reject privatization a priori out of ideological motives' but preferred to approach it pragmatically, he explained in a lecture.[53] The policy preference shifted from full privatization to hiving off public services to independent organizations – and decentralizing them to local government. As a result, in more cases than initially envisaged, the privatization process only went halfway: activities were placed at a distance, but the government retained political oversight.[54]

In this way, Kok took the ideological sting out of the privatization debate. The decision to privatize became a technocratic matter on which economists gave the final verdict. However, this tended to displace the problem, because the benefits of introducing market incentives were difficult to estimate in advance and depended heavily on economists' a priori assumptions about the effectiveness of the market mechanism.[55] This displacement of politics into the technocratic domain was characteristic of the Third Way policy paradigm that arose under Wim Kok. While the Labour Party thus had a moderating influence on the neoliberal agenda, it simultaneously contributed to the mainstreaming of market-based solutions.

A typical example of halfway privatization was that of social housing. The Netherlands had a strong tradition of providing social housing through state subsidization of the Dutch housing corporations. Due to the housing crisis of the 1980s, which was accompanied by a formidable squatter movement in the largest Dutch cities, public spending on social housing was still at an all-time high in the 1980s. During the second Lubbers cabinet, the Ministry of Economic Affairs and the Central Economic Committee started beating the drum to rein in spending on public housing.[56] In April 1989, the Christian Democratic state secretary of housing, Enneüs Heerma, published a policy paper, 'Public Housing in the 1990s', which proposed a fundamental liberalization of the Dutch

---

53   Cited in ibid., 291.

54   Eric van Damme, 'Pragmatic Privatization: The Netherlands 1982–2002', in M. Kothenburger, W. Sinn and J. Whalley, eds, *Privatization Experiences in the European Union* (Cambridge, MA: MIT Press, 2006), 289–337.

55   Eric van Damme, 'Marktwerking vereist maatwerk', *Maandschrift Economie* 65, no. 3 (2001): 185–207.

56   See Frans Rutten, 'Economie en openbare financiën', in W. van Lieshout, ed., *Bestuur en meesterschap: Opstellen over samenleving, staat en sturing* (The Hague: Staatsuitgeverij, 1988), 14.

housing sector. It advised cuts in state subsidies to housing corporations, reserve social housing for those on lower incomes and the deregulation of the private rental market, while promoting home ownership.[57]

In 1995, in a historic operation, state subsidies to the housing corporations were cut, and they were paid a one-time fee. While the corporations were still non-profits with a public task, they were now independent and incentivized to become more profit-oriented. The idea was to finance social housing provision by selling off part of the social housing stock and operating on the private rental market. Taking the housing subsidies off the state ledger in this way was an important step towards meeting the EMU accession criteria. While its approach was more moderate than the radical flash sale of social housing under Margaret Thatcher, the Netherlands still saw a significant reduction of social housing, from 40 per cent of total stock in the 1980s to 28 per cent in the early 2020s. The Dutch housing ministry was reduced to little more than half its size, while the share of the Dutch population qualifying for social housing was reduced from 51 per cent in 1991 to 29 per cent in 2009.[58]

Besides privatization, the labour market was a major bone of contention. The left blamed high unemployment on the neoliberal policies of the 1980s – especially the lack of an active labour market policy. For free market thinkers, the problem was the other way around. Rather than more government intervention, they believed more deregulation was the solution. They identified the high minimum wage, limited dismissal options and binding collective bargaining agreements as the real problem. These labour market 'rigidities' prevented the price mechanism from doing its job. The ideal was the American model, with its low wages and flexible dismissal rules. Gerrit Zalm, who had risen to director of the CPB in 1989, emerged as the main advocate of this perspective.

Zalm was constantly in the news in the early 1990s and was considered one of the most influential CPB directors ever. Economists spoke of 'the Planning Bureau paradox'.[59] The models of the CPB had lost much

---

57   Ministry of Housing and Spatial Planning, *Volkshuisvesting in de jaren negentig. Van bouwen naar wonen* (The Hague: SDU, 1989).

58   Naomi Woltring, 'De marktconforme verzorgingsstaat 1989–2008' (Utrecht: Utrecht University Press, 2023), 100.

59   Wiemer Salverda, 'De Planbureau-paradox: Minder gezag en meer invloed', *Tijdschrift Voor Politieke Economie* 15, no. 3 (1993): 106–11.

of their scientific authority in the 1980s and 1990s. Time and again, they had proved incapable of predicting changes in the economy. The leading economic think-tank had failed to foresee the economic recession of the early 1990s. 'In uneventfulness, the CPB thrives best,' the press observed witheringly in 1992.[60] The think-tank was like a weatherman who could not predict a change of weather.

At the same time, however, the CPB's political influence had risen to unprecedented heights. The governing coalition of Christian Democrats and the Labour Party had committed itself to the models, and so had the other political parties: the CPB had begun calculating the economic impact of election programmes in the late 1980s, and its predictions on employment and growth had become important talking points in election debates. All party programmes from now on were dependent on the blessing of the CPB.[61] Zalm played an important role in the newfound prominence of the CPB. 'Sometimes it seems as if the CPB is really Gerrit Zalm with an entire department backing him. That is how intensely he manifests and profiles himself on television, in the [Social and Economic Council] and in the newspapers,' wrote an economist in 1993.[62]

In a 1990 lecture at the Vrije Universiteit Amsterdam, Gerrit Zalm advocated the abolition of binding collective agreements. 'A large proportion of workers on unemployment and disability benefits are fit and willing to go to work, yet wages largely ignore the laws of supply and demand,' he stated bluntly.[63] In his view, trade unions and employers' associations formed cartels that set wages and restricted free competition through collective labour agreements. This made it impossible for the unemployed to work for lower wages. The government had made itself complicit by declaring these collective agreements legally binding for the entire sector. Lowering the minimum wage – a key neoliberal policy plank in reducing unemployment

60   Harko van den Hende, 'CPB krijgt het heen en weer van zwaar weer' [CPB cannot deal with heavy weather], *De Volkskrant*, 14 November 1992, 33.

61   Uwe Becker and Corina Hendriks, ' "As the Central Planning Bureau Says": The Dutch Wage Restraint Paradigm, Its Sustaining Epistemic Community and Its Relevance for Comparative Research', *Review of International Political Economy* 15, no. 5 (1 December 2008): 826–50.

62   Salverda, 'De Planbureau-paradox', 107–8.

63   Gerrit Zalm, *Mythen, paradoxen en taboes in de economische politiek*, inaugural lecture (Amsterdam: Free University Amsterdam, 1990), 26.

– made little sense as long as the unions negotiated a higher minimum through collective agreements.

In his interventions on this issue, Zalm teamed up with Eduard Bomhoff, who had long made the same case.[64] In his newspaper column, Bomhoff reported on his visit to an IMF conference in Washington, DC. For him, the many immigrants he encountered in taxis and in hotel lobbies exemplified America's success in providing jobs for immigrants and the less educated.[65] There was so much demand for workers that Burger King even recruited seniors. In western Europe, however, high benefits and the still unbroken power of trade unions with their collective agreements made this impossible. Bomhoff believed this was anti-social: 'At least here everyone has a chance, even if it's at Burger King,' he wrote from his hotel room in Washington. Gerrit Zalm agreed: 'We have seen no signs of the emergence of a Dutch hamburger economy. Given the large number of unskilled workers, it would be nice if we did.'[66] In this way, the abolition of binding collective agreements became a prominent national debate in the early 1990s.[67]

In an influential article in the economics journal *ESB*, Zalm wrote that binding collective agreements had come about in 1937 as part of the rise of Keynesianism.[68] The Keynesian insight was that wage competition in times of crisis led to lower wages, which, in turn, caused falling demand and further stagnation. Binding collective agreements could prevent such a negative spiral. Referring to Milton Friedman's monetarist analysis of the crisis of the 1930s, Zalm contended that the Great Depression 'is no longer seen as caused by the market mechanism'.[69] The

---

64   See Eduard Bomhoff, 'Betere kansen voor laaggeschoolden en immigranten' [Better chances for the less educated and immigrants], *NRC Handelsblad*, 19 August 1987, 14; Eduard Bomhoff, 'CAO's zijn te dwingend' [Collective agreements are too powerful], *NRC Handelsblad*, 9 September 1987, 18; Eduard Bomhoff, 'Neo-corporatisme' [Neo-corporatism], *NRC Handelsblad*, 9 December 1987, 22.

65   Bomhoff, 'Betere kansen voor laaggeschoolden en immigranten'.

66   Broer Akkerbook en Detlev van Heest, ' "Het mooie weer kan zo weer omslaan" ' [Nice weather can turn in an instant], *Het Parool*, 19 September 1989, 30.

67   Joop Meijnen, 'Schisma over verbindend verklaren van cao's' [Schism over declaring collective agreements binding], *NRC Handelsblad*, 20 December 1991; Ton Damen, 'Is monopolie van vakbonden en werkgevers achterhaald?' [Is monopoly of unions and employers obsolete?], *Het Parool*, 5 February 1992, 17.

68   Gerrit Zalm, 'Betekenis en toekomst van de algemeen-verbindendverklaring', *ESB* 77, no. 3,842 (15 January 1992): 60–4.

69   Ibid., 62.

real culprit was the 'faulty response of monetary and fiscal authorities'. There was no need for binding collective agreements. The Keynesian idea that employment was primarily determined by effective demand was also outdated, Zalm suggested, and had been replaced by the neoclassical theory that focused on labour costs. In short, binding collective agreements could be consigned, along with Keynesianism itself, to the dustbin of history.

Some feared, however, that this would put a bomb under Dutch industrial relations.[70] The trade union movement in the Netherlands had a relatively low level of membership (around 25 per cent of the workforce in 1991). It was able to play a major role in the labour market only because it was allowed to make binding agreements for entire sectors. If companies were able to ignore those agreements at will and compete on lower standards, this could eventually undermine the entire collective bargaining system. Trade unions, in that case, also had a strong incentive to become much more militant. Abolishing binding collective agreements could therefore lead to a much more unpredictable environment for employers.

Employers and trade unions unanimously turned against Zalm and Bomhoff's campaign in the Social and Economic Council. Hans Weitenberg of the Christian Employers' Association criticized their proposal as a 'fundamental attack on the position of the trade union movement'. The Netherlands, Weitenberg clarified in an opinion piece, was 'not a full-blown free market economy'. It was a 'coordinated market economy' in which there had always been room for social dialogue. 'Those who want to scrap binding collective agreements, and thus undermine the sectoral collective agreement, open the way to American industrial relations, with a much harsher social climate and much greater social contradictions,' Weitenberg warned. Opposition from employers ultimately forced Gerrit Zalm to cut his losses in the Social and Economic Council. The debate on collective bargaining illustrated that neoliberalism was more than just a rationalization of corporate interests. The neoliberal fight against 'cartels' had to be waged against the Dutch business community itself, whose interests weren't always aligned with increased deregulation and competition.

70   Meijnen, 'Schisma over verbindend verklaren van cao's'.

A final controversial issue was that of social security. The Lubbers cabinets of the 1980s had restricted themselves to cutting public sector wages and benefit levels; there had been little opportunity for a more fundamental reform of social security. With the recession of the early 1990s, the already high unemployment numbers began to rise further. The number of workers on disability benefits (WAO), a generous benefit for the incapacitated, rose to more than 800,000. Employers and trade unions had used the WAO to smooth the restructuring process during the crisis: companies could fire such workers without arguing their case before a judge, while workers could claim generous benefits. This had never been the intention of the disability benefit, and in the early 1990s the situation became untenable. Of the 17.5 billion guilders of planned cuts, 3.8 billion now had to come from disability benefits.[71]

The Labour Party had promised in the 1989 elections not to cut the height or duration of the disability benefit but only to reduce the number of benefit claimants – but this was not enough to bring down costs. Wim Kok therefore had to renege on his campaign promise. This produced a huge crisis within the party, which almost toppled Kok. He considered resigning but managed to defend the reforms at a special party congress on 28 September 1991. In his speech, he pleaded for a 'Third Way' between 'the disintegration in countries governed by the right' and 'the reduced commitment and personal responsibility in countries like ours'.[72] A month later, the trade unions organized one of the largest demonstrations since the Second World War, under the slogan 'Hands Off the WAO'.[73] The Labour Party lost half of its votes in the polls and a third of its membership – many of them the traditional trade union left. It would take until January 1993 for the centre-left government to finally settle the issue and avert its own collapse.

The crisis over disability benefits further strengthened the critique of the 'sluggish state'. The institutions that decided on benefit claims were governed by employers and trade unions. A parliamentary inquiry found in 1993 that the social partners had neglected reintegration and showed little interest in cutting costs: they were free-riding on public

71   Duco Hellema and Margriet van Lith, *Dat hadden we nooit moeten doen: De PvdA en de neoliberale revolutie van de jaren negentig* (Amsterdam: Prometheus, 2020), 73.

72   Krop, *Wim Kok: Een leven op eigen kracht*, 323.

73   Ibid., 76.

welfare.[74] The Labour Party wanted to reform the system and move towards an active welfare state, inspired by the Swedish model. The right, however, preferred the free market alternative: the 'mini-system'. The alluring idea behind this proposal was that the patchwork of benefits that made up the Dutch welfare state could be replaced by one simple scheme. Those who became unemployed or could not support themselves for some other reason would receive an income at the social minimum. For anything above that, people had to rely on private insurance. This idea had already been put forward in 1984 by the Teldersstichting, the think-tank of the VVD, but at the time it had been a bridge too far.[75] In the 1990s, calls for the mini-system became ever louder.[76]

Elco Brinkman, the heir-apparent for the Christian Democratic leadership, took up a position to the right of Ruud Lubbers and the embattled coalition government. Its collapse was expected at any moment, and Brinkman was not afraid to give it a final shove. On the advice of his spin doctor, Brinkman travelled to the small Dutch island of Texel in February 1992 to put pressure on the government in what seemed like a campaign speech. In this 'Texel Speech', Brinkman advocated a mini-system in social security, the freezing of the minimum wage and unemployment benefits, abolition of the wealth tax and introduction of a deductible in health insurance.[77] 'Playtime is over,' Brinkman told the assembled press. Frits Bolkestein, for his part, declared two months later at the VVD party council that 'the Lubbers-Kok cabinet is done for'.[78] The VVD was ready to govern and wanted to replace the corporatist welfare state with a liberal 'guarantor state', in which the government focused on core tasks.[79]

---

74   Ibid., 80.

75   Hans Heijmans, *Grenzen aan sociale zekerheid*, Geschrift 52 (The Hague: Teldersstichting, 1984).

76   Robert van der Veen, 'Hoe minimaal is de waarborgstaat van de vvd?' [How minimal is the VVD's guarantor state?], *De Volkskrant*, 8 February 1992, 18; Anton Knoester, 'Verzorgingsstaat toe aan fundamentele herziening' [Welfare state needs fundament revision], *De Telegraaf*, 12 December 1992, 51.

77   Hans Goslinga, 'Brinkman zet coalitie onder druk' [Brinkman puts coalition under pressure], *Trouw*, 4 February 1992, 1.

78   Karel Groenveld, 'Van verzorgingsstaat naar waarborgstaat', *ESB* 76, no. 3,828 (2 October 1991): 986–9.

79   'Bolkestein: "Kabinet heeft zijn tijd gehad"' [Bolkestein: 'Government has run its course'], *De Telegraaf*, 6 April 1992, 4.

Officials from the Ministry of Economic Affairs also jumped in. In 1992, the Royal Dutch Economics Society devoted its annual meeting to the mini-system. One of the contributions was by former Secretary-General Frans Rutten.[80] Together with two AEP officials, he contended that a revision of the welfare state was now inevitable. They had worked out a proposal for a mini-system, in which the government provided only a social minimum, while all other (quasi-)public goods such as healthcare, education, public transport and public housing could be left to the market. The abolished subsidies would go to tax cuts. They calculated that, as a result, the tax burden would fall by 10 per cent and employment would increase by 10 per cent.[81] The proposal made headlines in the press. Together with Arie van der Zwan, whom he still knew from the Wagner Committee, Rutten called for a 'new elite', who could 'lead the population in redressing the welfare state'.[82] The Central Economic Committee adopted the AEP proposal for a mini-system in its influential advice leading up to the 1994 elections.

In short, when it came to state bureaucracy, industrial relations and social security, a fundamentally different society was on the agenda in the first half of the 1990s. The push for social transformation had changed sides. It was no longer the left that wanted to change the world – a motley coalition of economists, businessmen, bankers and politicians sought a fundamental break with the status quo. Party intellectuals were now busy trying to provide such a market-oriented order with ideological legitimation.

80   Cees Kortleve, Frans Rutten and Cees Oudshoorn, 'Herijking van de verzorgingsstaat', in B. M. S. van Praag, P. J. Vos and H. P. van Dalen, eds, *De toekomst van de welvaartsstaat (Preadviezen van de Koninklijke Vereniging voor de Staathuishoudkunde)* (Leiden: Stenfert Kroese, 1992), 267–301.

81   Frans Rutten, 'Verzorgingsstaat moet en kan fors afslanken' [Welfare state can and should be cut back significantly], *De Telegraaf*, 30 December 1992, 19; 'Vijftig miljard besparen behoort volgens Rutten tot de mogelijkheden' [Fifty billion in savings are possible according to Rutten], *De Volkskrant*, 13 March 1993, 9.

82   'Groeiende bijval voor Brinkmans bezuinigingsplan' [Growing support for Brinkman's austerity plans], *Het Parool*, 13 March 1993, 13.

The Responsible Society

While Wim Kok had renounced the leftist pursuit of 'the Alternative' in his Nijmegen speech, the right-wing parties were hotly debating the alternative social order that had to replace the corporatist welfare state. Frans Rutten's 'new businesslike politics' provided a sense of direction but was far too technocratic to serve as a political compass. The same applied to the CPB's influential 1992 studies *Scanning the Future* and 'The Netherlands in Triplicate', in which the economic think-tank had worked out a 'free market' scenario for the Netherlands based on the neoliberal ideas of Hayek and Röpke.[83] A more political narrative was needed. The VVD and the Christian Democrats each tried to combine the neoliberal turn with their own political tradition. In both parties, this led to great controversy.

The first move in this direction was made by the Christian Democrats in the 1980s. Within the party, the technocratic nature of Lubbers's no-nonsense policy soon sparked criticism. The concern was that the policy shift would be unsustainable in the long term if the electorate was not actively persuaded of the need for 'more market, less government'. Herman Wijffels, a prominent party member and CEO of the large agricultural bank Rabobank, warned his party colleagues: 'If your main argument to cut spending is "People, it's unfortunate, but the money has run out", then you are on dangerous ground. The implication is that if there is money again, then all cuts can be reversed.'[84] Together with the Wetenschappelijk Instituut voor het CDA, the think-tank of the Christian Democrats, Wijffels was involved in a series of reports in which Christian Democratic thought was given a neoliberal twist.

It was not the first time that Christian democracy and neoliberalism had crossed paths. In the 1940s and 1950s, Christian neoliberals such as Wilhelm Röpke and Alfred Müller-Armack successfully brought the two traditions together, laying the intellectual foundation for the 'social market

---

83   There was also a rational expectations 'equilibrium' scenario and a Keynesian-corporatist 'coordination' scenario. CPB, *Scanning the Future: A Long-Term Scenario Study of the World Economy 1990–2015* (The Hague: CPB, 1992), 45–6; CPB, *Nederland in drievoud: een scenariostudie van de Nederlandse economie, 1990–2015* (The Hague: SDU, 1992).

84   Max van Weezel and Joop van Tijn, *Inzake het kabinet-Lubbers* (Amsterdam: Sijthoff, 1986), 74.

economy' of the West German CDU.[85] Most famously, Wilhelm Röpke developed such a synthesis in his 1944 book *Civitas Humana*, a classic text that was also influential in the Netherlands. Röpke combined a conservative Christian critique of large-scale statism and modernity with a neoliberal plea for the virtues of market forces and decentralization. According to Röpke, the welfare state and the growing centralization of state power resulted in anomie and a 'fading sense of responsibility', with the 'collectivist state' as the ultimate result.[86] By the same logic, more markets and decentralization could restore a sense of community and responsibility. In essence, Röpke had developed a Christian neoliberal communitarianism. Christian social thought in the Netherlands had previously been influenced by Röpke's ideas, though always in conjunction with other, more corporatist inspirations.

The think-tank of the CDA developed a similar narrative, harking back to Christian social thought of the 1950s. It began in 1978 with the report 'Devolved Responsibility', authored by CDA godfather Piet Steenkamp and think-tank staffer Hans Borstlap. According to the report, the Keynesian welfare state encouraged workers and companies to offload their own responsibilities to the government, 'an approach that offers little resistance to an encroaching totalitarian state'.[87] Only cutting back and decentralizing the state could restore the lost sense of responsibility.

Wijffels and Borstlap continued this discourse on responsibility in the 1984 report 'Unemployment and the Crisis in Our Society'.[88] In their view, the economic crisis was not just a socioeconomic issue; the towering unemployment had a deeper cultural cause. The expansion of the welfare state in the 1960s and 1970s had stifled societal initiative. The government had taken on ever more tasks that had previously been performed by (Christian) civil society. The culture of personal responsibility that pervaded civil society had gradually disappeared. Instead, a 'consumerist

---

85   Serge Audier, 'A German Approach to Liberalism? Ordoliberalism, Sociological Liberalism, and Social Market Economy', *L'Economie Politique*, no. 4 (2013): 48–76; Anthony James Nicholls, *Freedom with Responsibility: The Social Market Economy in Germany, 1918–1963* (Oxford: Oxford University Press, 2000).

86   Wilhelm Röpke, *Civitas Humana* (London: William Hodge, 1948), 95.

87   Piet Steenkamp, ed., *Gespreide verantwoordelijkheid: Een christen-democratische bijdrage aan de discussie over de economische orde, Rapport van een commissie van de wetenschappelijke instituten van KVP, ARP en CHU* (The Hague: KVP/ARP/CHU, 1978), 87.

88   CDA, *Werkloosheid en de crisis in onze samenleving* (The Hague: Wetenschappelijk Instituut voor het CDA, 1984).

culture' had emerged, focused on self-realization in the here and now. 'Entrepreneurship, profit-making, hard work, taking risks' had been 'pushed aside as reprehensible, harmful and unnecessary', Wijffels and Borstlap believed.[89] Bringing back that entrepreneurial culture would require a deliberate increase in inequality. 'Like a steamroller, egalitarianism . . . has flattened diversity and multiformity', the pair wrote. 'We will have to abandon the egalitarian drive as it has taken shape over the past twenty years.' The state should step back and adopt a policy 'through which societal responsibility is supported and, if necessary, provoked'. This required a 'policy of confrontation': 'creating the conditions that allowed people to face up to their responsibilities and obligations towards their fellow human beings'.[90] The government had to actively encourage communitarianism, filling in the gaps left by state retrenchment.

This vision was embraced by the Christian Democratic leadership as 'the responsible society'.[91] It was seen as a major ideological innovation by friend and foe alike. 'We provided an ideological legitimation for dismantling the welfare state', Wijffels would later tell his biographer.[92] Initially, the narrative of the 'responsible society' was so hazy that both wings of the CDA could identify with it; but soon it became clear that it primarily served the party's right wing. 'Christian-democratic ideology, [when] practically applied, leads to forms of right-wing liberal state abstinence and/or corporatism', journalists observed.[93] Left-leaning Christian Democrats soon turned against the new ideology. At a party conference in 1988, Bert de Vries warned his colleagues not to turn the responsible society into an ideology.[94] In his view, it was the aversion to ideology that characterized Christian democracy.

---

89   Ibid., 26.

90   Ibid., 34–6.

91   CDA, *Discussienota over de verantwoordelijke samenleving* (The Hague: Partijbestuur CDA, 1987).

92   Jan Smit, *De opdracht: De vele gezichten van Herman Wijffels* (Amsterdam: Balans, 2014), 182.

93   'De nieuwe machtsstrijd in het CDA' [The new power struggle within the CDA], *De Volkskrant*, 11 February 1989, 19.

94   'De Vries waarschuwt voor nieuwe ideologie' [De Vries warns of new ideology], *NRC Handelsblad*, 14 November 1988, 3; Willem Breedveld, 'De overheid als schild voor de sterken' [Government as a shield for the strong], *Trouw*, 19 November 1988, 4; Petra van Alten, 'CDA-concept is verzet tegen armetierigheid' [CDA concept is resistance to poverty], *Het Parool*, 17 December 1988, 2.

Academics also joined the fray. Sociology professor Godfried Engbersen observed that the new Christian Democratic ideology was built on two images: 'society as a business and society as a village'.[95] The two were at odds with each other, however, since business was focused on internationalization and scaling up, thereby eroding community. In the end, it was society as a business that dominated; the image of the village acted 'mainly as ideological legitimation' for cutting back the welfare state. Labour Party intellectual Paul Scheffer saw a very similar tension between economic globalization and community spirit in the Christian Democratic narrative.[96] He noted sharply that 'the very same community that Wijffels wants to defend as a conservative cultural critic, he demolishes as an internationally oriented entrepreneur'.[97]

Elco Brinkman, meanwhile, was readying himself to take over the reins from Lubbers, whose term was ending in 1994. As Brinkman was gearing up for his campaign, the 'responsible society' became increasingly synonymous with privatization and marketization. Important in this process was 'The Coming Government', an influential report edited by Christian Democrat heavyweight and former central bank president Jelle Zijlstra, with assistance from Herman Wijffels. 'Public finances will increasingly have to be aligned with the policy concept of a responsible society,' they wrote. 'This implies that parts of public welfare should henceforth be realized in the private sector.'[98]

While the welfare state had been retrenched somewhat in the 1980s, globalization required 'a real cultural shift' in policy, a 'turning point'.[99] The report referred to Frans Rutten's 'mini-system' and argued that a 'minimal welfare state' would cost only 65 per cent of the existing system.[100] In the coming government term, public debt needed to be

95   Godfried Engbersen and Aafke Komter, 'Schuivende verantwoordelijkheden. De verdeling van lasten en lusten in een verantwoordelijke samenleving', *Beleid en Maatschappij*, no. 5 (1988): 246.

96   Arjan de Visser, 'Verdwijning maatschappelijk middenveld kwelt grote partijen' [Disappearance of civil society torments major parties], *Nederlands Dagblad*, 20 October 1987, 3.

97   Paul Scheffer, 'Op voor het plan!' [Forwards with the plan!], *NRC Handelsblad*, 7 February 1994, 9.

98   Jelle Zijlstra, *De komende kabinetsperiode: enkele financieel-economische kanttekeningen* (The Hague: Wetenschappelijk Instituut voor het CDA, 1993), 21.

99   Ibid., 19.

100   Ibid., 41.

reduced to 50 per cent of national income, while public spending as percentage of GDP and the top tax rate needed to be cut back to the same percentage. This set the tone for Brinkman's campaign, as 'that report by those two [Zijlstra and Wijffels] was the starting point for the party's thinking', Brinkman later confirmed.[101] The result was a draft programme that, according to Christian Democratic insiders, was 'one-sidedly neoliberal' in tone.[102] After Lubbers's move to the centre in 1989, the party had once again shifted to the right. 'Onno Ruding got his way after all,' Bert de Vries remarked bitterly.[103] The Christian Democratic election programme of 1994 formed the historical climax of the ideology of the responsible society. The word 'responsible' appeared more than eighty times in the text.[104] As it turned out, it was not the magic formula that Christian Democrats had hoped for.

The Guarantor State

For its part, the VVD developed a more explicit neoliberal vision. Given the VVD's status as the party of business, this seems unsurprising, but it was not. Traditionally, the party had had an influential progressive-liberal wing. It identified itself in the late 1970s with the progressive-liberal philosophy of John Rawls, who argued that inequality can only be legitimized if it benefits the least well-off. Frits Bolkestein and a group of neoliberal intellectuals at the Teldersstichting had long resented this progressive profile of the party. They sought to transform Dutch liberal-ism with the help of the ideas of Friedrich Hayek.

Bolkestein, a former manager at oil giant Shell, was a somewhat un-Dutch politician. He had a pronounced dislike of Dutch consensus culture and an uncommon affection for intellectual debate. While work-ing for Shell in London in the 1970s, he had become familiar with the Institute of Economic Affairs (IEA), the famous neoliberal think-tank founded on Hayek's personal advice. Bolkestein later stated in a lecture at the IEA that he owed the institute 'a lot of gratitude'. 'As a beginning

101   Kroeger and Stam, *De rogge staat er dun bij*, 294.
102   Ibid.
103   Ibid., 316.
104   CDA, *Wat echt telt: werk – veiligheid – milieu. Landelijk verkiezingsprogramma CDA 1994–1998* (The Hague: CDA, 1994).

member of parliament' in the VVD in the late 1970s, he had decided to 'subscribe to the publications of the free market think-tank'.[105] The IEA provided him with the 'intellectual ammunition to engage and win the great debates of the 1980s and 1990s'. Bolkestein declared himself to be a big fan of Hayek, in his estimation 'perhaps the most important liberal political philosopher of the twentieth century'.[106]

Similar sympathies could be found within the Teldersstichting. Its director, the economist Klaas Groenveld, specialized in the Austrian school and was an admirer of both Hayek and Ludwig von Mises.[107] The young philosopher Andreas Kinneging was a rising star within the think-tank and the party. During his studies, Kinneging had been inspired by the libertarianism of Murray Rothbard and Robert Nozick. In the 1990s, he would become Bolkestein's speech-writer and the party's leading intellectual. In 1985, Groenveld and Kinneging together published the report titled 'Liberalism and Political Economy', in which they offered a historical overview of liberal economic thought, giving leading roles for the German neoliberals Walter Eucken, Alexander Rüstow and Wilhelm Röpke, as well as the American neoliberalism of Chicago school economists such as Milton Friedman, Gary Becker and George Stigler.[108]

Kinneging then worked as lead author on the report 'Liberalism: A Search for Philosophical Foundations', published in 1988. He was assisted by a working group of political heavyweights, including upcoming party leader Frits Bolkestein and the banker and former Economic Affairs Minister Harrie Langman. The study was written in honour of the VVD's fortieth anniversary and was accompanied by a more practical discussion paper. A leadership crisis within the VVD had created tensions between the progressive and conservative wings of the party, and the party chairman had thought that a debate on the party's

---

105   Frits Bolkestein, 'The EU's Economic Test: Meeting the Challenges of the Lisbon Strategy', speech, 17th Annual State of the International Economy Conference, London, 19 November 2001, available at ec.europa.eu.

106   Bolkestein, *Het heft in handen*, 15.

107   For example, Groenveld organized an international symposium on the Austrian School in 1986. See K. Groenveld, J. A. H. Maks and J. Muysken, eds, *Economic Policy and the Market Process: Austrian and Mainstream Economics* (Amsterdam: North-Holland, 1990).

108   Karel Groenveld and Andreas Kinneging, *Liberalisme en politieke economie*, Geschrift 54 (The Hague: Prof. Mr. B.M. Teldersstichting, 1985).

direction would restore calm. But the effect was just the opposite. Kinneging had written something of a neoliberal manifesto, which took a militant stand against progressive-liberal ideas.

The report divided the liberal political tradition into two parts. On the one hand, there was a progressive 'liberalism of personal development', which was at the root of the welfare state – a current represented by John Stuart Mill. The report gave it a cold shoulder. The other pole was 'utilitarian liberalism', of which Hayek was deemed the figurehead. The report committed itself to this second current and posited the 'guarantor state' as the political ideal. Philosophically, this was modelled on Hayek's ideal state, as described in his book *The Constitution of Liberty*. According to Hayek's vision, the state would not be allowed to engage in economic redistribution; only guaranteeing a social minimum was allowed.

The report was particularly controversial because the working group in the preface explicitly endorsed the neoliberal vision of the guarantor state 'as the basis for political action'.[109] The accompanying discussion paper pushed a similar line. It opened with a quote from *The Constitution of Liberty* and sided with the guarantor state.[110] The reactions to the report were intense. If the VVD really meant this, one commentator wrote, the entire party programme could be binned.[111] Another leading newspaper described the report as 'unfiltered bourgeois conservatism', and 'a return to Dickens'.[112] In an academic review essay, two Leiden philosophy professors argued that the think-tank had stripped liberalism of 'all the social guises in which this ideology has robed itself since the middle of the last century'.[113] The reaction from the centrist and progressive wing of the party was not long in coming. At the VVD party congress in May 1988, 2,000 amendments were tabled, effectively burying both publications.

109   Andreas Kinneging, *Liberalisme: een speurtocht naar de filosofische grondslagen*, (The Hague: Prof. Mr. B.M. Teldersstichting, 1988), v.

110   VVD, *Discussienota liberaal bestek '90: Een kansrijke toekomst, verantwoorde vrijheid* (The Hague: VVD, 1988), 3.

111   Hubert Smeets, 'VVD staat pal voor waarborgstaat' [VVD defends the guarantor state], *NRC Handelsblad*, 1 February 1988, 9.

112   'Restauratie' [Restoration], *De Volkskrant*, 23 January 1988, 3.

113   Hans Charmant and Percy B. Lehning, 'De kaalslag van het liberalisme: een analyse van "Liberalisme, een speurtocht naar de filosofische grondslagen"', *Beleid en Maatschappij* 15, no. 5 (1988): 248–60.

Still, Bolkestein was elected leader of the VVD in 1990 and resumed his advocacy of the guarantor state. In a 1993 essay, Bolkestein explained that the guarantor state was actually a step 'back to the future', as it meant going back to a moment in Dutch history before the expansion of the welfare state.[114] Rather than referring to Hayek or Friedman, he now claimed inspiration from the sober social democratic Prime Minister Willem Drees, who in the 1950s had coined the term 'guaranteeing state': a state that provided only minimal social security. In a newspaper interview in May 1995, Bolkestein provocatively argued: 'The old left was neoliberal,' and he continued: 'We propagate Drees's guarantor state in which a subsistence level income is guaranteed for everyone . . . We also propagate the same down-to-earth pragmatism.'[115] Bolkestein hoped that Labour Party leader Wim Kok, too, would turn out to be a Dreesian social democrat. Although Bolkestein had to accommodate the progressive-liberal wing of his party, the VVD came up with an outspoken neoliberal programme in 1994, increasing income inequality, radically reducing the number of civil servants by gutting ministries, abolishing property and transfer taxes and pursuing more privatization and marketization. The guarantor state was included as a 'basic welfare system'.[116] Roughly speaking, one can say that the VVD advocated a more individualist and the CDA a more communitarian form of neoliberalism.

A New Market-Based Consensus

In the early 1990s, the Netherlands found itself at a crossroads. Due to the disability benefit crisis, it seemed for a long time that a right-wing majority was within reach, allowing for a fundamental shift in socio-economic policy. With this assessment in mind, Lubbers's successor Elco Brinkman had increasingly distanced himself from the third Lubbers cabinet. He already had an agreement in principle with the VVD to find a right-wing resolution of the disability crisis. Unexpectedly,

---

114   Frits Bolkestein, 'Modern liberalisme', in *Het heft in handen*, 16–41.

115   Kees Versteegh, 'Het sociaal-democratische verleden van de vvd-top. De linkse wortels van het liberale succes' [The social democratic past of the VVD party elite], *NRC Handelsblad*, 13 May 1995, 4.

116   VVD, *Nederland weer aan de slag* (The Hague: VVD, 1994), 13.

however, Bert de Vries (CDA) and Wim Kok (PvdA) managed to reach a last-minute deal in January 1993. In the so-called 'Noodles Agreement', named after the takeaway food the negotiators had consumed, they found a formula for cutting disability benefits. This was a bitter disappointment for the right, which feared the Netherlands would miss the opportunity to make a clean break with the welfare state and the polder model.

The CDA party programme for the 1994 elections was presented by Elco Brinkman as a 'watershed'.[117] This created bad blood with Lubbers, who saw it as an attack on his legacy. However, it was the logical consequence of the earlier plea by Jelle Zijlstra and Herman Wijffels for a 'turnaround' in socioeconomic policy. The austerity policy Brinkman proposed proved wildly unpopular with Christian Democratic voters, especially the elderly. The party took a nosedive in the polls, and the election campaign went disastrously. The death blow for Brinkman was that Ruud Lubbers told the press he wouldn't vote for Brinkman but rather the number three on the Christian Democratic candidate list. In the elections, the CDA saw its vote share fall from 36 per cent to 22 per cent. The desired watershed remained out of reach.

Still, much had changed. Wim Kok had been a Keynesian economist during the 1980s and had noted that the austerity of the first Lubbers cabinets 'had a two-thirds leakage effect', as the cuts caused effective demand to slump and the crisis to deepen.[118] The 1987 Labour Party report 'Sliding Panels' argued that the supply-side policies of the 1980s had failed to prompt private investment. The report called for demand stimulus by 'increasing the spending opportunities of the large group of lower-income earners' and 'more government spending'.[119] As finance minister, however, Kok ultimately came to embrace the austerity and supply-side policies of his predecessor Ruding.

The disability crisis marked an important turning point for Kok: Keynesian thinking was buried for good. 'In the current electoral climate, tax increases and income levelling are tantamount to political suicide. In today's international market economy, vulgar Keynesianism

---

117   Kroeger and Stam, *De rogge staat er dun bij*, 300–1.

118   Kok, '60%: nieuwe normen en gedachten', 83–5.

119   PvdA, *Schuivende panelen. Continuïteit en vernieuwing in de sociaaldemocratie* (Amsterdam: PvdA, 1987), 86.

(increasing government spending, running up a budget deficit, fighting inflation with devaluation) equals economic suicide,' read the 1994 Labour Party election programme. Moreover, with the Maastricht Treaty concluded in 1992, member-states of the European Union had committed themselves to a maximum 3 per cent budget deficit and a public debt of no more than 60 per cent of GNP. These were the entry requirements for European Monetary Union, and they effectively made a Keynesian cyclical policy impossible.

But change also came from within. Under Kok's leadership, the Labour Party underwent a process of 'modernization'.[120] Control of the party was centralized, new marketing techniques were introduced, links with the trade unions were loosened and new faces were sought from outside traditional social democratic circles. As a result, a new generation of market-minded politicians emerged in the Labour Party. They came to play a central role in crafting the economic policies of the Dutch Third Way. The so-called Purple cabinets (1994–2002), which formed the Dutch equivalent of the Third Way, were to become the high point of the agenda of privatization, marketization, deregulation and flexibilization.

In the end, the neoliberal turn in the Netherlands was a gradual affair. The historical caesura never materialized, the longing for a Dutch Thatcher was never fulfilled and – during the Third Way cabinets – ultimately proved unnecessary. A new market-based consensus had quietly emerged.

---

120   Hellema and Lith, *Dat hadden we nooit moeten doen*, 108–23.

6

The Colour Purple (1994–2002)

In the mid-1990s, the Netherlands was getting to grips with globalization. As a result of the Maastricht Treaty, on 1 January 1993, the European single market went into force – the world's largest free trade zone. Goods, workers, services and capital could now cross Europe's internal borders without tariff walls. One year later, on the other side of the Atlantic Ocean, Canada, the US and Mexico signed the North American Free Trade Agreement (NAFTA). That same year also saw the revision of the General Agreement on Tariffs and Trade (GATT), resulting in the founding of the World Trade Organization (WTO). More than a hundred countries participated, and the negotiations resulted in a global free trade agreement of unprecedented scope. Tariff walls were abolished for a wide range of products: from toothbrushes to pleasure boats, financial services to telecoms, wild rice DNA to AIDS drugs. Sociologist Abram de Swaan expressed the prevailing sentiment by noting that the Netherlands had become a 'platform in the world'.[1]

The European single market, the NAFTA free trade zone and the WTO were products of the free market revolution of the 1980s.[2] But the intensified economic globalization triggered by these agreements in turn strengthened the neoliberal agenda. In a world where everyone was

---

1 Abram de Swaan, *Perron Nederland* (Amsterdam: Meulenhoff, 1991).

2 Quinn Slobodian, *Globalists: The End of Empire and the Birth of Neoliberalism* (Cambridge, MA: Harvard University Press, 2018), 218–62.

competing with everyone else, individual countries had less leeway to pursue independent economic policies. There were growing fears that the Netherlands, with its corporatist labour market and top-heavy welfare state, was not up to par with its competitors. The crisis atmosphere that prevailed among policymakers in the early 1990s was reminiscent of the early 1980s, when the Wagner Committee had managed to dominate the debate. Although corporate profits had recovered and the Dutch economy was performing better, there remained great concern among Dutch economic elites as to whether the Netherlands was ready for the new era of globalization.

'National Elite Must Save Economy', read the front-page headline of liberal newspaper *NRC Handelsblad* on 5 February 1994.[3] Editor-in-chief Ben Knapen had asked the secretary-general of economic affairs, Ad Geelhoed, economics professor Arie van der Zwan, Rabobank chairman Herman Wijffels, VVD leader Frits Bolkestein and Philips CEO Jan Timmer to share their concerns about the Dutch economy. The tone was grim. The Dutch have a nautical saying for a late confrontation with reality: 'The shore will turn the ship.' According to Geelhoed, there was an outright emergency: 'The shore has already penetrated the ship's hull and the water level has risen above the shoes.' Timmer predicted that, with the rise of Asia, Europe was in danger of being demoted 'to the status of a technological colony'. Wijffels wanted to reduce the welfare state to a 'mini-system' and believed that the Dutch corporatist model had 'run its course' if trade unions did not play along. Van der Zwan noted that one should strike the iron while it was hot: 'If you want to achieve something, you must do it in the period of cabinet formation. After that, it's too late.' Bolkestein called on everyone to come to the globalization debate convened by Koos Andriessen and to lobby politicians. After all, elections were due in May that year.

Koos Andriessen, the Christian Democratic minister of economic affairs, had organized a 'Globalization Platform' just before the end of his term. What was soon dubbed 'the Koos Show' took the form of a national debate on the challenges of globalization, broadcast in prime time on Dutch public television. On 24 March 1994, Dutch business leaders gathered in a Philips exhibition centre in the industrial city of

---

3   Ben Knapen, 'Nationale elite moet de economie redden', *NRC Handelsblad*, 5 February 1994, 1.

Eindhoven, in 'an attempt to make the Dutch national character ready for globalization'.[4]

The location was heavy with symbolism. The Dutch electronics giant Philips – in the 1980s still the third-largest electronics company in the world, with over 350,000 employees globally – had trouble keeping up with Asian competitors. Plunging share prices and pressure from shareholders led to the launch in the autumn of 1990 of 'Operation Centurion', modelled on the radical downsizing of American behemoth General Electric in the 1980s.[5] Timmer, nicknamed 'the butcher', was assisted by the Indian-American management guru Coimbatore Krishnarao Prahalad. The latter advised Timmer that management and workers had to be taken to 'the Valley of Death', convinced of the imminent demise of Philips.[6] Using a fake article from the *Financial Times*, Timmer convinced senior management in a closed session that bankruptcy was around the corner. He then fired over 45,000 Philips employees, an across-the-board cut of one out of every seven workers. Though the Centurion operation was originally credited as a success in averting bankruptcy, Philips never recovered and gradually devolved into a mere shadow of its former self. Understandably, the plight of Philips was all over the Dutch news in the early 1990s – a dire warning of the perils of globalization and the power of financial markets.

In the hometown of Philips, Andriessen held his debate. The event was inspired by US President Bill Clinton, who had centred his 1992 campaign on the need to boost American competitiveness in the face of economic globalization. After winning the presidency, Clinton organized a two-day televised conference in his former hometown of Little Rock, Arkansas. Together with business leaders and civil society organizations, he sought to build support for his economic agenda. It formed

---

4   Cees Banning, 'Andriessen: Schouders er onder' [Andriessen: Get a move on], *NRC Handelsblad*, 15 March 1994, 18.

5   Luchien Karsten et al., 'Leadership Style and Entrepreneurial Change: The Centurion Operation at Philips Electronics', *Journal of Organizational Change Management* 22, no. 1 (2009): 73–91.

6   Nigel Freedman, 'Operation Centurion: Managing Transformation at Philips', *Long Range Planning* 29, no. 5 (1 October 1996): 607–15. Presently, this type of unfocused downsizing is seen as counterproductive, due to bad publicity, loss of knowledge, weakened worker engagement and lower innovation. See Shalene Gupta, 'Layoffs That Don't Break Your Company', *Harvard Business Review*, May–June 2018: 122–9.

the beginning of the American Third Way.[7] Andriessen wanted a similar 'Clinton-like setting' in the Netherlands. The Globalization Platform became a great publicity success and was the talk of the town for many weeks. From a practical point of view, the platform gave Dutch business an excellent opportunity to restate its demands a week before the start of the 1994 election campaign. Timmer called for a 20 per cent reduction in wage costs, the easing of employment protection, longer working hours and the cutting of red tape. The Dutch trade unions were also allowed to participate but had to content themselves with a role on the margins.[8]

It almost seemed as if the Ministry of Economic Affairs had organized its own election campaign. Alongside Andriessen, there was an important role for Frans Rutten's successor, Secretary-General of Economic Affairs Ad Geelhoed. Since his appointment in 1989, Geelhoed had been sounding the alarm about the coming European single market and European monetary integration (EMU). He warned that, due to European unification, there was 'no room for our political folklore', such as consensual Dutch decision-making.[9] He contended that 'EMU forces us to lower labour costs' and cut social security, so as to not lose out to other member-states with lower taxes.[10] In his eyes, 'the Netherlands was not yet ready for EMU' and 'the Dutch welfare state was no longer tenable'.[11] These pronouncements by Geelhoed often became front-page news. 'Prof. Geelhoed: European Race to Lowest Taxes', *De Telegraaf*, the largest Dutch newspaper announced on its front page in January 1992.[12] While officially a member of the Labour Party, Geelhoed wasn't seen as a typical social democrat. 'You have to redefine social democracy if you want to call Geelhoed a social democrat,'

---

7   Later, Clinton's free-trade policy, and the unemployment in the American rust belt would be seen as a cause of Donald Trump's election victory. See Nelson Lichtenstein and Judith Stein, *A Fabulous Failure: The Clinton Presidency and the Transformation of American Capitalism* (Princeton, NJ: Princeton University Press, 2023).

8   '"Katerig" gevoel bij vakbonden na debat' ['Hangover' feeling among unions after debate], *Nieuwsblad van het Noorden*, 25 March 1994, 21.

9   'Geelhoed: Geen plaats voor onze bestuurlijke folklore' [Geelhoed: No room for our political folklore], *Het Parool*, 12 December 1991.

10   'EMU dwingt ons tot verlagen arbeidskosten' [EMU forces us to lower labour costs], *De Volkskrant*, 16 December 1991.

11   'Nog niet klaar voor EMU' [Not ready for EMU], *Trouw*, 3 January 1992.

12   'Wedloop in EG om laagste belasting', *De Telegraaf*, 3 January 1992.

leading party intellectual Jos de Beus remarked.[13] But the 1990s were a time of political redefinition. Geelhoed would be appointed as Wim Kok's right-hand man at the end of the decade.

As secretary-general of economic affairs, Geelhoed chaired the Central Economic Committee (CEC). Under Frans Rutten, this so-called 'cockpit' of economic policymaking, which prepared the agenda for the Council of Ministers, had grown into a powerful advocate of 'more market and less government'. It comprised senior officials from the Ministries of Finance, Economic Affairs and Social Affairs, together with the directors of the Dutch Central Bank and the CPB. During the 1980s and 1990s, the CEC was at the peak of its powers; some journalists described it as a 'shadow government'.[14] A sign of the influence the CEC exerted was that newspapers had a tendency of covering its advice in front-page headlines: 'Senior Officials: Fundamental Reconsideration of Social System Needed'; 'Senior Officials: Lower Tax Burden to Curb Unemployment'.[15] Most influential, however, were its confidential recommendations on economic policy, which were given to the political parties during the formation of new coalition governments.[16]

There had been important ideological disagreements between the Labour Party and the CEC. In 1989, for instance, Wim Kok had turned down CEC advice in which the committee had advocated a hefty tax cut of 4.5 billion guilders. According to the supply-side theory then in vogue, such a tax cut would contribute to wage moderation and help strengthen incentives to work. Kok, at a press conference during the formation of the third Lubbers cabinet, spoke of an 'astonishing' study, adding that 'this way of limiting the available fiscal space . . . does not meet with my approval'.[17] In the run-up to the elections of 1994, the CEC recommended cuts of 20 billion guilders, or 10 per cent of total

---

13   Cees Banning, 'De rationaliteit van topambtenaar Geelhoed' [The rationality of senior official Geelhoed], *NRC Handelsblad*, 5 January 1998.

14   'Waakhond CEC' [Watchdog CEC], *Nieuwsblad van het Noorden*, 2 July 1991.

15   'Topambtenaren: Fundamentele herbezinning op sociaal stelsel nodig', *Trouw*, 22 December 1990; 'Topambtenaren: Verlaag belastingen om werkloosheid te verminderen', *Trouw*, 10 December 1990, 1.

16   Wimar Bolhuis, 'Van woord tot akkoord. Een analyse van de partijkeuzes in CPB-doorrekeningen van verkiezingsprogramma's en regeerakkoorden, 1986–2017' (PhD diss., Leiden University, 2018), 59.

17   'Kok verrast door plan lagere BTW' [Kok surprised by lower VAT plan], *Het Parool*, 21 September 1989.

government spending, which meant heavy cuts in the social security system.[18] This was even more than the VVD (17 billion guilders) and the CDA (18 billion guilders) had planned in cuts.

The CEC raised the prospect of large job losses, since Dutch companies made products that could be produced more cheaply elsewhere. At the same time, it touted the opportunities of economic globalization: as the economies of developing countries grew, there would be a greater need for 'highly productive, knowledge-intensive activities' that the Dutch could supply.[19] If the Netherlands wanted to reap the benefits, it had to change direction in time, ensuring low labour and production costs for these activities. 'The biggest threat of the globalization process is that we do not seize these opportunities,' the CEC opined. 'The main threat lies with us.'[20] The CEC's recommended package included a tax cut worth 12 billion guilders, privatization of large parts of the social security system and replacement of the welfare state with a mini-system.[21]

When he later looked back at the crucial role of the Ministry of Economic Affairs, Geelhoed wrote that 'unilaterally changing the policy agenda in the Netherlands' was almost impossible, due to the many blockage points in the decision-making process: 'Such changes only have a chance if they have become inescapable in the direct perception of citizens themselves and of relevant civil society organizations.'[22] The Globalization Platform and the continuous media interventions of Geelhoed were an attempt by the ministry to create such a sense of inevitability. When asked to characterize his contribution to economic policy, Geelhoed later remarked: 'In economic terms, think of me as a neoliberal.'[23]

18   'Advies topambtenaren: Forse ingreep sociaal stelsel "noodzakelijk"' [Advice from senior officials: Major intervention in social system 'necessary'], *NRC Handelsblad*, 18 May 1994, 1.

19   National Archive, Archive Ministry of Economic Affairs: directie Algemene Economische Politiek, inv.nr. 1442, Centrale Economische Commissie, *Nota ten behoeve van de kabinetsformatie*, 16 May 1994, 1.

20   Ibid.

21   'Advies topambtenaren'.

22   Ad Geelhoed, 'Making a Difference: De beleidsagenda en AEP', *Tijdschrift Voor Politieke Economie* 24, no. 1 (2002), 66.

23   Jacques de Jong and Ed Weeda, *Dertig jaar Nederlands energiebeleid: van bonzen, polders en markten naar Brussel zonder koolstof* (The Hague: Clingendael International Energy Programme, 2005), 443.

Naturally, the Labour Party was not happy with the CEC advice. The party had only 9 billion guilders in cutbacks in its election platform, and Wim Kok promised during the campaign that, after the disability crisis, there would be no major restructuring of the welfare state. Referring to projected economic growth of 2 per cent and a reduction in unemployment of between 5,000 and 10,000 jobs a month, Kok dismissed the suggested 20 billion guilders in cuts as 'out of proportion'.[24] He reminded the CEC of its status as a bureaucratic body: 'We make policy, civil servants implement it.' The article cited an anxious senior civil servant who feared for the future: 'When Wim Kok becomes prime minister, the CEC can pack it up.'

The Primacy of Finance

The elections of May 1994 turned out differently than the proponents of neoliberal reform had hoped. As we have seen, the centre-right parties CDA and VVD had campaigned for a 'watershed' in socioeconomic policy in the run-up to the elections. But the harsh austerity policies that Christian Democratic leader Elco Brinkman insisted on led to a historic electoral defeat. Of the 54 seats (out of 150) the Christian Democrats had won in 1989, only 34 remained in 1994. The Labour Party experienced a reverse trajectory. After the 1991 disability crisis, the party was expected to lose half of its 49 seats. Months before the 1994 elections, the party was still in fourth place in the polls, behind the CDA, VVD and the progressive-liberal D66.[25]

Wim Kok originally intended to run a centrist campaign focused on his newly acquired reputation for sound fiscal policy. Internal polling however, showed that Labour Party voters found social justice far more appealing than budget discipline. On the advice of his campaign managers, Wim Kok launched a more traditional left-wing election campaign.[26] In this way, the Labour Party put some colour back in its cheeks. Ultimately, the fear of a hard swing to the right brought many left-wing voters back to

24   Cees Banning, 'Ivloed topambtenaren afgenomen onder Kok' [Influence of senior officials declined under Kok], *NRC Handelsblad*, 18 May 1994, 3.

25   Marnix Krop, *Wim Kok: Een leven op eigen Kracht*, part 1, *Voor zijn mensen 1938–1994* (Amsterdam: Prometheus, 2019).

26   Ibid.

the party. It lost 'only' twelve seats, becoming the largest party as a result. Behind Labour, with thirty-seven seats, followed the CDA with thirty-four, the VVD with thirty-one and D66 with twenty-four.

A new coalition was in the making. D66 leader Hans van Mierlo, who had emerged as kingmaker, had set his sights on a government without the Christian Democrats – for the first time since the introduction of the franchise in 1918. Such a cabinet made it possible to introduce new progressive legislation on 'social issues' such as abortion, euthanasia and gay marriage. The Labour Party had a choice: tie their fate to that of the Christian Democrats, who had lurched to the right, or team up with Bolkestein's VVD, which was on a 'veritable crusade' to liberalize the economy.[27] After tense negotiations, the latter option was chosen, leading to a historic 'Purple' cabinet: a combination of red (PvdA), blue (VVD) and green (D66).[28]

The coalition agreed to 18 billion guilders' worth of cuts, with 9 billion guilders in tax relief and privatization of a large part of the social security system. Although the Labour Party had run a left-wing campaign around social justice, it quickly transformed into a centrist party when governing. The CEC could breathe a sigh of relief, but the left wing of the Labour Party was not amused. Paul Kalma, director of the Wiarda Beckman Stichting, the social democratic think-tank, wrote of 'the primacy of the Ministry of Finance' and criticized the Purple cabinet as the culmination of the neoliberalism of the Lubbers cabinets.[29] Bart Tromp, a leading Labour Party intellectual, spoke of a 'democratic deficit'.[30] When forming his Purple government, Wim Kok had 'strongly minimalized the importance of the election programme, arguing that six months had already passed since its adoption' – as if the

---

27   These were the words of the future right-wing populist Pim Fortuyn, who meant them as a compliment: 'The VVD and especially its political leader Frits Bolkestein have been on a veritable crusade for over a decade, for more market and less regulation.' Pim Fortuyn, 'Marktordening', *ESB* 80, no. 4,029 (27 September 1995): 923.

28   Peter Maas, 'PvdA en VVD: Polarisatie en profilering', in Peter Maas and Fred Lafort, *Illusie of monsterverbond: mogelijkheden en grenzen van een PvdA-VVD coalitie*, Nederlandse Parlementaire Reeks 1 (Amsterdam: De Bataafsche Leeuw, 1984); Jouke de Vries, *Paars en de managementstaat: het eerste kabinet-Kok (1994–1998)* (Leuven: Garant, 2002).

29   Paul Kalma, 'Het primaat van Financiën', *Socialisme en Democratie* 51, no. 9 (1994): 393. See also Paul Kalma, *De wonderbaarlijke terugkeer van de solidariteit* (Amsterdam: Wiardi Beckman Stichting, 1995).

30   Bart Tromp, 'Democratisch Tekort', *Socialisme en Democratie* 51, no. 10 (1994): 441.

world had fundamentally changed after six months. Kalma and Tromp were joined by Labour MP Frans Leijnse, who believed that Kok had 'made financial norms predominate over any policy consideration'.[31] This was precisely the accusation Kok had levelled at the 1980s 'no-nonsense' cabinets. In the party journal, Leijnse lamented the rise of

> a type of politician who can no longer even be called 'opportunistic', having never had an outspoken political opinion. A type that has internalized the predominance of financial-technical dogma to such an extent that it regards political vision and political debate as an inconvenient complication. This aversion to ideological precepts has led to a completely apolitical politics; nowhere has technocratic thinking acquired such a dominant position as in The Hague.[32]

While Kok stood accused of subordinating his political ideology to fiscal discipline, former CPB director Gerrit Zalm became the face of the Purple cabinet's fiscal policy. His appointment as finance minister for the VVD came as a surprise to many. Zalm's name was not initially considered during the formation of the 1994 government, since VVD leader Frits Bolkestein did not know the CPB director was a member of his party. This false start, however, did not stand in the way of a brilliant political career: Zalm instantly became a leading figure within the right-wing liberal VVD, even making it to party leader (2002–04).

In the 1980s, budget policy had been organized around an 'actual deficit norm' – which meant that the coalition agreement stipulated the reduction of the deficit to a certain absolute level. This arrangement had considerable downsides: whenever a setback occurred, new cuts had to be planned. Conversely, when the economy picked up, politicians were tempted to spend more money. With the new Zalm-norm introduced by the liberal finance minister, a ceiling on government spending was agreed in advance, based on conservative estimates of expected economic growth. While setbacks at the ministries had to be compensated by additional cuts in departmental budgets, financial windfalls had to be spent on paying off the national debt or lowering taxes. This

31   Frans Leijnse, 'De CDA-isering van de PvdA: Een kritiek op het regeerakkoord', *Socialisme en Democratie* 51, no. 10 (1994): 442–54.

32   Ibid., 452.

norm would grow into a prominent liberal achievement: it made reduction of public spending the norm. Economist Bas Jacobs called it a 'brilliant liberal accomplishment'.[33]

Zalm explained the intellectual background of his norm at an academic symposium to mark the retirement of his former boss, Frans Rutten. Zalm invoked the work of the new-classical economists Robert Lucas and Robert Barro (also a member of the Mont Pelerin Society). Both were leading critics of Keynesianism, who argued that the 'activist government policies advocated by Keynesians were not the solution but partly the cause' of the economic malaise of their time.[34] Frans Rutten's plea for 'businesslike politics', with a focus on technocratic budgeting rules rather than political discretion, was inspired by this new-classical critique and by public-choice theory, Zalm reminded his audience. Politicians could not be trusted with the budget, Rutten had argued, because they faced pressures from interest groups and ministries seeking to expand their budgets. Zalm presented his fiscal norm as the culmination of Rutten's long-term vision. Also at the European level, Zalm worked on the consolidation of an austere fiscal policy. Together with the German finance minister, Theo Waigel, Zalm was a leading proponent of 1997 Stability and Growth Pact, which tried to enforce a maximum 3 per cent budget deficit and a ceiling of 60 per cent on public debt. For the Dutch Finance Ministry, the European budget rules also meant a substantial strengthening of its domestic position. 'If we have an economic and monetary union,' the former Finance Minister Onno Ruding declared in 1990,

a country like the Netherlands can no longer freely cook up budget deficits at its own pleasure. Brussels is going to dictate what can and cannot be done. Some lament losing that freedom. Not me, I applaud it. Of course, it strengthens the position of the finance minister. You can use Brussels to make ministers and parliament toe the budgetary line.[35]

---

33   Bas Jacobs, 'De Zalmnorm en het begrotingsbeleid 1994–2007', *Tijdschrift Voor Openbare Financiën* 39, no. 1 (12 July 2007): 4.

34   Gerrit Zalm, 'Budgettaire coördinatie. To Be or Not to Be?', in R. S. G. Lenderink, Arie Ros and Jarig van Sinderen, *Langs lijnen van geleidelijkheid. Opstellen aangeboden aan prof. dr. F. W. Rutten* (Groningen: Wolters Noordhoff, 2000), 4.

35   Onno Ruding, 'Er moet meer gebeuren', in Jarig van Sinderen, ed., *Het sociaal-economisch beleid in de tweede helft van de twintigste eeuw* (Groningen: Wolters-Noordhoff, 1990), 60.

The Ministry of Finance had concluded its war against the pressure groups – a conflict it had been embroiled in ever since the 1970s – with a resounding victory.

Shedding Ideological Feathers

'Jobs, jobs, jobs' – that was the motto of the Purple coalition sworn in by Queen Beatrix on 22 August 1994. It promised 'work that significantly improves safety on the streets, public supervision, childcare [and] better health services, especially for the dependent elderly'. It sounded like a familiar social democratic message.[36] Those who read further, however, saw that the cabinet wanted to achieve these goals through wage restraint, tax cuts, deregulation, privatization of sick pay, labour market flexibilization and the lowering of the minimum wage. It was a supply-side policy, focused on improving business incentives.

The Purple coalition marked the beginning of a sustained compromise between social democracy and neoliberal ideals – what came to be called the 'Third Way'. The neoliberal approach was to replace the corporatist welfare state with a 'guarantor state' while lowering wages, tax burdens and regulatory pressure to create more jobs. The Labour Party instead proposed an 'active' welfare state. Social democrats favoured public investments in childcare, training and reintegration and thus made a case for a state that actively improved the functioning of the labour market. But the amount of public investment turned out to be rather disappointing. The Purple coalition decided to cut 18 billion guilders during the cabinet period, while only 4 billion guilders was invested. In this version of purple, blue was the dominant colour.

This was not simply because the Labour Party ruled in a coalition with two liberal parties. The Labour Party itself had undergone an ideological transformation, in line with the international trend. US President Bill Clinton, who took office in 1993, and UK Labour leader Tony Blair, elected as prime minister in 1997, had openly broken with Keynesianism and traditional social democratic politics. 'It is not

---

36 Coalition agreement of the first Kok cabinet, year 1993–1994, Kamerstuk 23.715, 11, 6.

tired. It is dead,' Tony Blair said of the socialist tradition in an interview with *Newsweek*.[37] Clinton and Blair advocated a Third Way between social democracy and neoliberalism. Wim Kok made a similar grand gesture in a landmark speech that he delivered in an old Amsterdam conventicle in December 1995. In the lecture, he spoke of the 'liberating effect of shedding one's ideological feathers' and distanced himself from old-school social democracy: 'A true renewal of the PvdA begins with a definitive departure from socialist ideology; with a definite severing of the ideological ties with other heirs of the traditional socialist movement.'[38] This separation, he noted, was by then almost complete.

In contrast to the US and the UK, however, where the Third Way was loudly proclaimed as the new party ideology, Kok took a more cautious approach.[39] It was somewhat of a paradox. On the global stage, Kok was celebrated as a pioneer of the Third Way. When Clinton organized a global Third Way conference in Washington, DC, in 1999, he introduced the Dutch Labour leader glowingly: 'Wim Kok, from the Netherlands, actually was doing all this before we were. He just didn't know that – he didn't have anybody . . . who could put a good label on it.'[40] In response, Kok reluctantly agreed that he 'put it into practice without having the label on it, the Third Way'. What Clinton did not know was that Kok had political reasons to spurn good labels: he feared internal controversy with the more traditional social democratic wing of his party. And in the Dutch proportional voting system, if the Labour Party was seen as moving too much to the centre, there was the threat of left-wing competitors such as the GreenLeft and the Socialist Party. Instead, Kok insisted there was no need for new grand narratives. Prominent Third Way social democrats later accused him of changing the course of the party by stealth:

---

37   Michael Elliott, 'What's Left? The Socialist Dream Is Dead Throughout Europe', *Newsweek*, 10 October 1994.

38   Wim Kok, *We laten niemand los* (The Hague: Stichting 'Dr J. M. den Uyl-lezing', 1995).

39   See Merijn Oudenampsen, 'The Riddle of the Missing Feathers: Rise and Decline of the Dutch Third Way', *European Politics and Society* 22, no. 1 (1 January 2021): 38–52.

40   Staff blogger, 'Revealed: The Way They Want to Go . . . Or What Tony and Bill Said to Ger and Wim', *New Statesman*, 24 May 1999.

The economically liberal policy of this government could be attributed to the VVD, so that the PvdA apparently could stay true to its
traditional positions, albeit diluted to social-liberal government
policy. In so doing the PvdA, under the leadership of former trade
union leader Wim Kok, entered a completely new path in the nineties,
without any serious internal debate.[41]

Meanwhile, Bolkestein claimed the ideological space that Kok left
open. In a speech in the Belgian city of Bruges in December 1994, the
VVD leader observed that 'even more moderate forms of socialism
have gradually entered a terminal phase'.[42] He noted a 'fundamental
reorientation in the leftist camp' and wondered 'what still distin-
guishes social democrats from liberals'. Bolkestein then appropriated
the coalition agreement: 'In my estimation, there is very little distance
between the VVD election manifesto and the content of the coalition
agreement.'[43] This was a striking affront to the largest coalition partner. It was also an exaggeration; after all, the VVD had wanted a
more radical break with the corporatist welfare state, as indicated in
its plea for a 'guarantor state' and a wholesale departure from corporatism. Moreover, it was highly questionable whether the VVD was
able to take credit for this ideological shift. After all, the right-wing
liberals were a relatively minor force until 1994, with limited influence on the policy debate. The new global economic realities and
pressure from economic policymakers had a much more significant
impact.

In hindsight, the two Purple cabinets (1994–2002) have often been
seen as the high point of Dutch neoliberalism, in which the Labour
Party allowed itself be taken for a ride by the right-wing liberals.[44] Some
authors even argue that 1994, rather than 1982, was the real neoliberal

---

41   Paul de Beer, 'Het debat over sociaalliberalisme op herhaling', *Socialisme en
Democratie* 5–6 (2004): 68.

42   Frits Bolkestein, 'Hoe liep de weg naar paars?', in Patrick van Schie, ed., *Tussen
polarisatie en paars: De 100-jarige verhouding tussen liberalen en socialisten in Nederland*
(Kampen: Kok Agora, 1995), 174.

43   Ibid., 179.

44   Enneus Heerma, 'Eerste honderd dagen leiden niet tot Paars élan' [First hundred
days do not lead to purple élan], *Trouw*, 10 December 1994; De Vries, *Paars en de
managementstaat*.

breakthrough.[45] But that flattens the politics of the Purple cabinets and paints neoliberalism as a more moderate force than it really was. Like the Anglo-American Third Way, the Purple cabinets were a response to neoliberalism, a new social contract between capital and labour that was still a far cry from the ideals of card-carrying neoliberals such as Bolkestein (who would soon become a member of the Mont Pelerin Society and the German Friedrich Hayek Stiftung).[46] The still common perception of social democratic naivety also underplays the fact that the Purple agenda was not some hasty political bargain but a deliberate and well-considered technocratic policy agenda that was actively pursued by the Labour Party leadership – in reality the dominant force in the Purple cabinets.

One of the main public advocates of the social-liberal compromise was the British-Dutch economist Rick van der Ploeg. He was described in the press as the 'John Cleese of professors', due to his uncanny physical resemblance to the British *Monty Python* star.[47] Known by colleagues as a brilliant, prolific, arrogant and eccentric figure, Van der Ploeg had pursued his PhD in applied macroeconomics at Cambridge and lectured at the London School of Economics, where he picked up an interest in public-choice theory.[48] He soon became a rising star on the Dutch economics scene, was appointed full professor at the University of Amsterdam in 1991 and became an influential advisor within the Dutch Labour Party.

His inaugural lecture, 'Is the Economist an Enemy of the People?', was a qualified appraisal of the 'freshwater economics' of the Chicago school. It was a provocation of sorts. Referring to the 'neoclassical school of

---

45   De Vries, *Paars en de managementstaat*; Duco Hellema and Margriet van Lith, *Dat hadden we nooit moeten doen: De PvdA en de neoliberale revolutie van de jaren negentig* (Amsterdam: Prometheus, 2020).

46   Robert Schuettinger, 'Washington, D.C. 1998 Golden Anniversary Meeting', *Mont Pelerin Society Newsletter* 51, no. 1 (February 1999).

47   Dick van Eijck, 'Rick van Der Ploeg: The John Cleese Among Professors', *NRC Handelsblad*, 26 August 1991.

48   See Vani K. Borooah and Rick Van der Ploeg, *Political Aspects of the Economy* (Cambridge: Cambridge University Press, 1983); Frederick van der Ploeg, 'Election Outcomes and the Stockmarket', *European Journal of Political Economy* 5, no. 1 (1989): 21–30; Rick van der Ploeg, 'Government Ideology and Re-Election Efforts', *Oxford Economic Papers* 36, no. 2 (1984): 213–31; Roel M. W. J. Beetsma and Rick van der Ploeg, 'Does Inequality Cause Inflation? The Political Economy of Inflation, Taxation and Government Debt', *Public Choice* 87, nos 1/2 (1996): 143–62.

political economy (public choice)', Van der Ploeg described Dutch corporatism and collective labour agreements as a cartel that needed to be abolished.[49] He agreed with Milton Friedman that housing shortages were caused by rent control, denied the existence of a multiplier for public investments and argued that right-wing economic policy was inherently more efficient, but that a large class of poor people was also bad for the economy, because they tend to vote for left-wing parties whose policies of redistribution were distortionary.

The title of his lecture was a reference to Henrik Ibsen's famous play *An Enemy of the People*, in which a doctor in a small spa town finds out that the water of the baths is contaminated. The mayor and the towns-people stop him from disclosing this information, for fear of losing customers. In a meeting with the local townsfolk, the doctor launches a passionate tirade against the democratic majority that opposes new ideas:

> Who are the people that make up the biggest proportion of the popu-lation – the intelligent ones or the fools? I think we can agree it's the fools, no matter where you go in the world, it's the fools that form the overwhelming majority. But I'll be damned if that means it's right that the fools should dominate the intelligent . . . I'm thinking of the few, the genuine individuals in our midst, with their new and vigorous ideas. These men stand in the very forefront of our advance, so far ahead that the compact majority hasn't even begun to approach them – and here they fight for truths too newly born to have won any support from the majority.[50]

The economist, Van der Ploeg told his University of Amsterdam audi-ence, faced a similar obstruction to the one experienced by the doctor in the play. 'The thinking minority of economists are portrayed as an enemy of the people', he complained – while the real enemy of the people were the politicians and interest groups that dominated Dutch policy-making, to the detriment of the public interest. 'The economist is left as

---

49   Rick Van der Ploeg, *Is de econoom een vijand van het volk?* (Amsterdam: Prometheus, 1992), 72.

50   Henrik Ibsen, *An Enemy of the People: A Play in Five Acts*, transl. James Walter McFarlane (London: Oxford University Press, 1960), 74–5.

a voice crying in the wilderness, since the people simply can't and won't understand that you sometimes have to be cruel in order to do good.'[51]

In 1994, during the first Purple cabinet, Van der Ploeg entered parliament, becoming the financial spokesperson of the Labour Party. In a series of essays, later published as the book *A Sheep in Wolf's Clothing*, he discussed how privatization, marketization and deregulation could be made to serve the public interest. Taking an intermediate position, Van der Ploeg criticized both the 'market fundamentalists' on the right and his statist critics on the left:

> The Netherlands wants neither politicians that unthinkingly follow the market, nor politicians that structurally praise the government as the solution for all ills. What we need are good cocktails of market and state . . . [Marketization] provides ample opportunity for left-wing policy because the government can (and should) guarantee that no-one is excluded.[52]

A Social-Liberal Compromise

In short, Van der Ploeg argued that the Purple cabinet represented a new 'social-liberal' compromise. But what, concretely, did this compromise consist of? A first important controversy was over the future of the welfare state. The neoliberal ideal of the 'guarantor state' or 'mini-system' that Bolkestein, Wijffels, Rutten and Geelhoed had campaigned for was quietly abandoned. In a concession to the Labour Party, the generosity and range of benefits was left untouched. Instead, it was the governance of the welfare state that was liberalized. A more economic approach to the governance of welfare, seeing it in terms of incentives and disincentives, had come to predominate over the traditional, juridical vision of welfare as a social right.[53] In the past, the institutions determining social security provision had been governed in corporatist fashion by representatives of

---

51   Van der Ploeg, *Is de econoom een vijand van het volk?*, 90.

52   Rick van der Ploeg, *Een schaap in wolfskleren. Opstellen over politiek en economie* (Amsterdam: Prometheus, 1997), 20.

53   Romke van der Veen and Willem Trommel, 'Managed Liberalization of the Dutch Welfare State: A Review and Analysis of the Reform of the Dutch Social Security System, 1985–1998', *Governance* 12, no. 3 (1999): 289–310.

trade unions and employers. A parliamentary inquiry in 1993 concluded that employers and trade unions had neglected prevention and reintegration, offloading problems to the state.[54] By 1990, almost 16 per cent of the Dutch working population was receiving disability benefits, and almost 6 per cent were on sickness benefits.

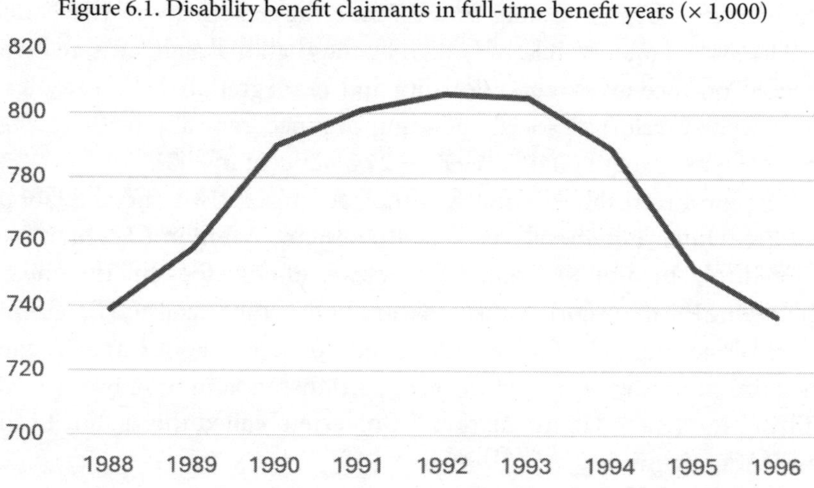

Figure 6.1. Disability benefit claimants in full-time benefit years (× 1,000)

Source: Van der Veen and Trommel, 'Managed Liberalization', 302.

The first Purple cabinet moved quickly to privatize sick pay and disability benefits. Responsibility for paying the first year of sickness – at 70 per cent of the normal wage – now shifted to employers, who could insure themselves against that risk with private insurers.[55] This gave employers an incentive to develop policies to prevent sickness on the work floor. Conditions to apply for disability benefits were tightened, and re-examinations were made obligatory. Employers began receiving rewards when engaging partially disabled people and had to pay penalties when an employee became disabled.

At the same time, the government turned to active labour market policies, in a more liberal version of the Swedish model. Access to unemployment benefits was restricted and was increasingly geared towards reintegration through job training, obligation to accept employment

---

54   See Chapter 5, above.

55   Mara Yerkes and Romke van der Veen, 'Crisis and Welfare State Change in the Netherlands', *Social Policy and Administration* 45, no. 4 (2011): 430–44.

offered and subsidy schemes for employers to hire vulnerable jobseekers. Social security also became more punitive, with a new law stipulating penalties against abuse. Finally, the social security institutions responsible for collecting contributions, providing benefits, tracking fraud and examining and retraining workers were first privatized altogether and, in the early 2000s, renationalized and brought under the responsibility of a semi-autonomous governing body. While the generosity of the Dutch welfare state remained relatively high by international standards, reforms focused on incentives, conditionality and reintegration.[56] As a result of these welfare reforms, social spending declined radically in the 1990s, from 27.6 per cent of GDP in 1990 to 21.8 per cent in 2001.[57]

A second unresolved issue was that of corporatism and the labour market. Dutch neoliberals such as Bolkestein, Zalm and Fortuyn had wanted to get rid of 'the mouldy structures of corporatism'. This meant abolishing the main corporatist advisory body – the Social and Economic Council; getting rid of state-sanctioned collective labour agreements, the minimum wage and protection against dismissal; and radically flexibilizing the Dutch labour market.[58] Bolkestein called this a shift to the 'mid-Atlantic model'.

Certainly, the weight of corporatism was reduced through the above-mentioned welfare state reforms and by downgrading the status of the Social and Economic Council. What ultimately happened, however, was more of a neoliberal restructuring of corporatism – a move towards 'competitive corporatism' rather than its wholesale abandonment.[59] The basis for this was provided by the landmark 1992 advice of the Social and Economic Council, *Convergence and Corporatism*.[60] In light of the Maastricht Treaty and the European single market, Dutch employers and trade unions had agreed to modernize corporatism rather than abandon it. The trade unions offered to moderate wages and reduce

---

56 Uwe Becker, 'Welfare State Development and Employment in the Netherlands in Comparative Perspective', *Journal of European Social Policy* 10, no. 3 (1 August 2000): 219–39.

57 Wim van Oorschot, 'The Dutch Welfare State: Recent Trends and Challenges in Historical Perspective', *European Journal of Social Security* 8, no. 1 (2006): 61.

58 Frits Bolkestein, 'Modern liberalisme', in Bolkestein *Het heft in handen*.

59 Uwe Becker, 'An Example of Competitive Corporatism? The Dutch Political Economy 1983–2004 in Critical Examination', *Journal of European Public Policy* 12, no. 6 (2005): 1078–102.

60 SER, *Convergentie en overlegeconomie* (The Hague: SER, 1992).

social spending while increasing flexibilization and pay differentials in the labour market; and employers committed themselves to carrying part of the burden of social security.[61]

The trade union leadership had moved in a more neoliberal direction in the 1990s, abandoning its earlier insistence on wage-led growth and job redistribution. It now accepted the need for sustained wage restraint – keeping wage growth below productivity growth – as a prerequisite for international competitiveness.[62] 'Competitiveness is improving because wage costs per unit of product in Dutch industry lag far behind its competitors. The controlled development of labour costs is an important driver,' wrote the Trade Union Confederation (FNV) in a 1993 report.[63] The FNV went on to introduce a 'maximum wage demand': wage increases above a predetermined maximum percentage were not allowed. This deeply entrenched wage restraint in the collective bargaining strategy of the FNV. The largest Dutch trade union would adhere to the maximum wage demand until 2015.

The renewed relevance of corporatism was evinced in the agreements 'A New Course' (1994) and 'Flexibility and Security' (1996). Since the 1980s, the number of flexible and part-time jobs had grown massively. The trade unions had opposed the wholesale flexibilization of the labour market but turned a blind eye to employers creating a flexible pool of (mostly female) workers outside the core segment of workers with permanent contracts. In a largely unplanned development, the Dutch male-breadwinner model gradually morphed into a 'one-and-a-half' model, in which men worked mostly full-time while women worked mostly part-time.[64] Between 1987 and 1996, the Dutch labour market added 937,000 jobs, of which 777,000 were flexible and/or part-time

---

61   Joop Meijnen, ' "Sociale partners vrezen Europese CAO's" ' [Social partners fear European collective labour agreements], *NRC Handelsblad*, 11 March 1993.

62   Saskia Boumans, 'Did Trade Unions Reinforce the Neoliberal Transformation? The Dutch Case', *Journal of Industrial Relations* 65, no. 2 (1 April 2023): 134–55. On the Dutch wage-restraint paradigm, see also Uwe Becker and Corina Hendriks, ' "As the Central Planning Bureau Says": The Dutch Wage Restraint Paradigm, Its Sustaining Epistemic Community and Its Relevance for Comparative Research', *Review of International Political Economy* 15, no. 5 (1 December 2008): 826–50.

63   Cited in Boumans, 'Did Trade Unions Reinforce the Neoliberal Transformation?', 143.

64   Uwe Becker, 'A "Dutch Model": Employment Growth by Corporatist Consensus and Wage Restraint? A Critical Account of an Idyllic View', *New Political Economy* 6, no. 1 (2001): 19–43.

jobs. The real key to Dutch employment growth were flexibilization and women's entry into the labour market, rather than wage restraint. In less than a decade, the Netherlands became the European leader in part-time and flexible employment. The problem was that this new segment of workers had far fewer social rights.

Since PvdA and VVD disagreed over how to proceed with the flexibilization of the labour market, Wim Kok and the minister of social affairs, Ad Melkert, proposed to leave the decision to the social partners. In the spring of 1996, employers and trade unions gathered at the kitchen table of FNV trade union leader Lodewijk de Waal and signed the 'Flexicurity Pact'. They agreed to make it easier for employers to hire and fire workers on flexible contracts. In exchange, discrimination in wage levels and by labour conditions was legally prohibited and equal treatment of full-time and part-time work mandated. While this prevented a lapse into American labour market conditions, at the same time it further encouraged the growth of temporary and freelance employment in the Netherlands. In twenty years, the number of workers on temporary contracts had risen from 6 per cent of the working population in 1983 to 14 per cent in 2002, and still further to 23 per cent in 2022 – the highest number in Europe.[65] The other major drawback to this new model was that the most vulnerable and long-term unemployed hardly benefited from the economic upturn. While overall income inequality in the Netherlands remained relatively low by European standards, the lowest-earning workers lagged behind.[66] From 1981 to 2021, the disposable income of the poorest 10 per cent of households declined by 35 per cent, while the entire upper half of the Dutch income distribution saw gains of between 60 and 70 per cent in the same period.[67] The social-liberal compromise thus failed to stem rising inequality.

A third important pillar of the social-liberal compromise was a renewed privatization offensive, legitimized by the idea of 'privatization under social conditions'. The Labour Party had long been critical of the privatizations of the 1980s, which had been pursued by the Ministry of

---

65   Eurostat, 4 April 2024, ec.europa.eu.

66   Monique Kremers et al., *Economic Inequality in the Netherlands in 8 Figures* (The Hague: WRR, 2014).

67   Heike Vethaak and Egbert Jongen, *Stille wateren hebben diepe gronden: Een analyse van de inkomensverdeling en haar determinanten over de afgelopen veertig jaar* (Leiden: Leiden University, 2024); Wiemer Salverda, 'The Netherlands: Is the Polder Model Behind the Curve with Regard to Growing Household Income Inequality?', in Daniel Vaughan-Whitehead, ed., *Reducing Inequalities in Europe* (Cheltenham: Edward Elgar, 2018), 368–423.

Finance for accounting reasons: to bring down the budget deficit and public debt levels.[68] As Rick van der Ploeg pointed out, this had no real effect on the net income of the government, since the assets that were sold off also brought in profits. According to Van der Ploeg, privatization had to be judged by whether it improved economic efficiency and lowered prices for consumers, which was dependent on a strong state that fostered competition and countered monopolistic practices. To this end, the first Purple cabinet introduced the Competition Law forbidding price agreements, market concentration and the abuse of market power, while creating a National Competition Authority to oversee that. As Geelhoed and Van der Ploeg both continued to stress: 'Marketization needs to be enforced; a weak government cannot do that.'[69] Public utilities such as electricity, the national railways, local transport and telecommunications were partially privatized in the second half of the 1990s.[70]

Privatization and marketization were also introduced to the public sector – a development made possible by the voucher, or individual subsidy. Rather than subsidizing social housing, childcare centres, reintegration services, education or elderly care directly, the government would facilitate market competition and provide lower-income citizens with an individual subsidy or grant. As Van der Ploeg argued, this allowed citizens to choose as sovereign consumers, rather than being subject to bureaucratic paternalism.[71] For the Labour Party, the crucial precondition was that lower-income workers and vulnerable groups would not be excluded from these new quasi-markets.

The upshot of the social-liberal compromise was a broad,

68   Van der Ploeg, *Een schaap in wolfskleren*, 26. See also Hugo A. Keuzenkamp and Frederick van der Ploeg, *Saving, Investment, Government Finance and the Current Account: The Dutch Experience*, CEPR–Bank of Greece Conference, 'Macroeconomics and the External Constraint: The European Experience', Athens (1990).

69   Paul Wessels and Roel Janssen, 'Topambtenaar Ad Geelhoed: "Marktwerking moet je afdwingen. Dat kan een softe overheid niet"' [Senior official Ad Geelhoed: 'Marketization has to be enforced; a weak government cannot do that'], *NRC Handelsblad*, 1 March 1997. See also Ad Geelhoed, '1996: Geloofwaardigheid en vertrouwen', *ESB* 81, no. 4,039 (1996): 4.

70   Eric van Damme, 'Pragmatic Privatization: The Netherlands, 1982–2002', in Marko Köthenbürger, Hans-Werner Sinn and John Whalley, eds, *Privatization Experiences in the European Union* (Cambridge, MA.: MIT Press, 2006), 289–337.

71   Van der Ploeg, *Een schaap in wolfskleren*, 20.

market-based consensus and the deep depoliticization of the market-based policies of the Purple cabinets: they were seen as politically 'neutral' and 'pragmatic'. On the one hand, this was the side effect of policy developments taking place within the ministries rather than in private think-tanks or political parties. As we have seen, Dutch economic policymakers traditionally refrain from normative considerations and belief in 'objective' solutions. But depoliticization was also a conscious strategy pursued by political and economic elites. Minister of Economic Affairs Hans Wijers argued in parliament that 'a broad ideological discussion over the design of the economic order' could only 'hinder the necessary deregulation efforts'.[72]

When resistance to privatization emerged in the early 2000s, Coen Teulings, director of the prestigious Tinbergen Institute and future director of the CPB, advised policymakers to stay clear of politicians:

> There are still far too many topics on which parliament has to offer its opinions, and those opinions are time and again rather arbitrary . . . For the time being, the prevailing sentiment runs counter to depoliticization and decentralization. But sooner or later, that wind will change direction, for there is simply too much to gain from a more efficient design of society.[73]

As the Dutch political economist Uwe Becker later wrote, 'in most other countries liberal supply-side theories also became dominant, but economic debate continued there. In the Netherlands however, it died.'[74] The new market-based consensus was widely celebrated as an end of ideology.

<hr>

72   Cited in Naomi Woltring, 'De marktconforme verzorgingsstaat 1989–2008' (Utrecht: Utrecht University, 2023), 88–9.

73   Coen Teulings, 'Niet ontpolderen maar depolitiseren', *ESB* 86, no. 4,325 (27 September 2001): 31.

74   Uwe Becker, '"Miracle" by Consensus? Consensualism and Dominance in Dutch Employment Development', *Economic and Industrial Democracy* 22, no. 4 (2001): 475.

The Birth of the Polder Model

As we have seen, the atmosphere was grim at the start of the first Purple cabinet in 1994, with 18 billion in cuts to come and dire assessments of the state of the Dutch economy. The mood soon changed, however, as the economy started to boom and reforms in social security began to pay off. During the first Purple cabinet, the deficit fell from 4 per cent to 1.5 per cent, and the economy grew at around 3.5 per cent a year. Inflation was low, and 500,000 new jobs had been created since the coalition came in and official unemployment was at 5.5 per cent. Of course, real unemployment was almost double that figure, due to the hidden unemployment of those on disability benefits. But here, too, there was good news: for the first time in the 1990s, the number of people on disability benefits was slowly declining. After a decade of dramatic underperformance, the Netherlands was now outperforming other European countries. Contributing to this buoyant mood was the beginning of a housing boom, triggered by a liberalization of mortgage financing; banks were allowed to count the income of women and lend more. Housing prices doubled in the 1990s, the OECD concluded that private consumption had been boosted by the 'wealth effect stemming from the boom in housing prices'.[75] Internationally, the Dutch economy became the subject of considerable hype. Newspapers and magazines such as *Le Nouvel Observateur*, *Le Monde*, *Business Week*, the *Economist* and *Die Zeit* spoke of 'Le Miracle néerlandais', 'the Dutch Miracle' and 'Das Wirtschaftswunder'.[76]

In January 1997, as the Netherlands assumed the presidency of the European Council, the minister of social affairs, Ad Melkert (PvdA), seized the moment. In the former nineteenth-century city hall in the Amsterdam canal district, now transformed into the luxurious Grand Hotel, Melkert had organized a conference on social policy and economic performance.[77] With hundreds of international journalists

---

75   OECD, *Economic Outlook* (Paris: OECD, 2000), 117.

76   Cited in Becker, ' "Miracle" by Consensus?', 455; Luchien Karsten, Kees van Veen and Annelotte van Wulfften Palthe, 'What Happened to the Popularity of the Polder Model? Emergence and Disappearance of a Political Fashion', *International Sociology* 23, no. 1 (2008).

77   Marcella Breedeveld and Robert Giebels, 'Melkert wil poldermodel aan Europa verkopen' [Melkert wants to sell the polder model to Europe], *NRC Handelsblad*, 23 January 1997.

flocking to the Netherlands, Melkert used the Dutch presidency to sell the success story of the Dutch corporatist polder model. He promoted it as an alternative to the 'cold' neoliberal restructuring undertaken by Thatcher and Reagan. His efforts were part triangulation, part national myth-making. Melkert projected the polder model back in time, portraying the recent economic resurgence as the fruit of the 1982 Wassenaar Accord and the wage-moderation strategy of three successive Lubbers cabinets. Not for nothing, Melkert had invited the former Christian Democrat prime minister to preside over the conference. This was a remarkable turnaround. Until the early 1990s, the no-nonsense austerity policies of Lubbers had been deemed a failure, or a mixed bag at best.[78] Now they were seen as having planted the seeds of the success of the polder model in the 1990s. What is more, until the early 1990s, corporatism was widely perceived to be in crisis, perceived as a drag on the economy. Now, it was suddenly argued that there had been a corporatist consensus ever since the Wassenaar Accord of 1982 – and that it had been a big success.

Was corporatist wage moderation really the key to the recovery of the 1990s? Scholars later pointed out that there was little evidence for this assertion.[79] It was not the Dutch export sector that was driving renewed growth. Far more important was the rise in consumption made possible by women's entry into the labour market and a credit-fuelled Dutch housing boom. Politically, however, the idea that the belt-tightening of the 1980s ultimately paid off was very attractive. It provided the Purple coalition with a convincing argument to pursue further cuts of its own. The polder model was hyped both internationally and domestically, even though proof of its existence before the mid-1990s was rather thin. The Dutch press was not oblivious to this fact and initially wrote

---

78　Representative of that general sentiment was an opinion piece by Flip de Kam, a leading public finance professor and political commentator. He wrote in 1994 that the Lubbers cabinets had aimed for three things: smaller government, restored profitability and lower unemployment. Only profitability had been achieved. 'The inevitable conclusion is that Lubbers hasn't been able to do the job.' Flip de Kam, 'Afrekenen met kabinetten Lubbers' [Evaluating the Lubbers cabinets], *NRC Handelsblad*, 6 April 1994. See also Eduard Bomhoff, *Een Haagse Lente?* (Schoonhoven: Academic Service, 1994).

79　Wiemer Salverda, 'The Dutch Model: Magic in a Flat Landscape?', in Uwe Becker and Herman Schwarts, eds, *Employment 'Miracles': A Critical Comparison of the Dutch, Scandinavian, Swiss, Australian and Irish Cases versus Germany and the US* (Amsterdam: Amsterdam University Press, 2005), 39–64; Becker, 'A "Dutch Model"'.

sceptically of the 'polder myth'.[80] But it proved to be a highly seductive saga that mobilized powerful historical clichés relating to the dikes and Dutch national character.

Propelled by the Dutch presidency of the European Council, the polder model became an influential mascot of Third Way social democracy. In June 1997, Wim Kok was invited to give a speech on the Dutch approach at the G8 summit held in Denver. At the meeting, US President Bill Clinton praised the Dutch model as a 'success story' deserving of imitation.[81] There were various political motives at play for hyping the polder model. Some, particularly in France and Germany, latched on to the polder model to make market-based reforms palatable to unwilling domestic electorates and trade unions. Conservative central bankers Jean-Claude Trichet and Hans Tietmeyer stepped in to recommend the Dutch model to their French and German compatriots.[82] The awarding of the German Carl Bertelsmann prize in September 1997 to the Dutch polder model could be understood in this light: as a subtle hint to the German trade unions to be more flexible.

But in the Netherlands itself the polder model had an opposite function, too. It served as a tool for Third Way social democrats to sideline free market critics such as VVD leader Frits Bolkestein, who wanted market-based reform to go much further. In response to the Labour Party's public relations offensive surrounding the polder model, Bolkestein wrote a disgruntled opinion piece in the *Economist*, where he argued that market reform in the Netherlands had been achieved largely in opposition to the polder model and went on to stress that the social-liberal compromise did not go far enough, adding that 'more liberal reforms [were] needed everywhere in Europe'.[83]

Not that the polder model formed an effective bulwark against further neoliberal reform. As Lei Delsen has argued, it never reflected a stable compromise.[84] Due to ongoing labour market flexibilization and

---

80   Gijsbert van Es and Robert Giebels, 'Poldermodel als modeverschijnsel' [Polder model as a fashion phenomenon], *NRC Handelsblad*, 25 November 1999.

81   Karsten, Van Veen and Van Wulfften Palthe, 'What Happened to the Popularity of the Polder Model?', 48.

82   Eric le Boucher, 'Le modèle hollandais', *Le Monde*, 29 October 1996.

83   Frits Bolkestein, 'The High Road That Leads Out of the Low Countries', *Economist*, 20 May 1999.

84   Lei Delsen, *Exit Poldermodel? Sociaal-economische ontwikkelingen in Nederland* (Assen: Van Gorcum, 2000).

increasing global competition, the balance of power between capital and labour was gradually shifting in favour of the former. Trade unions had a more compliant role in this new form of corporatism. 'Nous avons des syndicats magnifiques,' Finance Minister Gerrit Zalm proclaimed in November 1996 to the French daily *Le Figaro*.[85] The Purple cabinets also led to a rightward drift in the Labour Party itself, reflecting the formative experience of a new generation of Third Way politicians – Wouter Bos, Diederik Samsom, Jeroen Dijsselbloem, Frans Timmermans – who believed the socioeconomic opposition between left and right to be a relic of the past.[86] Finally, the profound depoliticization of socio-economic issues opened the door to the rise of right-wing populism, tilting the entire political landscape further to the right from 2002 onwards.

The Neoliberal Roots of Right-Wing Populism

On Friday, 1 May 1998, a large crowd queued before the entrance of Nighttown, the famous Rotterdam nightclub. It was not a party as usual. The Labour Party was celebrating Labour Day, which happened to fall six days before the national elections. The queueing crowd had come to see the British prime minister, Tony Blair, who was there to lend Wim Kok a hand on the last leg of his election campaign. Blair had won the British elections in a landslide the year before and had achieved rock-star status in the Netherlands. 'Today is Labour Day,' Kok said while introducing Blair. 'Today is also New Labour Day.' The crowd in the nightclub chanted: 'Tony! Tony! Tony!' Also present was Kok's future successor, the fresh thirty-four-year-old MP Wouter Bos, soon dubbed 'the Prince of Purple' and 'darling of the Third Way' by the New Labour spin doctor Peter Mandelson. 'I feel nothing,' Bos answered when asked by a journalist what Labour Day meant to him.[87] In this, he was considered a typical representative of his generation, who no longer believed in ideology. Anyway, the atmosphere was festive. The speeches of Kok and

---

85   Cited in Van Es and Giebels, 'Poldermodel als modeverschijnsel'.

86   Oudenampsen, 'Riddle of the Missing Feathers'.

87   '"Sorry", zegt ze. "Maar ik kom voor Wim"' ['Sorry,' she says, 'but I'm here for Wim'], *NRC Handelsblad*, 2 May 1998.

Blair had been preceded by a fashion show accompanied by loud electronic music. Unemployment was down, the Dutch economy was performing surprisingly well and the budget deficit had been brought back down to 1.5 per cent of GDP. Kok, long scarred by the disability crisis of the early 1990s, had transformed into a popular prime minister. In the 1998 elections, six days later, voters rewarded the PvdA and the VVD with fifteen additional seats, a 10 per cent increase in their vote share. The Purple coalition went on to govern for a second term. The most prevalent critique of the Purple cabinets was one of profound boredom: with the new market-based consensus, the opposition between left and right seemed to have lost its salience. Political struggle had been replaced by technocratic management.

But the lull was brief. In 1999, VVD leader Frits Bolkestein unexpectedly departed for Brussels, to become the European commissioner for the internal market. In speeches at neoliberal think-tanks such as the British Institute of Economic Affairs and the German Walter Eucken Institute, he presented his work in Brussels as leading towards a neoliberal Europe.[88] His sudden exit from Dutch politics, however, left a vacuum on the Dutch right. During his leadership of the VVD, Bolkestein had pioneered a winning formula of economically liberal and culturally conservative positions, becoming the country's foremost critic both of the corporatist welfare state and of Islam, immigration and multiculturalism.[89] After Bolkestein's departure, the VVD moved back to the centre, leaving its conservative flank wide open.

In this flattened political landscape, the right-wing populist Pim Fortuyn entered the stage. During the Purple coalitions, Fortuyn had

88   See Pierre Dardot and Christian Laval, *The New Way of the World: On Neoliberal Society* (London: Verso, 2013), 480–4; Frits Bolkestein, 'The EU's Economic Test: Meeting the Challenges of the Lisbon Strategy', speech, 17th Annual State of the International Economy Conference, London, 19 November 2001, available at ec.europa. eu; Frits Bolkestein, 'Building a Liberal Europe in the 21st Century', speech, Walter Eucken Istitut Freiburg, 10 July 2000; Angela Wigger, 'Competition for Competitiveness: The Politics of the Transformation of the EU Competition Regime' (PhD diss., Vrije Universiteit, 2008), 72.

89   Merijn Oudenampsen, *The Rise of the Dutch New Right: An Intellectual History of the Rightward Shift in Dutch Politics* (London: Routledge, 2021), 90. The term 'winning formula' comes from Herbert Kitschelt, who uses it to explain the success of the European radical right, but a similar combination could be found on the centre-right. Herbert Kitschelt and Anthony J. McGann, *The Radical Right in Western Europe: A Comparative Analysis* (Ann Arbor: University of Michigan Press, 1995).

become the voice of right-wing opposition against the social-liberal compromise.[90] A radical critic of both the corporatist welfare state and of Islam and multiculturalism, he occupied the ideological space vacated by Bolkestein. He founded the List Pim Fortuyn (LPF) to compete in the 2002 Dutch elections. Nine days before the elections, Fortuyn was fatally shot by an animal-rights activist while on the campaign trail. When the elections were held, Fortuyn's orphaned party won twenty-six seats, or 17 per cent of the vote – a historic turnaround known as 'the Fortuyn revolt'.[91] It broke the spell of the politics of Purple, inaugurating a new era in Dutch politics marked by the dominance of anti-immigrant sentiment and right-wing populist parties.[92]

Right-wing populism is known above all for its strident positions on Islam and immigration.[93] The neoliberal roots of Dutch right-wing populism have garnered less attention. But the radicalization of future right-wing populist leaders Pim Fortuyn and Geert Wilders took place long before immigration and integration came to dominate the debate. Both entered the political fray in the first half of the 1990s and earned their stripes campaigning against the corporatist welfare state.

Fortuyn, a flamboyant former Marxist sociologist, had become a free market convert at the end of the 1980s.[94] He left his tenured job at the University of Groningen, exchanged his jeans and denim jacket for tailored suits and brightly coloured silk ties and embarked on a free-lance career as a political commentator, consultant and public speaker in small-business circles. By the time Fortuyn underwent this conversion, however, the momentum of neoliberal reform had stalled. As noted, Wim Kok proclaimed in 1989, after ten years of neoliberal policy, that 'the pendulum had swung too far'. He had promised a

---

90   Cas Mudde, 'A Fortuynist Foreign Policy', in Christina Schori Liang, ed., *Europe for the Europeans* (Aldershot: Ashgate, 2007), 210.

91   Oudenampsen, *Rise of the Dutch New Right*.

92   H. Pellikaan, S. L. de Lange and T. W. G. van der Meer, 'The Centre Does Not Hold: Coalition Politics and Party System Change in the Netherlands, 2002–12', *Government and Opposition* 53, no. 2 (2018): 231–55.

93   Merijn Oudenampsen, 'From Clashing Civilizations to the Replacement of Populations: The Transformation of Dutch Anti-Immigration Discourse', in Sarah Bracke and Luis Manuel Hernández Aguilar, eds, *The Politics of Replacement* (London: Routledge, 2023).

94   Merijn Oudenampsen, 'Neoliberal Populism: The Case of Pim Fortuyn', *Political Studies*, 14 July 2023.

return of consensus politics, involving the trade unions once more in policymaking.

Fortuyn had joined the chorus of disappointed neoliberals, turning his fire on the new consensus politics. 'Why my plea to remove the wonderfully warm consensus blanket from our little Dutch bed?' wrote Fortuyn in 1991 on the opening pages of his first neoliberal pamphlet, 'Without Civil Servants'. 'Our country is faced with the heavy task of drastically modernizing itself. Globalization of culture and economy requires a different management of the economy and society, which is enforced by the free movement of people, money and goods after 1993 in the European Community.'[95] Fortuyn proposed to downsize Dutch central government to 5 per cent of its former size, subcontracting and outsourcing public tasks to either market actors, local government or NGOs. All permanent contracts of civil servants were to be prohibited and exchanged for flexible contracts. This urgent modernization project, however, was obstructed by public sector unions and entrenched elites who were trying to conserve the corporatist institutions of yesteryear. Fortuyn pleaded for a 'Dutch Margaret Thatcher', for 'our own Iron Lady to convince the public sector unions it's time for sweeping changes'.[96]

But the private sector also needed a shakedown. The main problem was the paternalistic power of the government to declare collective labour agreements generally binding. This imposed centralized salary scales and labour conditions, while businesses and employees were better off negotiating the value of work individually. Inspired by Silicon Valley management gurus who prophesized the end of the traditional nine-to-five job, Fortuyn wanted to prohibit all centralized wage bargaining and permanent contracts; new labour contracts would have a maximum duration of five years. The Dutch worker had to become 'an entrepreneur of the self'.[97] Meanwhile, the welfare state could be abolished and replaced with a negative income tax, as proposed by Milton Friedman.

The Dutch neoliberal turn up to this point had been a highly technocratic affair. Fortuyn was the first to provide it with a populist energy. As

---

95   Pim Fortuyn, *Zonder ambtenaren: De ondernemende overheid* (Amsterdam: Van Veen, 1991), 8.

96   Pim Fortuyn, *Het zakenkabinet Fortuyn* (Utrecht: Bruna, 1994), 113.

97   Pim Fortuyn, *Uw baan staat op de tocht! De overlegeconomie voorbij* (Utrecht: Bruna, 1995), 161.

is well known, populism is a politics that invokes an opposition between the 'true people' and the 'estranged elite', criticized for being in league with 'freeloading' immigrants and outsiders. In the neoliberal populism of Fortuyn, 'the people' were equated with entrepreneurs and the marketplace. The 'estranged elite' was a parasitic class of bureaucrats and corporatist paternalists, allied with the unemployed. In his 1992 book *To the People of the Netherlands*, Fortuyn sarcastically dubbed this elite 'Our Kind of People' ('Ons Soort Mensen'). The expression was taken from Bram Peper, then mayor of Rotterdam and a leading social democrat. In a private conversation at the end of the 1980s, Peper had purportedly told the budding consultant Fortuyn that he would never become part of 'our kind of people' – the ones 'that really mattered'.[98] For Fortuyn, the problem with this paternalistic caste was that it blocked innovation: 'Our country has been held for decades already in the iron grip of a thin upper layer, which hinders radical interventions in social security and public administration, but also in the corporatist economy and the way in which large and vital companies are managed.'[99] In his eyes, all major political parties belonged to this cartel or 'partocracy', but the Labour Party received his particular scorn. 'Voters of the Netherlands,' Fortuyn proclaimed, 'unite and wipe them out, these representatives of a no-longer-existing working class!'[100]

This neoliberal populism took centre stage in Fortuyn's bestselling manifesto accompanying his 2002 election campaign, *The Disasters of Eight Years Purple*.[101] The book was a synthesis of Fortuyn's writings over the course of the 1990s and was advertised on the cover as a 'ruthless analysis of the public sector'. In the eyes of Fortuyn, neoliberal reform during the Purple cabinets had been far too limited in scope. While the business world was adapting smoothly to the New Economy and the digital age, the public sector was still living in the industrial age, with its anonymous, large-scale production. 'The consumer-citizen is only paid

98   Pim Fortuyn, *Aan het volk van Nederland: De contractmaatschappij, een politiek-economische zedenschets* (Amsterdam: Contact, 1992), 53.

99   Fortuyn, *Het zakenkabinet Fortuyn*, 28.

100   Fortuyn, *Zonder ambtenaren*, 22.

101   Pim Fortuyn, *De puinhopen van acht jaar paars: Een genadeloze analyse van de collectieve sector en aanbevelingen voor een krachtig herstelprogramma* (Uithoorn: Karakter Uitgevers, 2002).

lip service to,' Fortuyn complained.[102] 'There is no democracy, unless one sees democracy as marking a box red once every four years.' Citizens had no say in the products the government provided to them. All this was exacerbated by the tripartite polder model, 'a kind of *musyawarah* [deliberative] system in which people talk to each other until they more or less agree and responsibilities have evaporated'.[103] This culture needed to be transformed through privatization, marketization, the introduction of wage and pay differentials and the wholesale abolition of the corporatist institutional legacy. The welfare state, Fortuyn asserted, 'had given birth to a monster'.[104] By that he meant the unemployed, 'a dead weight in society' with 'a big mouth'.[105] Since unemployment and disability were problems of mentality, he proposed to solve them by lowering benefits, abolishing rent subsidies and cutting disability benefits.

This neoliberal agenda was also central to the 2002 and 2003 party platforms of the LPF, which pleaded for the marketization of healthcare and education, Reaganesque tax cuts, curtailment of disability benefits and the wholesale elimination of housing subsidies and family allowances.[106] In newspaper interviews during his campaign, Fortuyn stated that 'the poor should learn to care for themselves', that the welfare state 'took people's soul'. He warned that 'not only Dutch politics is hopeless, but many Dutch citizens are, too'.[107]

The politician who would eventually claim Fortuyn's mantle, the anti-Islam firebrand Geert Wilders, had a similar origin story. He had started his career in 1991 as an assistant to Frits Bolkestein, working as a specialist on the terrain of corporatist social security. One of his first feats of arms was helping write an opinion piece for Bolkestein that proposed abolition of the Social and Economic Council and corporatist control over social security.[108] In 1998, when Wilders entered parliament as an MP for the VVD, he was assigned social security as his portfolio, where

---

102　Ibid., 9.

103　Ibid., 17.

104　Ibid., 103.

105　Ibid., 104.

106　LPF, *Politiek is passie: Verkiezingsprogramma Lijst Pim Fortuyn 2003–2007* (Rotterdam: LPF, 2003); LPF, *Zakelijk met een hart* (The Hague: LPF, 2002).

107　Bart Jan Spruijt, 'Gentleman in de politiek' [Gentleman in politics], *Reformatorisch Dagblad*, 8 September 2001.

108　Meindert Fennema, *Geert Wilders: Tovenaarsleerling* (Amsterdam: Prometheus, 2010), 14–15.

he made a name for himself as a right-wing critic of the Purple cabinet. Wilders called the Netherlands the 'village idiot of Europe' and disability benefit a 'directionless supertanker heading unavoidably towards a sandbank'. On issues of social security, he called Dutch politics a 'socialist feast'.[109] In 2001, Wilders wrote an opinion piece, 'Stop Trade Union Power', in which he argued that 'the exaggerated pursuit of societal consensus takes the dynamism out of socioeconomic activities, which the Netherlands can hardly afford'.[110] Wilders pleaded for a smaller welfare state and the curbing of trade unions, in order to restore the entrepreneurial freedom of the Dutch citizen. When Wilders left the VVD and founded his own Freedom Party in 2006, he published a *Plan for a New Golden Age*. It contained a Reagan-inspired €16 billion tax cut, bringing 'freedom, responsibility, creativity, innovation and entrepreneurialism'. 'Lowering taxes, reducing the role of government, and minimal regulation,' the plan stated, had proved 'the only engine of economic growth'.[111] Gradually, in the decade that followed, Wilders abandoned this agenda and tactically moved to the socioeconomic centre, making aversion to Islam and immigration his defining issues.

Radical right-wing populism has often been presented as a reaction against neoliberalism and globalization. In his 1998 book *False Dawn*, the philosopher John Gray argued that the idea of a global free market was a dangerous utopia.[112] He predicted that neoliberal globalization would mobilize all sorts of countertendencies: populist, xenophobic, fundamentalist and neo-communist. This became a popular framework for understanding the rise of right-wing populism in the Netherlands. Politics was defined no longer by the opposition between left and right – or so this idea went – but rather by the distinction between 'open' and 'closed'. Fortuyn and Wilders, however, like many radical right-wing populists in the 1990s, stood for a combination of economic openness and cultural closure.

From the very beginning, Fortuyn defended his agenda as pursuing a

---

109   Bert Snel, 'Zijn Wilders en Fortuyn vergelijkbaar?', *Civis Mundi Digitaal* 5 (2011).

110   Geert Wilders, 'Stop de vakbondsmacht' [Stop trade union power], *NRC Handelsblad*, 15 February 2001.

111   PVV, 'Plan voor een nieuwe gouden eeuw', Partij voor de Vrijheid, 2006, pvv.nl.

112   John Gray, *False Dawn: The Delusions of Global Capitalism* (New York: New Press, 2000).

modernization that was necessary in light of 'the globalization of culture and economy'.[113] Only on cultural issues did Fortuyn come to oppose globalization – particularly the freedom of movement it entailed. He spoke out against further immigration and threatened to close the Dutch borders, while promising a strict regime of assimilation into the dominant Dutch culture for immigrants already present in the Netherlands. It was this cultural agenda that later led leading commentators such as the British journalist David Goodhart to think of Fortuyn's right-wing populism as a reaction against neoliberal globalization.[114] But, rather than a reaction or revolt, the populist wave of the 1990s and 2000s represented an insurgent offshoot of neoliberalism.

113   Fortuyn, *Zonder ambtenaren*, 8.
114   David Goodhart, *The Road to Somewhere: The Populist Revolt and the Future of Politics* (Oxford: Oxford University Press, 2017). For similar narratives in the Netherlands, see Gabriël van den Brink, *Ruw ontwaken uit de neoliberale droom* (Amsterdam: Prometheus, 2020).

7

Never Let a Good Crisis Go to Waste (2008–17)

In the spring of 2007, a silverback gorilla named Bokito escaped its quarters in the Rotterdam zoo. The gorilla had jumped over the moat and attacked a frequent female visitor, dragging her by her hair and biting her over a hundred times. Bokito then ran off to one of the zoo restaurants, where some more people were hurt. The zoo, with thousands of visitors present at the time, had to be evacuated. Eventually, zookeepers managed to put down the animal with a tranquilizer gun. In the hospital, the assaulted female visitor said of the gorilla: 'He is and continues to be my darling.' Understandably, this became a viral story and a favourite topic of conversation at Dutch coffee machines.

After the 2008 financial crisis, Bokito turned into a metaphor for the dangers of deregulated capitalism. In January 2010, Wouter Bos, minister of finance and leader of the Labour Party at the time, gave a landmark speech, soon dubbed 'the Bokito lecture'. Bos reflected on what the financial crisis meant for Third Way social democrats such as himself and their relation to the free market. He concluded that 'the market sometimes behaves like a Bokito. For a long time, it seems like you have it under control, but one day it will do what its reflexes tell it to.' Bos called it the 'big tragedy of the Third Way' that 'social democrats embraced the free market at the very moment that modern capitalism was changing form': 'Third Way progressives went to bed with a reasonably tame free market, but were woken with a beast unleashed.'[1]

---

1 Wouter Bos, 'De derde weg voorbij. 21e Den Uyl-Lezing', 25 January 2010.

As the minister of finance in a centrist coalition under Christian Democratic Prime Minister Jan Peter Balkenende (2006–10), Bos had been responsible for the bailout of the Dutch banks. The highly leveraged banks had billions of investments in the American subprime mortgage market and now stood on the brink of bankruptcy. The most dramatic intervention was the bailout of the Belgian–Dutch banking and insurance giant Fortis in September 2008. Shortly before the financial crisis, Fortis had acquired large parts of the Dutch bank ABN AMRO, in a $72 billion deal involving Royal Bank of Scotland and Banco Santander.

For both ABN AMRO and Fortis, it was a classic story of financial hubris.[2] ABN AMRO had been one of the ten largest European banks and the crown jewel of the Dutch banking sector. In an attempt to raise its stock market valuation, ABN AMRO had lowered its defences against hostile takeovers. The idea was to raise capital and buy up other banks – but ABN AMRO was itself bought up and taken apart. It soon turned out, however, that the Belgian–Dutch Fortis had bitten off more than it could chew. As a result of the credit squeeze in the wake of the financial crisis, Fortis was unable to meet its financing needs. For a total that eventually amounted to €30 billion, the Dutch state acquired the Dutch activities of Fortis and ABN AMRO. Former VVD leader Gerrit Zalm became the new CEO of ABN AMRO. The Dutch government also had to vouch for ING, another major Dutch bank exposed to the American subprime mortgage market.

The political lessons derived from this financial fiasco, however, were not immediately apparent. Bos had continued the implicit Third Way politics of Wim Kok under the anodyne slogan 'pleasant pragmatism': 'no fancy words, just solving problems of ordinary people'.[3] Since the Third Way had never been presented as a new party ideology in the Netherlands, there was not that much to renege on. Indeed, Bos was rather non-committal in his Bokito lecture. He denied any responsibility of Third Way social democracy for liberalizing the market and warned of 'a return to the old belief in state intervention'. In fact, after

---

2   Jeroen Smit, *De prooi: Blinde trots breekt ABN AMRO* (Amsterdam: Prometheus, 2009).

3   Hans Goslinga, 'Met de VVD indien mogelijk, met de PvdA indien noodzakelijk' [With the VVD if possible, with the PvdA if necessary], *Trouw*, 19 September 2006.

some soft-spoken self-criticism, Bos pleaded for a 'sympathetic re-appraisal' of the much-maligned Third Way.[4]

The right-wing liberals of the VVD, meanwhile, seemed unfazed by the financial crisis. With the assistance of the former European Commissioner Frits Bolkestein and former elite banker and Wagner Committee member Harrie Langman, the Teldersstichting (the think-tank of the VVD) published a report that blamed the financial crisis on an excess of state intervention. It was the American government's support of home-ownership that had led to the crisis, the report suggested, 'illustrating how market-distorting government policy can be'.[5] Citing neoliberal stalwarts Friedrich Hayek and Ludwig von Mises and an anti-stimulus manifesto by the American neoliberal CATO think-tank, the report stated that the government should refrain from any further stimulus, as the 'automatic stabilizers' of increased social spending were already more than enough. The VVD, however, was in the opposition.

The CDA–PvdA government took a middle course. As a result of the financial crisis, world trade collapsed, and the open Dutch economy went into recession. With a 4 per cent contraction of Dutch GDP in 2009, this was the single largest economic downturn since the Second World War. In March 2009 Balkenende presented a set of measures to combat the crisis. It involved a stimulus of €4 billion in that year and the next, with another €4 billion per year in social spending to cover for rising unemployment. In short, the 'automatic stabilizers' were given free rein to do their work, the budget deficit was allowed to rise to 5 per cent and the government would only begin cutting back the budget deficit from 2011 onwards, by half a percentage point per year.[6]

An important moment in defining the response was a closed 'inspiration session' that took place at the Ministry of Finance. Those present included Finance Minister Bos, some senior civil servants and a few prominent economists of various political backgrounds. The economists agreed that blunt cuts and tax increases could be avoided in the

---

4   Bos, 'De derde weg voorbij', 1.

5   F. A. Engering, *Krachtproef voor het kapitalisme: een liberale reflectie op de kredietcrisis*, (The Hague: Prof. Mr. B. M. Teldersstichting, 2010), 6.

6   Ministry of General Affairs, *Werken aan toekomst: Een aanvullend beleidsakkoord bij 'samen werken, samen leven'* (The Hague: Ministry of General Affairs, 2009).

short term. Among them was the Tilburg economics professor Lans Bovenberg, an influential advisor to the Christian Democrats.

In an opinion piece in February 2009, Bovenberg had urged the government to 'resist the pressure from interest groups' to seek short-term solutions.[7] He proposed a trade-off between an expansionary budgetary policy in the short term and long-term structural reforms, such as the raising of the state pension age from sixty-five to sixty-seven years. He coined the motto that inspired the government's approach: 'Lenient in the short term, responsible in the long term.' Later that year, as the immediate impact of the crisis subsided, Bovenberg suggested saving €30 billion through a few high-stakes structural reforms, avoiding across-the-board budget cuts. 'Never let a good crisis go to waste is not only a slogan for Obama; it can also become reality in the Netherlands,' he wrote.[8]

Since the Christian Democrats and the Labour Party disagreed on long-term reforms, senior financial officials proposed a solution: initiating a 'broad review'. In the 1980s, Zalm had acquired fame with this operation. It consisted of expert committees led by the Ministry of Finance that compiled an extensive austerity menu, with proposals for spending cuts and tax increases on a wide range of policy terrains. Political parties were then able to draw on this document for their election programmes. This time around, the nineteen expert committees were asked to include an option with a 20 per cent budget cut. In an interview, Wouter Bos referred to it as 'a foot in the door': 'At that time, I was perfectly capable of filling the financial holes, but not in a way that the Christian Democrats liked. A broad review is a great way to get reforms on the agenda. And then you can't get rid of them that easily.'[9]

In a parliamentary debate on the broad review, the opposition accused the government of outsourcing its responsibility. It was criticized as a 'displacement of politics, leaving the big political questions to be resolved by bureaucrats'.[10] The cuts were thus reduced to an accounting question, rather than a long-term vision on where to spend and where to cut.

7   Lans Bovenberg, 'Crisis versnelt aanpassing aan nieuwe wereld' [Crisis makes faster adjustment to new world], *NRC Handelsblad*, 11 February 2009.

8   Lans Bovenberg, 'Het kabinet kan de kaasschaaf in de la laten' [The government can leave aside across-the-board cuts], *NRC Handelsblad*, 14 September 2009.

9   Ibid.

10   Parliamentary records, HTK, 2009/2010, TK 34, 3315–39, p. 3315.

Prime Minister Balkenende responded by praising the approach of the 1980s: 'A fundamental revision of the design of the public sector is needed. That demands well-founded choices and reflection. The exceptional circumstances have led us to deploy a tested instrument. The broad review from the 1980s has proved its worth.'[11]

Meanwhile Mark Rutte, the new leader of the VVD, started beating the drum of austerity. A former human resources manager at the Anglo-Dutch multinational Unilever, Rutte had acquired the reputation of a 'man without qualities': a brilliant communicator with an ever-present mask of feigned enthusiasm.[12] After seeing off a right-wing populist challenge within the VVD, he continued Frits Bolkestein's strategy of combining neoliberal and culturally conservative views.

Even though he was not a man of ideas, Rutte was quite open about his neoliberal sympathies. In a 2007 essay for the right-wing weekly *Elsevier*, Rutte praised Friedrich Hayek, calling *The Road to Serfdom* 'essential reading for liberals'.[13] After the financial crisis, Rutte became the country's foremost critic of budgetary leniency. 'You look more and more like a father of an overweight child who says: Here's another lollipop, and tomorrow we're going on a diet,' he admonished Prime Minister Balkenende in parliament in September 2009.[14] Rutte then tabled a motion of no confidence. 'You're not even the captain of the *Titanic*,' he sneered. 'You are the conductor of the orchestra on board, starting a new tune.' The motion did not receive enough support to pass, but Rutte went on to win the 2010 elections.

The right-wing liberal VVD emerged for the first time in Dutch history as the country's largest political force, with thirty-one seats – only just beating the Labour Party, who came in second with thirty seats. The largest winner of the elections, however, was anti-Islam firebrand Geert Wilders, whose right-wing populist Freedom Party (PVV) almost trebled its score, its twenty-four seats making it the third-largest party. Rutte then formed a right-wing minority government with support

11   Ibid., 3323–4.

12   Sheila Sitalsing, *Mark: portret van een premier* (Amsterdam: Prometheus, 2016).

13   Mark Rutte, 'Betutteling: Politiek van wantrouwen', *Elsevier Weekblad*, 11 August 2007.

14   Parliamentary records, HTK, 2009/2010, Algemene politieke beschouwingen 13-10-2009, 126.

from Wilders's Freedom Party, the most right-wing government in post-war Dutch history.

For the VVD, austerity was not merely a question of economic efficiency but also an opportunity to realize the cherished ideal of smaller government – especially in those parts of the public sector where there was a lingering left-wing legacy: public education, social housing, welfare, culture. 'We want a smaller and especially more efficient government,' Rutte declared in a government policy statement in October 2010. 'The Netherlands suffers from administrative obesity, and it's about time we put the state on a diet. Bureaucracy is a tax on growth. Society itself can do things better if the government steps back.'[15]

The broad review initiated under the previous government handed Rutte an ideal opportunity to pick and choose what to cut back on. The Dutch turn to austerity was given further intellectual support by advice from the Study Group Fiscal Space, a high-level committee from the Ministry of Finance that also had an important role in the 1980s. In the run-up to the 2010 elections, the Study Group advised €29 billion in cuts, of which €18 billion was to be achieved in the coming government's term. The official aim was to reach a balanced budget in four years' time.[16] The first Rutte cabinet heeded this advice. 'We have to cut our way to growth,' Rutte said in the government policy statement.[17]

The government then froze public sector wages, reduced the budgets of ministries, abolished the ministry of Housing, Spatial Planning and Environment, downsized the cultural sector, raised the price of childcare, replaced student grants with loans and introduced a more repressive welfare regime. At the same time on the European stage, the first Rutte government presented itself as an ardent advocate of austerity and structural reform. In a hard-hitting piece in the *Financial Times*, Mark Rutte and Finance Minister Jan Kees de Jager pleaded for stricter enforcement of budget norms and tougher sanctions, with expulsion

---

15   Ministry of General Affairs, 'Regeringsverklaring 2010', 3.

16   Studiegroep Begrotingsruimte, *Risico's en zekerheden: Dertiende rapport studiegroep begrotingsruimte* (The Hague: Ministry of Finance, 2010), 11. For a critique, see Bas Jacobs, 'Studiegroep begrotingsruimte is de kluts kwijt', *Politieke Economie – Bas Jacobs* (blog), 2 April 2010, basjacobs.wordpress.com.

17   Ministry of General Affairs, 'Regeringsverklaring 2010', 3.

from the euro as the ultimate penalty for countries such as Greece.[18] Not for the first time, the Netherlands outflanked Germany in its fiscal hawkishness. De Jager explained this as part of a good cop–bad cop negotiation strategy. Germany had difficulty imposing its will on other European countries for historical reasons; it needed to play the friendly police officer. De Jager happily assumed the role of bad cop on behalf of the Netherlands. 'I always say: I am Dutch, so I can be blunt.'[19]

The Dutch 2010 elections formed part of a broader right-wing shift in Europe. Angela Merkel's centre-right cabinet of Christian Democrats (CDU) and right-wing liberals (FDP) took office in Germany in October 2009, while David Cameron's coalition of Conservatives and Liberal Democrats assumed power in the UK in May 2010. From the summer of 2010 onwards, European governments collectively switched to austerity and market-led reform.

To many international commentators, this was a surprising development. In the immediate aftermath of the financial crisis, leading scholars had anticipated the imminent breakdown of neoliberalism. 'We shall not soon hear again from the ideologues of free market dogma,' the British historian Tony Judt wrote in his book *Ill Fares the Land*.[20] Speaking two weeks after the bankruptcy of Lehman Brothers, the Nobel Prize–winning economist Joseph Stiglitz proclaimed that 'just as the fall of the Berlin Wall marked the end of communism', the financial crash signalled the end of neoliberalism.[21] Robert Skidelsky, the biographer of John Maynard Keynes, saw a revival of Keynesianism and wrote of 'the Return of the Master'.[22] These predictions proved false: after a short-lived Keynesian revival, free market ideas emerged surprisingly unscathed from the financial disaster.

One of the more convincing explanations for this apparent invulnerability is that neoliberalism is an institutional phenomenon. As the historian Quinn Slobodian has written, it is not 'in the realm of ideas

---

18   Mark Rutte and Jan Kees de Jager, 'Expulsion from the Eurozone Has to Be the Final Penalty', *Financial Times*, 7 September 2011.

19   Caroline de Gruyter and Jeroen Wester, ' "I'm Dutch, So I Can Be Blunt" ', *NRC Handelsblad*, 6 July 2011.

20   Tony Judt, *Ill Fares the Land* (New York: Penguin, 2010), 220.

21   Joseph Stiglitz, 'Moving Beyond Market Fundamentalism to a More Balanced Economy', *Annals of Public and Cooperative Economics* 80, no. 3 (2009): 345.

22   Robert Skidelsky, *Keynes: The Return of the Master* (New York: Public Affairs, 2009).

but in the scrum of interests and institutions that neoliberalism lives on'.[23] As we will see in this chapter, ideas still mattered, but an important part of the explanation for the neoliberal revival after the financial crisis in the Netherlands was the way in which ideas had been institutionalized. A new generation of economists and politicians had grown up with the dominant ideas of the 1980s. And entities such as the broad review and the Study Group Fiscal Space shaped Dutch fiscal policy, while internationally, there was the framework of the European Monetary Union (EMU) and the European fiscal rules. The neoliberal turn of the 1980s provided a powerful intellectual and policy legacy, a common sense to which leading politicians and economists could simply defer.[24]

The European Turn to Austerity

The unexpected return of fiscal orthodoxy was also a result of the changing face of the crisis. In the spring of 2010, Greece was on the brink of bankruptcy and proved unable to pay the interest on its sky-high public debt. The uncertainty this caused in bond markets soon spread across the entire periphery of the Eurozone. Due to the no-bailout clause and the prohibition of monetary financing in the Maastricht Treaty, the European Central Bank was unable to act as a lender of last resort, and this absence of a failsafe undermined the confidence of investors. Ireland, a country with a much lower public debt than the Netherlands on the eve of the crisis, was getting into trouble, as were Portugal and Spain, as interest rates on their public debts were rising.

Attention was now shifting from fumbling bankers to excessive government debt, even though that debt was largely a result of the bank bailouts. This development strengthened the hand of the fiscal hawks. They argued that the problem was not so much located in the financial

---

23   Quinn Slobodian, 'Is Neoliberalism Really Dead?', *New Statesman*, 27 October 2020.

24   For more on the powerful role of political legacies, see Margaret Weir and Theda Skocpol, 'State Structures and the Possibilities for "Keynesian" Responses to the Great Depression in Sweden, Britain and the United States', in Peter B. Evans, Dietrich Rueschemeyer and Theda Skocpol, eds, *Bringing the State Back In* (Cambridge: Cambridge University Press, 1985).

sector and the architecture of the euro but rather in the state. Excessive public debt and budget deficits were deemed risky by the financial markets and therefore led to higher interest rates. From this viewpoint, any Keynesian stimulus was considered fruitless. The crisis was now reframed by European politicians and economic policymakers as a 'sovereign debt crisis'. While rising public debt had been a result of the crisis, it was now presented as its root cause.[25]

The turning point was the G20 meeting in Toronto, in June 2010. It marked the moment when the Keynesian approach to the financial crisis was replaced with a more austere policy, spearheaded by the European Central Bank (ECB) and Germany. The final communiqué of the Toronto meeting called for 'growth-friendly fiscal consolidation'.[26] After the meeting, Jean-Claude Trichet wrote a much-discussed opinion piece in the *Financial Times*, titled 'Stimulate No More – It Is Now Time for All to Tighten'. 'The idea that austerity measures can lead to stagnation is incorrect,' wrote the ECB president. 'Anything that increases the confidence of households, companies and investors in the sustainability of public finances is good for growth and employment.'[27]

Closer to home, the Ministry of Finance and the Dutch Central Bank were selling the same message. 'So, the irony is that, thus far, the crisis has been fought with the problem that caused it: excessive debt creation,' wrote central bank president Nout Wellink in the introduction to the bank's 2010 annual report. 'The debt level of many countries must be reduced, otherwise you will not solve the problems that caused the crisis.'[28] The minister of finance, Jan Kees de Jager, repeatedly appeared on Dutch public television to explain that public debt levels were at the root of financial turmoil: 'We have a high level of debt. Financial markets look closely at that debt, so you cannot continue to expand your debt endlessly. The financial markets want the debt to go down.'[29] Mark Rutte and Jan Kees de Jager laid out this argument in the *Financial Times* piece

---

25   Mark Blyth, *Austerity: The History of a Dangerous Idea* (Oxford: Oxford University Press, 2013), 51–96.

26   Ibid., 61.

27   Jean-Claude Trichet, 'Stimulate No More – It Is Now Time for All to Tighten', *Financial Times*, 22 July 2010.

28   De Nederlandsche Bank, *Jaarverslag 2010* (Amsterdam: De Nederlandsche Bank, 2011), 20.

29   'Minister De Jager on Mortgage Deduction and Austerity', *Buitenhof*, 11 December 2011.

mentioned before, erroneously claiming that government profligacy was at the root of the crisis:

> We all know the saga of the last decade. Strict budgetary rules were laid down in the Stability and Growth Pact, a no-bail-out clause was included in the relevant treaty. So far, so good. But the main cause of the current problems is that some countries played fast and loose with the very rules designed to guarantee budgetary discipline.[30]

In terms of the ideas behind austerity, there was a central role for the Italian Bocconi school, which had acquired fame for producing a particular strand of public-choice theory. The origins of this tradition lie in the Public Finance Department of the Bocconi University of Milan, founded in the inter-war period by the neoliberal economist (and MPS member) Luigi Einaudi, president of the Italian Republic in the post-war period. In the 1980s and 1990s, a new generation of Bocconi graduates became international figureheads of the economics discipline – especially Alberto Alesina, Guido Tabellini, Roberto Perotti and Silvia Ardagna. They specialized in the political economy of public debt and deficits and played a crucial role in building the argument for growth-friendly austerity: the idea that one could cut one's way to growth.

The core idea was that cutting public spending, especially welfare and public sector wages, could trigger an economic recovery by changing expectations. The expectation of lower taxes, lower interest rates and lower wages in the near future would boost consumption and investment in the present.[31] While this theory had been developed in the 1980s and 1990s, Alesina updated his argument in the wake of the financial crisis.[32] He made the case for expansionary austerity at the ECOFIN meeting, where European ministers of finance and economic affairs gathered in April 2010.[33] Even though the empirical evidence for this idea was weak, and it was soon shown to be false, it became a standard

---

30   Rutte and De Jager, 'Expulsion from the Eurozone Has to Be the Final Penalty'.

31   Blyth, *Austerity*, 170–7.

32   Alberto Alesina, Silvia Ardagna and Jordi Galí, 'Tales of Fiscal Adjustment', *Economic Policy* 13, no. 27 (1998): 489–545.

33   Peter Coy, 'Keynes vs. Alesina. Alesina Who?', Bloomberg, 1 July 2010, bloom berg.com.

reference in the crisis narrative of politicians, economic policymakers and central bankers.[34]

The Netherlands was no exception. Alesina's work quickly became front-page news. When asked by the Dutch press about his plans to cut spending, Finance Minister Jan Kees de Jager referred to Alesina's lecture at the ECOFIN meeting in Madrid: 'Recently we were given a presentation by Harvard economist Alberto Alesina. He argues that it is a myth that austerity hurts the economy.'[35] More significantly, the Budget Memorandum for 2011, presented by the Dutch Ministry of Finance in September that year, extensively made the case for expansionary austerity. It cited the work of Alberto Alesina and Silvia Ardagna. 'Several studies show that consolidation of public finances under certain circumstances has a positive effect on growth,' it stated promisingly.[36]

The Finance Ministry claimed that 'exactly the current situation, in which lots of debt has accumulated, where confidence is frail and the financial markets are already counting on strong interventions, meets the conditions in which austerity can go hand in hand with economic recovery.'[37] Apart from the economic efficacy, it was also a question of timing and opportunity. The Budget Memorandum referred to public choice theory and stated that a crisis provides a rare opportunity to make deep cuts: 'Insights from political economy plead for starting now with the necessary consolidation. In practice, cutbacks and important structural reforms are only feasible in bad times.' A hackneyed Dutch metaphor of dikes and floods clinched the argument: 'It only becomes clear that the dikes are too weak when there is a flood. And if the water is gone again, people prefer to restore their houses and gardens, rather than strengthening the dikes.'[38]

The cuts turned out to be a dramatic exercise in self-harm, dragging the Dutch economy into a double-dip recession. Balancing the budget

---

34   Anis Chowdhury, 'Revisiting the Evidence on Expansionary Fiscal Austerity: Alesina's Hour?', *VoxEU*, 28 February 2012; Anis Chowdhury and Iyanatul Islam, 'The Debate on Expansionary Fiscal Consolidation: How Robust Is the Evidence?', *Economic and Labour Relations Review* 23, no. 3 (1 September 2012): 13–38.

35   Douwe Douwes, '"Er blijven altijd zorgen, maar die 750 miljard heft goed gewerkt"' [Concerns remain, but those 750 billion euros have worked well], *De Volkskrant*, 5 June 2010.

36   Parliamentary records, HTK, 2010–2011, 32 500, nr. 1, p. 35.

37   Ibid., 37–8.

38   Ibid., 38.

in four years, as Prime Minister Rutte set out to do, proved untenable. In the spring of 2012, the first Rutte cabinet had to deepen its austerity drive to conform to the European budget norms that Rutte and De Jager had been insisting on. From 2010 to 2017, subsequent coalition governments led by Mark Rutte implemented an extensive austerity programme, amounting to an estimated €50 billion euros, including the blunt cuts and tax hikes that had originally been advised against by leading economists. CPB estimates of the economic damage of austerity under Rutte range from 7.5 per cent to 10 per cent of Dutch GDP, with an extra 365,000 unemployed and long-term damage to the public sector that would later result in major crises at the Dutch tax service, as well as in childcare, social housing, youth care and education.[39]

Figure 7.1. The Dutch double-dip recession

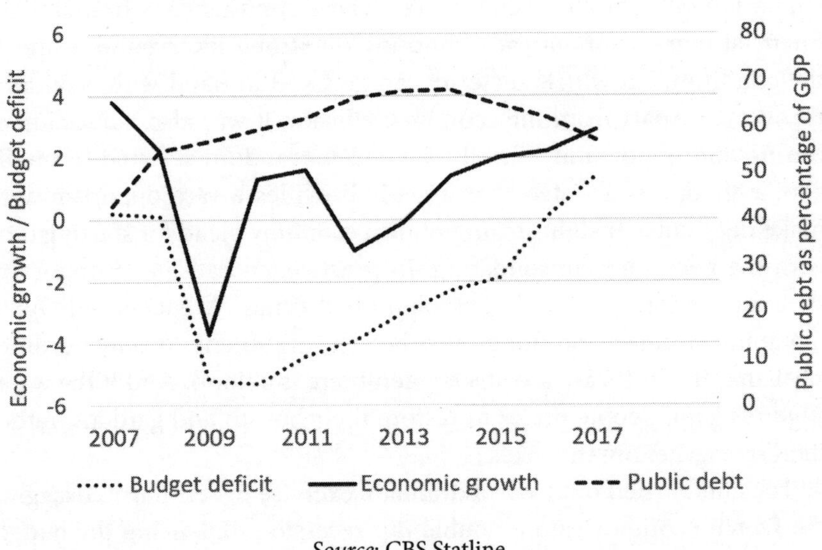

Source: CBS Statline

A Re-Run of the 1980s

That the Netherlands was at the forefront of the European turn to austerity should come as no surprise. The country has long had a reputation as

---

39   CPB, *Middellange-Termijnverkenning 2018–2021* (The Hague: CPB, 2016).

Europe's leading fiscal hawk. Already in the late 1990s and early 2000s, the Dutch VVD finance minister, Gerrit Zalm – nicknamed 'Il duro' by the Italians – was known for his insistence on budget discipline.[40] He famously chastised Germany and France for transgressing European budget norms in 2003.[41] And during the Eurozone crisis, the Netherlands again lived up to its reputation for stringency. Dutch Finance Ministers Jan Kees de Jager, Jeroen Dijsselbloem and Wopke Hoekstra lectured Southern European countries for their lack of fiscal discipline.

In the international financial press, Dutch hawkishness has often been associated with deep-seated Calvinism. Publications such as the *Financial Times* and the *Economist* have described the Netherlands as a 'prosperous Calvinist country', 'committed to austerity', and 'a famously thrifty people' with 'Calvinist attitudes'.[42] The obvious problem with this cultural trope is that the Netherlands is one of the most secularized countries in the world. Far more important than any lingering residue of Calvinism was the legacy of the 1980s. The Eurozone crisis saw a harkening back to the austerity policies of that time. Of course, the crisis of the 1980s had been very different in nature; high wages, high inflation and high interest rates were not present in the 2010s. Still, for politicians and policymakers, the no-nonsense policies of the 1980s served as an all-important reference point for dealing with an economic crisis. 'It's not about what Brussels wants,' Prime Minster Mark Rutte told the press at a Euro Summit in Brussels in March 2012. 'I value fiscal discipline because I think it's important. It's the lesson of the 1980s.'[43] It became the basis for the political belief in expansionary austerity, which defined the Dutch position during the Eurozone crisis. As the aforementioned Budget Memorandum for 2011 stated:

The Dutch experiences of the 1980s showed that while consolidation

---

40   Jouke de Vries and Ton Bestebreur, 'Budget Reform in the Netherlands: Sadder but Much Wiser Now', in John Wanna, Lotte Jensen and Jouke de Vries, eds, *The Reality of Budgetary Reform in OECD Nations: Trajectories and Consequences* (London: Edward Elgar, 2010), 221–39.

41   Martin Heipertz and Amy Verdun, *Ruling Europe: The Politics of the Stability and Growth Pact* (Cambridge: Cambridge University Press, 2010), 144.

42   Matt Steinglass, 'Dutch Mood Shifts Against Austerity and the EU', *Financial Times*, 8 August 2013; 'Not So Calvinist Anymore', *Economist*, 3 October 2013.

43   Cited in Coen Teulings, *Over de Dijken: Tien Jaar Na Het Uitbreken van de Financiële Crisis* (Amsterdam: Prometheus, 2018), 103.

can indeed hurt, it can also provide the basis for economic recovery. The government decided to intervene vigorously: industrial subsidies were halted; unemployment benefits lowered; public sector wages cut. With the Wassenaar Accord, the social partners and the government agreed to moderate wages in the private sector. This contributed in subsequent years to lower inflation and the recovery of Dutch competitiveness.[44]

In making this point, the Budget Memorandum referred to a book on the 1980s reforms of Frans Rutten, the powerful neoliberal head of the Ministry of Economic Affairs at the time. Similarly, in a 2012 book on the Eurozone crisis, director of the CPB Coen Teulings held up the Dutch response to the crisis of the 1980s as a model for the present: 'Experience teaches that often a large crisis is necessary before far-reaching reforms can be implemented to boost growth. The Netherlands successfully implemented such a policy in the 1980s and 1990s and is now reaping the benefits. Before that could occur, our country had to bite the bullet.'[45]

In terms of institutional practices, the 1980s were ever-present. As we have seen, institutional instruments from the 1980s, such as the broad review and the Study Group Fiscal Space, were again used in the 2010s to depoliticize austerity measures and generate political momentum for cuts. What by now seemed wholly forgotten was that the experiences with Dutch economic policy in the 1980s had not been all that positive. Even in the austerity-friendly work of Alberto Alesina, the Dutch austerity of the 1980s did not qualify as an economic success.[46]

Compared to the 1980s, however, there was also a novel institutional dimension to the eurocrisis austerity policies, and that was the fiscal framework established under EMU in the 1990s. As Kathleen McNamara has argued in her classic *The Currency of Ideas*, the Maastricht Treaty and EMU were built on an emerging 'neoliberal policy consensus that

---

44   Parliamentary records, HTK, 2010–2011, 32 500, nr. 1, 37.

45   Coen Teulings et al., *Europa in Crisis: Het Centraal Planbureau over Schulden En de Toekomst van de Eurozone* (Amsterdam: Balans, 2011), 147.

46   Alberto Alesina and Roberto Perotti, 'Fiscal Expansions and Adjustments in OECD Countries', *Economic Policy* 10, no. 21 (1995): 205–48. See also the discussion of this paper in the Dutch press: Flip de Kam, 'Links of rechts: lood om oud ijzer' [Left or right: lead for scrap iron], *NRC Handelsblad*, 17 September 1996.

elevated the pursuit of low inflation over growth or employment'.[47] To understand how this played out in the Netherlands, it is necessary briefly to take a step back in time.

How European Integration Entrenched the Dutch Neoliberal Turn

As the Labour Party intellectual Jos de Beus pointed out, the Netherlands was 'one of the member-states where the turn to European market liberalization went in tandem with a [domestic] turn to neoliberal ideas: deregulation; privatization; monetarism; retrenchment; tax reform; and market-simulation in the management of public services'.[48] The Dutch neoliberal turn started earlier, of course, but it received a powerful impulse from the process of European integration in the 1990s. As we saw in the previous chapter, the prospect of European integration (and globalization more broadly) became a crucial argument for market-based reform in the Netherlands. At the same time, the Netherlands developed into a leading fiscal hawk on the European stage.[49]

The European Union is not structurally neoliberal. Before the 1980s, there had been influential leftist visions of European integration.[50] The reality is more contingent: the European integration process gained momentum in a period when a neoliberal policy consensus emerged. As McNamara wrote, that consensus revolved around the belief that fiscal

47   Kathleen R. McNamara, *The Currency of Ideas: Monetary Politics in the European Union* (Ithaca, NY: Cornell University Press, 1998), 3. See also Peter A. Hall, 'The Economics and Politics of the Euro Crisis', *German Politics* 21, no. 4 (1 December 2012): 355–71.

48   Jos de Beus, 'Dutch Social Democracy and EMU', in Ton Notermans, ed., *Social Democracy and Monetary Union* (New York: Berghahn, 2001), 232.

49   Simon Otjes, 'From Eurorealism to Europhilia? The 2021 Dutch Elections and the New Approach of the Netherlands in EU Politics', *JCMS: Journal of Common Market Studies* 60, no. S1 (2022): 60–75.

50   Aurélie Dianara Andry, *Social Europe, the Road Not Taken: The Left and European Integration in the Long 1970s* (Oxford: Oxford University Press, 2022); J. Magnus Ryner, 'Is European Monetary Integration Structurally Neoliberal? The Origins of the EMS and the 1977–1978 Locomotive Conflict', *Comparative European Politics* 20, no. 6 (1 December 2022): 731–48; Laurent Warlouzet, *Governing Europe in a Globalizing World: Neoliberalism and Its Alternatives Following the 1973 Oil Crisis* (London: Routledge, 2017).

and monetary stimulus was counterproductive, due to inflationary expectations.[51] To achieve growth and employment, price stability had to be ensured, and the best way to achieve that was to have a rules-based monetary and fiscal policy, with a large degree of autonomy for technocrats and central bankers. States had to restrict themselves to 'structural reform' of the supply-side of the economy, improving competitiveness through infrastructure, education, labour market flexibilization and competitive wage levels. Some scholars have described the roll-out of this agenda as a European top-down process – the domain of unelected Eurocrats and business lobbies that impose budget discipline and neoliberal reform on unwilling nation-states.[52] In the Dutch case, however, these policy priorities were first the product of a largely domestic transformation, which was then transposed to the European level.[53]

European integration was seen by Dutch policymakers as both a problem and a solution. It was a problem because the European Union had expanded the challenge of maintaining budget discipline unto new terrains. The Institute for Research on Public Spending – the conservative fiscal watchdog founded in the 1960s by Willem Drees Jr and Theo Stevers – organized a symposium in the summer of 1988 titled 'Europe Without Frontiers, Budgets Without Frontiers?'[54] At the event, senior civil servants fretted about the ever-expanding European budget. They proposed to export the new Dutch budgeting standards to Brussels: strict norms and targets and a specialized taskforce to advise periodic cutbacks.[55] Then CPB director Gerrit Zalm compared the European budget, with its massive agricultural subsidies, to a heroin addiction:

51   McNamara, *Currency of Ideas*, 62.

52   Wolfgang Streeck, 'The International State System After Neoliberalism: Europe Between National Democracy and Supranational Centralization', *Crisis and Critique* 7, no. 1 (2020): 214–34; Bastiaan Van Apeldoorn, *Transnational Capitalism and the Struggle over European Integration* (London: Routledge, 2003).

53   It dovetails with portrayals of European neoliberalism as defined more by the particular trajectories, ideas and interests of different national elites, rather than a single supranational logic. See Perry Anderson, *The New Old World* (London: Verso, 2009); Nicholas Mulder, 'The Origins of European Neoliberalism', *N+1* (blog), 29 April 2019, nplusonemag.com; McNamara, *Currency of Ideas*.

54   Ronald Gerritse, ed., *Europa zonder grenzen, begroting zonder grenzen?* (The Hague: Instituut voor Onderzoek van Overheidsuitgaven, 1988). The editor of this special issue would become the treasurer-general of the Ministry of Finance during the Eurozone crisis years.

55   Ibid., 45.

'Someone in financial trouble can be helped with advice. They could keep a household ledger and make some price comparisons. But if he spends all his money on heroin, only one piece of advice counts: stop.'[56] The power struggle between the Ministry of Finance and the 'spending departments' appeared to be repeating itself once more, but this time on a European scale. As Finance Minister Onno Ruding wrote in his auto-biography, 'For Dutch budgeting policy, Europe became a permanent problem case.'[57] The growth of the European budget in the 1980s, Ruding explained, allowed national governments to escape their own budgeting constraints on the national level.

A similar anxiety took hold regarding the elimination of the national currencies and the establishment of the euro. Normally, if states spend too much or accumulate too much debt, they are punished by higher interest rates, since investing in that government's debt would become riskier. Alternatively, the value of their currency would decline relative to others. The fear was that the common European currency would weaken the disciplining role of the exchange rate mechanism, encourag-ing further fiscal profligacy. In the new situation, the costs of higher public debt – in terms of inflation or higher interest rates – could be partially displaced to other member-states.

In the Netherlands, the debate on European monetary policy had been the preserve of a small network of economists straddling the Ministry of Finance, the Ministry of Economic Affairs, the Dutch Central Bank and the Rotterdam pro-market think-tank OCFEB, founded by Frans Rutten. Leading Dutch economists involved in formulating the Dutch position on EMU, such as Lans Bovenberg, Jeroen Kremers, Rick van der Ploeg, Roel Beetsma and Jakob de Haan, used public-choice theory (most notably in the form expounded by Buchanan and Alesina) to argue that democracies had a 'deficit bias'.[58] Hence the perceived need for strict norms and targets

---

56   Paul Friese, 'De EG Als onbeheersbare kostenpost' [The EC as an unmanageable cost item], *NRC Handelsblad*, 3 June 1988.

57   Onno Ruding, *Balans: Het ging om meer dan geld alleen* (Amsterdam: Boom, 2020), 284.

58   Lans Bovenberg, Jeroen J. M. Kremers and Paul R. Masson, 'Economic and Monetary Union in Europe and Constraints on National Budgetary Policies', *IMF Staff Papers* 38, no. 2 (June 1991): 374–98. For the Dutch debate on public choice, fiscal norms and budget discipline, see also Harrie Verbon and Frans van Winden, *The Political Economy of Government Debt* (Amsterdam: North-Holland, 1993); Jakob de Haan, *De noodzaak van normen: een beschouwing over begrotingsbeleid* (The Hague:

on inflation, deficits and debt at the European level – most famously the 60 per cent ceiling on public debt and the 3 per cent limit on budget deficits as criteria for entering the euro.

At the same time, Dutch economists favoured prohibiting the European Central Bank from printing money to finance national debt and a no-bailout clause to prevent moral hazard. Even though, as some critics argued, the Maastricht norms on debt and deficits did not make macroeconomic sense and might work pro-cyclically, they made sense from a public-choice perspective focused on enforceability and the unreliability of political institutions. 'The criteria might very well be arbitrary, too restrictive, pro-cyclic, and resulting in a skewed composition of the public budget,' Rick van der Ploeg admitted in a 1992 meeting of the Royal Dutch Economics Association.[59] But the norms would serve both as artificial sources of European unity and as a big stick ensuring member-states would do what had to be done anyway – namely, put the house of the welfare state in order.

In this way, the euro also offered a solution to the problem of reconciling democracy with budget discipline. It tied budgetary decision-making to strict international rules, further depoliticizing economic policymaking. For this reason, leading public-choice theorists were enthusiastic about the possibilities of EMU. At a 1990 Mont Pelerin conference dedicated to the European Union, James Buchanan presented a paper in which he welcomed the 'genuine diminution of sovereignty that nation-states must experience' in the European Union. He believed 'the transference [of sovereignty] to the free play of competitive forces operating across and beyond national boundaries' would mark the end of the twentieth-century belief in state provision.[60] It was crucial,

---

Prof. Mr. B.M. Teldersstichting, 1987); Jakob de Haan, *Towards Budget Discipline: An Economic Assessment of the Possibilities for Reducing National Deficits in the Run-up to EMU*, Economic Papers (Brussels: Directorate-General for Economic and Financial Affairs, Commission of the European Communities, 1992); Roel M. W. J. Beetsma and A. Lans Bovenberg, *The Optimality of a Monetary Union Without a Fiscal Union*, Discussienota 9802 (The Hague: Ministry of Economic Affairs, 1998); Ministry of Finance, *Convergence with an Eye to EMU: EMU-convergentieprogramma voor Nederland* (The Hague: Ministry of Finance, 1992).

59   Koos Alders, ed., *Begrotingsbeleid en financiering Nederlandse staatsschuld: op weg naar de EMU* (Amsterdam: NIBE, 1992), 8.

60   James M. Buchanan, 'An American Perspective on Europe's Constitutional Opportunity', *Cato Journal* 10 (1990): 624.

however, to keep the federal state in check, with formal rules set out in a constitutional text and through 'an attitudinal climate that embodies generalized scepticism about both the motives of political agents and the working of political institutions, at all levels'.[61]

While more moderate in their political scepticism than Buchanan, Dutch economic policymakers saw European integration similarly as a welcome instrument to discipline spendthrift politicians further. As the second-highest public official at the Ministry of Finance argued in a lecture in 1988, 'European integration forces budget discipline and targets upon us.'[62] Naturally, the ministry was itself a strong proponent of such rules, but these new constraints could now be presented as an external reality that simply had to be complied with. Frans Rutten, the powerful head of the Ministry of Economic Affairs from 1973 till 1989, saw EMU in similar terms:

> The biggest disappointment and harshest lesson of the end of the seventies and beginning of the eighties was the impossibility of creating societal support for changing the policy paradigm in time, while it was obviously necessary to control public finances better. It is not unthinkable that in the nineties we will repeat old mistakes. It is now again the case that the financial-economic development and governability of our country are cause for concern. In the United States, Nobel Prize–winner Buchanan has argued that constitutional constraints are needed for good governance. In our country there is less enthusiasm for that, especially among politicians. I believe it isn't the core quality of a well-functioning democracy to leave as much as possible to the discretion of elected politicians. I am enthusiastic about the design of EMU, not solely because the exchange rates are fixed . . . I believe guaranteeing solid public finances by law or international treaty should be applauded.[63]

61 Ibid., 628. For the Mont Pelerin conference, see Roberto Ventresca, 'Neoliberal Thinkers and European Integration in the 1980s and the Early 1990s', *Contemporary European History* 31, no. 1 (2022): 31–47. See also Quinn Slobodian and Dieter Plehwe, 'Neoliberals Against Europe', in William Callison et al., *Mutant Neoliberalism: Market Rule and Political Rupture* (New York: Fordham University Press, 2019), 89–111.

62 Jan Postma, 'Europese integratie dwingt tot budgetdiscipline en normering' [European integration forces budget discipline and standardization], *Nederlandse Staatscourant*, 18 January 1989.

63 Frans Rutten, *Zeven kabinetten wijzer: de nieuwe zakelijkheid bij het economische beleid* (Groningen: Wolters-Noordhoff, 1993), 32–3.

There was much talk of the decline of the nation-state in the 1990s. But, as political scientists observed at the time, these fiscal rules also strengthened the state in ways that were not immediately obvious. In *Why the European Union Strengthens the State*, Andrew Moravcsik argued that integration empowered parts of the state apparatus in relation to others.[64] The technocrats at the Ministries of Finance and Economic Affairs, in particular, gained in power and prestige. Because these policymakers were closely involved with the closed Brussels meetings, they had an information advantage and could determine the national decision-making agenda. As a result, they came to decide what economic policy was necessary to achieve the convergence aims necessary to qualify for the euro. Politicians, meanwhile, were only too eager to outsource controversial policy decisions to technocrats. Edgar Grande called it 'the paradox of weakness'.[65] Nation-states saw strategic benefits in their own hands being tied – it gave them the power to push through unpopular reforms and outmanoeuvre the domestic opposition. It was a rerun of the depoliticization strategy of the 1980s, but now on an international footing.

Even the technocrats themselves were surprised about the lack of substantive public debate on European integration. Ad Geelhoed, the head of the Ministry of Economic Affairs and perhaps the most influential voice on reform and convergence, wondered about 'the acquiescent or lacklustre silence' on the Maastricht Treaty.[66] In public and parliamentary debate, 'there had been no thorough exploration of the consequences of a completed EMU' for national economic policy. The preparations for Maastricht had taken place under the third Lubbers cabinet, with Labour Party leader Wim Kok as finance minister. Especially for the Labour Party, the lack of debate was remarkable, since the new free market order enshrined in the Maastricht Treaty clashed with the party's legacy of state

64 Andrew Moravcsik, *Why the European Community Strengthens the State: Domestic Politics and International Cooperation* (Cambridge, MA: Minda de Gunzburg Center for European Studies, Harvard University, 1994).

65 Markus Jachtenfuchs and Edgar Grande, 'Das paradox der Schwäche: Forschungspolitik und die Einflußlogik europäischer Politikverflechtung', in Markus Jachtenfuchs and Beate Kohler-Koch, *Europäische Integration* (Opladen: Leske + Budrich, 1996), 373–99.

66 Ad Geelhoed, ' "Maastricht" en de Nederlandse sociaaldemocratie', in Bart Tromp et al., eds, *Nederland in de wereld: Het zestiende jaarboek voor het democratisch socialisme* (Amsterdam: De Arbeiderspers, 1995), 88.

intervention. The aforementioned social democrat intellectual Jos de Beus – lead author of the 1994 party programme – argued that this silence had been a deliberate choice of the party leadership:

> [The social democrats] did not want partisan politics, social contestation and public debate about EMU. The PvdA never installed a special government commission, as did the SAP, and as Dutch incumbent parties were used to doing when issues became constitutional or alien to traditional party ideology. Indeed, the PvdA leadership tried to avoid any well-considered standpoint on the future of EMU.[67]

As a result, even the ministers were poorly informed about the coming changes. As Jan Pronk, then Labour Party minister for foreign trade and development aid, observed in 1994: 'I think few in the government realized how far-reaching the consequences of the EMU convergence norms would be for national economic policy in the 1990s. I thought the approach was technocratic. The bureaucrats had seized the opportunity.'[68]

Indeed, the reflection on what the euro and the European single market would mean for Dutch economic policy was not much of a party-political affair. It was the preserve of a small circle of economic policymakers at the Ministry of Finance, the Ministry of Economic Affairs, the Dutch Central Bank and the Social and Economic Council.[69] Shortly after the signing of the Maastricht Treaty, the third Lubbers cabinet had sent a request to the Social and Economic Council to advise on future economic policy. The cabinet rejected 'a one-sided choice for the market mechanism' and asked the Social and Economic Council to develop a policy mix combining consultation and coordination with market reform.[70]

Made up of employers, trade unions and a group of economic experts,

---

67   De Beus, 'Dutch Social Democracy and EMU', 239.

68   Peter Rehwinkel and Jan Nekkers, *Regerenderwijs: De PvdA in het kabinet-Lubbers/Kok* (Amsterdam: Bert Bakker, 1994), 116.

69   Some key publications include: Jeroen J. M. Kremers, ed., *Inspelen op Europa: Uitdagingen voor het financieel-economische beleid van Nederland* (Schoonhoven: Academic Service, 1993); Ministry of Finance, *Convergence with an Eye to EMU*; Alders, *Begrotingsbeleid en financiering Nederlandse staatsschuld*; Ad Geelhoed, 'Het Europese integratieproces en het coördinatievraagstuk', in Kremers, *Inspelen op Europa*, 173–83.

70   SER, *Convergentie en overlegeconomie* (The Hague: SER, 1992), 154.

the Social and Economic Council agreed on a proto–Third Way strategy for dealing with European unification. The core argument was that European integration would intensify policy competition between member-states. The quality of human capital and of public goods would become a major competitive advantage in a globalizing world. After increasing labour market participation and reducing unemployment through an active labour market policy, the government should set aside money to invest in public goods, while modernizing the public sector through the introduction of market incentives. Since economic shocks and crises could no longer be remedied through the exchange rate or through Keynesian fiscal stimulus, adaptation had to come through the moderation of wages and the flexibilization of the labour market. After the 1994 elections, when the neoliberal challenge to corporatism quietened down, this became the Dutch competitive strategy in response to European integration, even though it was never really presented as such in public debate.

The Best Boy in Class

The same years saw the transformation of the Netherlands into Europe's leading fiscal hawk. Up to the early 1990s, the Netherlands was itself performing badly on deficits and debt and had little standing to lecture other countries. Moreover, Dutch political elites had long been proponents of European federalism.[71] The hawkish Dutch position on European fiscal policy was formed in the aftermath of Maastricht, during the Purple coalitions of social democrats (PvdA), right-wing liberals (VVD) and progressive liberals (D66) that governed from 1994 to 2002. Due to the economic recovery in the second half of the 1990s, the Dutch were able to pass the EMU convergence criteria with flying colours. The Netherlands formed an alliance with Germany on the Stability and Growth Pact in 1996, which tried to police the Maastricht fiscal rules after the establishment of the euro.[72]

71   Robert Harmsen, 'Euroscepticism in the Netherlands: Stirrings of Dissent', in Joachim Schild and Robert Harmsen, eds, *Euroscepticism* (Leiden: Brill, 2004), 99–126.
72   Mathieu Segers and Femke Van Esch, 'Behind the Veil of Budgetary Discipline:

In part, this simply reflected the Dutch national interest. As one of the hard-currency countries, the Netherlands believed that Southern European countries with weaker currencies should bear the costs of adjustment to the euro: they should not be allowed to free-ride on Dutch and German fiscal probity. 'We are not throwing our good guilder in the pond,' Prime Minister Wim Kok reportedly said in a private meeting with Zalm in November 1997, looking out over the small lake surrounding the seventeenth-century Dutch parliament building in The Hague.[73] Kok and Zalm campaigned in secret to force Italy's prime minister, Romano Prodi, to agree to more austerity, or else the Netherlands would veto Italy's entry into the Eurozone. Zalm even threatened to resign as finance minister over Italy's accession. It was the first time the Netherlands had positioned itself in this hawkish fashion. At this point, Germany was not sure it would meet the convergence criteria itself and was rather late in supporting the Dutch pressure on the Italian government. Prodi ultimately accepted the demands, and the Netherlands rescinded its veto.

While the PvdA and the VVD shared the same position on budgetary rigour, they had political disagreements about the future of European integration. The Labour Party believed that EMU and Dutch social democracy were mutually reinforcing, 'because EMU rewards the Dutch competitive strategy of wage moderation and punishes foreign strategies like industrial policy'; furthermore it prevented devaluation from Southern European competitors.[74] In other words, European integration vindicated the Third Way strategy of competitive corporatism. But the Labour Party also had a functionalist vision of EMU and European integration, which assumed that it would ultimately lead to the enlargement of European norms, budgets and competencies, which would in turn form an institutional counterweight to the neoliberal logic of the single market and the Stability Pact. The convergence generated by EMU, in other words, would be 'convergence around a social-democratic Europe'.[75]

The Political Logic of the Budgetary Rules in EMU and the SGP', *JCMS: Journal of Common Market Studies* 45, no. 5 (2007): 1089–109.

73   Roel Janssen, 'Nederland Gidsland' [The Netherlands takes the lead], *NRC Handelsblad*, 1 May 1998.

74   De Beus, 'Dutch Social Democracy and EMU', 237.

75   Ibid., 245.

The VVD, in contrast, was opposed to harmonization and the deepening of European integration. Frits Bolkestein, the leader of the VVD from 1990 to 1998, and the upcoming European commissioner for the Internal Market (1999–2004), was the first to politicize European integration in this way. He shared James Buchanan's scepticism towards politicians and the public purse, quipping that 'a dog can sooner build up a stockpile of sausages than a democratically elected politician can implement a sound budget policy'.[76] He proposed a 'liberal Europe' that limited itself to 'core tasks'.[77] In this project, neoliberalism and Dutch nationalism went hand in hand. Bolkestein introduced a Eurosceptic discourse in the Netherlands, mobilizing Dutch nationalist sentiment against the deepening of European integration. In a much-discussed party speech on foreign policy in February 1995, Bolkestein claimed that the Dutch position on European integration had been naive and idealistic. He roused controversy by calling for a European policy strictly based on the Dutch 'national interest':

> [Dutch] financial interests have been neglected . . . In Europe, around a hundred billion [guilders] in subsidies are pumped around yearly. That is bad enough in itself. But we do not seem able to pilot much of this silver fleet into the Dutch harbour. Over the coming five years, the Netherlands with its net contribution of 25 billion guilders is the largest contributor per inhabitant. While, partly with our money, highways are built in the holiday paradise of Tenerife, we must count every penny to strengthen our dikes.[78]

With its nostalgic nautical metaphors and its jealous evocation of southern holiday climates, the speech was a foreshadowing of Dutch sentiment during the Eurozone crisis, when Dutch television crews would descent on Athens to film ordinary Greeks sitting on sun-lit terraces

76   Willem Breedveld and Marcel Ten Hooven, 'Frits Bolkestein: Lubbers zit nu op de blaren' [Frits Bolkestein: Lubbers has made his bed and should lie in it], *Trouw*, 19 September 1990.

77   Frits Bolkestein, 'Europa zal liberaal zijn, of niet zijn' [Europe will be liberal, or won't be], *NRC Handelsblad*, 14 June 1996.

78   Frits Bolkestein, 'Herijking van het buitenlands beleid', in *Boren in hard hout* (Amsterdam: Prometheus, 1998), 163–71.

eating ice cream, implying that that was where Dutch bailout money was going. Bolkestein contended that European cultural diversity made further integration impossible, criticizing cohesion funds and transfers.[79] The position of the VVD, as set out in a 1992 party report, was that the ceding of Dutch sovereignty on differing policy terrains was predicated on 'the direction given to European integration' and 'whether that direction was liberatory' or not.[80] In this way, the VVD hewed close to Friedrich Hayek's original neoliberal vision of European integration in his 1939 essay on interstate federalism.[81] In this famous text, Hayek commended a European supranational institution that had the power to limit domestic political interference with the market but lacked the democratic legitimacy and popular support to develop a European social policy.

Leading Dutch economic policymakers tended to support the neoliberal vision. They argued that a small open economy like the Netherlands had a specific national interest in focusing on negative integration. Geelhoed, the influential head of the Ministry of Economic Affairs and from 1998 the senior assistant to Prime Minister Wim Kok, spelled out the argument: because smaller member-states had more limited means of intervention, they would lose out to the larger member-states when it came to industrial policy. Moreover, a small country such as the Netherlands would have little say in any European social or industrial policy. At the same time, as a country with a small domestic market and a large export sector, the Netherlands had much to gain from market integration and little from Keynesian stimulus to promote domestic demand. 'Pure market integration offers the Netherlands, from a strategic point of view, much more possibilities,' Geelhoed concluded.[82]

---

79   Samuel Rozemond, *Bolkestein en de Euroscepsis, Clingendael-notitie* (The Hague: Clingendael, 1996); Hans Vollaard, 'Dutch Discourses of a Small Nation in an Inefficient Europe: Cosmopolitanism, Pragmatism, and Nationalism', in Robert Harmsen and Joachim Schild (eds.) *The 2009 European Parliament Elections and Beyond* (Baden-Baden: Nomos Verlagsgesellschaft, 2011), 85–104; Harmsen, 'Euroscepticism in the Netherlands'.

80   Werkgroep van Aardenne, *Europa: Een volgende akte*, Geschrift 76 (The Hague: Teldersstichting, 1992), 70.

81   Friedrich A. Hayek, 'The Economic Conditions of Interstate Federalism', *New Commonwealth Quarterly* 5, no. 2 (1939): 131–49.

82   Geelhoed, 'Het Europese integratieproces en het coördinatievraagstuk', 181–2.

However, it was also the political dynamic of the European Union that favoured the neoliberal vision. European politics follows the logic of a two-level bargaining game.[83] Politicians use the domestic context to increase their leverage on the international stage, and vice versa. European rules strengthened the bargaining position of Dutch politicians and policymakers advocating austerity and structural reform at the domestic level. In their book on the Stability and Growth Pact, Martin Heipertz and Amy Verdun give the example of Zalm, who used European fiscal rules 'to contain the mounting pressures in his own country' against austerity measures.[84] At the same time, the aversion to Brussels among the Dutch public strengthened the bargaining position of Dutch politicians internationally, this time in opposing European fiscal solidarity and debt mutualization. In this way, the Eurosceptic vision of the Dutch centre-right took precedence over the functionalist ideals of the Labour Party, who favoured more European harmonisation and policy coordination. Increasingly, the dominant Dutch vision on European integration became a milder version of the Thatcherite maxim: to seek as much negative integration as possible, with as little positive integration as possible.

There was one problem, however. The Netherlands had little political clout to enforce its preferences on other member-states. To maintain fiscal discipline, it was dependent on its alliance with Germany. When Germany and France amassed large budget deficits and flouted the rules of the Stability and Growth Pact in 2003, the Dutch stood by empty-handed. What is more, leading political figures questioned the rules of the Pact. Romano Prodi, then president of the European Commission, called the rules 'stupid, like all rigid decisions'. Trade commissioner Pascal Lamy lambasted the pact as 'crude and medieval'.[85] In The Hague, this was widely felt as a betrayal. The Dutch had surrendered their hard guilder on the condition of strict rules – but, at the first sign of trouble, the rules were being called into question!

---

83   Kenneth Dyson and Kevin Featherstone, 'Italy and EMU as a "Vincolo Esterno": Empowering the Technocrats, Transforming the State', *South European Society and Politics* 1, no. 2 (1996): 272–99.

84   Heipertz and Verdun, *Ruling Europe*, 144.

85   Ibid., 135.

In an opinion piece, the influential Dutch economist Lans Bovenberg called on the Netherlands to take the lead in defending the Stability and Growth Pact, since stability was in the national interest of a small, open economy.[86] In his eyes, the pact was a crucial instrument to strengthen the position of the ministries of finance in the various member-states. It served to spread budgetary discipline from the north of Europe to the south and the east, by strengthening the position of those ministries. He called on the Netherlands to lead by example, by enforcing fiscal discipline and structural reform at home. 'To maintain our moral authority, our country has to conform to the rules of the Stability Pact and if possible to the 3 per cent norm of the Maastricht Treaty . . . Showing that good reforms work is more productive than lecturing Europe.'[87] The Netherlands, in other words, had to become the best boy in class. Rather than debating the wisdom of the European fiscal rules per se, making the grade became the dominant discourse in the Netherlands on European integration.

Austerity and the Left

This policy legacy made itself felt during the Eurozone crisis. 'It has rarely been as important to behave as the best boy in class,' former president of the Dutch Central Bank Nout Wellink said in an interview during the height of the Eurozone crisis, in May 2012.[88] Instead of recovering, Europe had slipped back into recession. The open Dutch economy took a hit, contracting by 1 per cent; the budget deficit for 2012 was an embarrassing 4.4 per cent of GDP, and a similar deficit was projected for 2013, in clear violation of the rules of the Stability Pact. Dutch politicians could have asked for leniency from Ollie Rehn, the newfound European budget tsar, whose appointment the Netherlands had pressed for. But the Dutch government had taken such a tough stance in Brussels that it felt it now needed to walk the walk to maintain its moral authority. In March 2012, negotiations had started on

---

86   Lans Bovenberg, 'Nederland moet Stabiliteitspact redden' [The Netherlands must save stability pact], *NRC Handelsblad*, 10 September 2003.

87   Lans Bovenberg, 'Nederland moet het goede voorbeeld geven' [The Netherlands should set a good example], *NRC Handelsblad*, 4 December 2003.

88   Geelhoed, 'Het Europese integratieproces en het coördinatievraagstuk', 181–2.

additional cuts. Weeks later, the government collapsed. The right-wing populist Geert Wilders, who until then had supported the minority coalition between the VVD and the Christian Democrats, decided he did not want to obey a 'Brussels diktat' and assume responsibility for additional cuts in healthcare and pensions. It meant new elections in the autumn of 2012. A panicky atmosphere descended on The Hague. Brussels expected an adjusted budget for 2013 at short notice, including austerity measures.

At this very moment, there was an international build-up of opposition to Europe's austerity policies. Leading economists questioned the rationale behind the cuts. Nobel Prize–winner Paul Krugman attacked the new-classical doctrines underlying the budget cuts and wrote scornfully of the 'confidence fairy' that would magically bring about recovery.[89] At the spring meeting of the IMF and World Bank in Washington on April 2012, where the global economic policymaking elite gathered, IMF president Christine Lagarde warned that 'a rush to austerity will ultimately prove self-defeating'.[90] She cited new empirical research by IMF economists Olivier Blanchard and Daniel Leigh, which found that fiscal multipliers were much larger in downturns than expected. In other words, spending cuts during an economic crisis had a much larger negative impact than previously thought. Lagarde warned that 'an overly aggressive adjustment today will hurt growth, and might actually also raise public debt ratios'.[91] In the Netherlands, this was a message the government did not want to hear. The financial press also weighed in. In a blistering editorial titled 'The Sinking Dutchman', the *Financial Times* portrayed the Dutch political crisis as an own goal:

> The Dutch case is a horrific display of Europe's self-harming. In pressurised states with no fiscal space, deficit cuts are of course imperative, but countries that can should let deficits widen to buoy aggregate demand in the eurozone until the recovery is firm. There is no reason for the Netherlands, whose 65 per cent debt to output ratio puts it

89   Paul Krugman, 'Death of a Fairy Tale', *New York Times*, 27 April 2012.
90   Christine Lagarde, 'Banque de France Financial Stability Review on Public Debt – Special Address to Panel Discussion', International Monetary Fund, 21 April 2012, imf.org.
91   Ibid.

among the eurozone's most solvent, to fear moderate deficits in a recession.[92]

The austerity debate manifested itself in the Netherlands too, though largely outside of the dominant institutions of Dutch economic policymaking.[93] The centre-left economics professor Bas Jacobs took the lead in making the case against austerity, taking up positions similar to those of Paul Krugman in the United States.[94] On the political front, the largest left-wing parties had taken a critical stance on austerity. The leftist Socialist Party (SP), for a long time the unexpected frontrunner in the polls for the upcoming elections, wanted to adjust European budget rules so that 'countries are not forced to destroy their economies'.[95] The SP proposed to delay the cuts for another two years and wanted to democratize the ECB and broaden its mandate to include employment.

The new centre-left Labour Party leader Diederik Samsom was somewhat more moderate, but still highly critical. In his leadership campaign in spring 2012, Samsom denounced the 'financial fetishism' of the VVD and the 'fiscal obsession' that had taken over Europe.[96] Samsom proposed to ally with the French president, François Hollande, who was elected in May 2012 and had centred his campaign on denouncing 'ruthless austerity'.[97] The European tide seemed to be turning: Hollande was forming an anti-austerity coalition to confront Germany. Samsom wanted to be part of that coalition and pleaded for a new approach to the Eurozone crisis: 'A

---

92   Matt Steinglass, 'Sinking Dutchman Haunts the Eurozone', *Financial Times*, 24 April 2012.

93   With the exception of CPB president Coen Teulings, who opposed the strict application of the 3 percentage norm and dissented on the 2012 report from the Studygroup Fiscal Space. See Jean Pisani-Ferry and Coen Teulings, 'Eurozone Countries Must Not Be Forced to Meet Deficit Targets', Breugel, 27 February 2012, bruegel.org.

94   Bas Jacobs, 'De blinde vlekken van Rutte' [The blind spots of Rutte], *NRC Handelsblad*, 17 January 2013.

95   Socialistische Partij, *'Nieuw vertrouwen': Verkiezingsprogramma Tweede Kamerverkiezingen 2012* (Amersfoort: Socialistische Partij, 2012), 60.

96   Diederik Samsom, 'Congrestoespraak Diederik Samsom', 17 March 2012, parlement.com; Derk Stokmans, ' "Ik kan het. Ik heb energie en ik kan keuzes maken" ' ['I can do it. I have energy and can make choices'], *NRC Handelsblad*, 23 February 2012.

97   Markus K. Brunnermeier, Harold James and Jean-Pierre Landau, *The Euro and the Battle of Ideas* (Princeton, NJ: Princeton University Press, 2018), 151.

Southern Europe stuck in recession will hit our exports and jobs too . . . Sticking to the neoliberal "we will cut our way to recovery" is not going to work. Europe needs something very different: growth and jobs for millions of Europeans now without work.'[98] A similar position was taken by the largest trade union, the FNV: 'The eurozone is in dire straits, but both the Netherlands and Germany are "surplus countries". They should cut back less and spend more in the interests of their own economies and the rest of the eurozone.'[99] Even the powerful Dutch employers' association VNO-NCW was hesitant about the strict application of the 3 per cent norm. It had called on the outgoing minority government to announce long-term structural reforms 'and to find flexibility in Europe for less austerity'.[100]

All in all, this amounted to a significant challenge to the dominant economic paradigm. As Frans Rutten had written at the end of his career, a central tenet of his 'businesslike' policy in the 1980s was to focus on easily enforceable 'rules of thumb' about budget deficits and public debt. The 'cerebral' Keynesian ideas about the macroeconomic function of public spending were to be 'dimmed down'.[101] This policy paradigm was still very much the norm at the Dutch Ministry of Finance. In the latest Budget Memorandum, published in August 2012, the Ministry of Finance cited the infamous and soon-to-be-discredited Reinhart–Rogoff paper on the dangers of excessive public debt. The memorandum went on to argue that a lack of budget discipline and structural reform in Southern European countries was at the root of the Eurozone crisis. 'The European rules on budget deficits and government debt haven't been sufficiently heeded,' it stated.[102] This flawed diagnosis

---

98   Parliamentary records, HTK, 2011/2012, 101–5, 53.

99   Cited in Saskia Boumans, 'Did Trade Unions Reinforce the Neoliberal Transformation? The Dutch Case', *Journal of Industrial Relations* 65, no. 2 (1 April 2023): 146.

100   Editorial Staff, 'Drie procent is geen heilig getal' [Three per cent is not a holy number], *NRC Handelsblad*, 26 March 2012.

101   Rutten, *Zeven kabinetten wijzer*, 99.

102   Parliamentary records, HTK, 2012–2013, 33 400, nr. 1, 15. As leading economists argued, this was confusing the symptoms (public debt) with the cause of the crisis (a European banking crisis). See Paul de Grauwe, 'The Eurozone as a Morality Play', *Intereconomics* 2011, no. 5 (2011): 230–31; Matthias Matthijs and Mark Blyth, 'When Is It Rational to Learn the Wrong Lessons? Technocratic

formed part of a much larger moralistic and nationalistic framing of the crisis, popularized by the Dutch centre-right parties. Framing the crisis in terms of saints and sinners, however, also strengthened the need for fiscal discipline at home.

After the withdrawal of Wilders, Rutte's outgoing minority government found enough support in parliament to realize a further €12 billion in cuts and tax increases. This so-called Spring Agreement of April 2012 included a VAT increase, a two-year freeze on the wages of civil servants, an increase in the healthcare deductible, an expedited rise in the pension age to sixty-seven and a faster reduction in interest deductions on mortgages. Among Dutch political and media elites, there was widespread relief that the political crisis had been averted. The response in the press was jubilant. The absence of the Labour Party was widely commented on. Samsom was under great public pressure to join in, also from within his own party, the majority of whose voters supported the Spring Agreement. Commentators wrote that 'the PvdA joined the populist naysayers of SP and PVV'.[103] Behind the scenes, Samsom was beset by doubts, changing his mind twice about participating in a mere twenty-four hours.

When economic forecasts appeared on the effects of the Spring Agreement, the initial enthusiasm soon faded. The CPB predicted an additional 100,000 unemployed. The FNV described the Spring Agreement as a 'sledgehammer', and the Christian trade union (CNV) referred to it as a 'social nightmare'.[104] In the run-up to the September 2012 elections, the Labour Party could claim to have been proved right. In their election programme, the Labour Party denounced the agreement as prolonging the 'vicious circle of austerity that prevents investments and purchases, causes job losses and sinks the Netherlands further into recession'.[105] Samsom warned in a major election debate that the obsessive focus on deficits would result in job losses. Ordinary

---

Authority, Social Learning, and Euro Fragility', *Perspectives on Politics* 16, no. 1 (March 2018): 110–26.

103   Derk Stokmans and Thijs Niemantsverdriet, 'De eerste tachtig turbodagen van de nieuwe PvdA-leider' [The first eighty dazzling days of the new PvdA leader], *NRC Handelsblad*, 9 June 2012.

104   'Lenteakkoord ligt onder vuur' [Spring Agreement under fire], *NRC Handelsblad*, 18 May 2012.

105   PvdA, *Nederland Sterker & Socialer: Verkiezingsprogramma 2012* (Amsterdam: PvdA, 2012), 5.

people were worried about their jobs, not the budget deficit. 'Austerity, austerity, austerity' was not the answer, Samsom argued forcefully: 'In these vulnerable times, you have to maintain employment.'[106] The Labour Party printed election posters with a large image of Samsom, accompanied by the text: 'How do we get the economy going? By not hurting families, so no higher VAT.'

'Samsom is then still on the right economic line,' said the Labour Party MEP Paul Tang. The macroeconomist and former financial spokesperson for the Labour Party thought it was commendable that Samsom had kept the party out of the Spring Agreement. 'But then something very strange happens.'[107]

For a long time, it seemed that the Socialist Party was going to become the largest party. The first stumbling block for party leader Emile Roemer was a controversial interview in the month before the election in which he took a stand against the European budget rules. 'Do I have to pay that ridiculous fine if the deficit is over 3 per cent? Over my dead body,' Roemer said.[108] In the following days, the entire political class attacked the leftist leader. The Socialist Party fumbled and backtracked in response. The most painful reaction came from the still powerful Socialist Party founder Jan Marijnissen, who publicly called Roemer's statement 'a mistake.'[109] It was the start of a dramatic campaign for Roemer.

---

106   PvdA, 'Samsom tijdens NOS-debat: de samenleving gaat over meer', 23 August 2012, youtube.com.

107   Paul Tang, telephone interview with author, 16 February 2023.

108   Klaas Broekhuizen and Laurens Berentsen, '"Moet ik die belachelijke boete betalen als het tekort groter is dan 3%? Over My Dead Body"', *Financieel Dagblad*, 16 August 2012.

109   Koen Haegens, 'Verboden terrein' [Forbidden terrain], *De Groene Amsterdammer*, 22 August 2012, 34th edn.

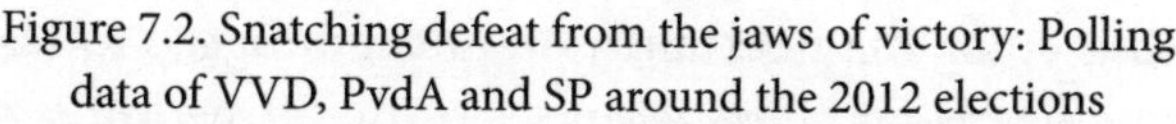

Figure 7.2. Snatching defeat from the jaws of victory: Polling
data of VVD, PvdA and SP around the 2012 elections

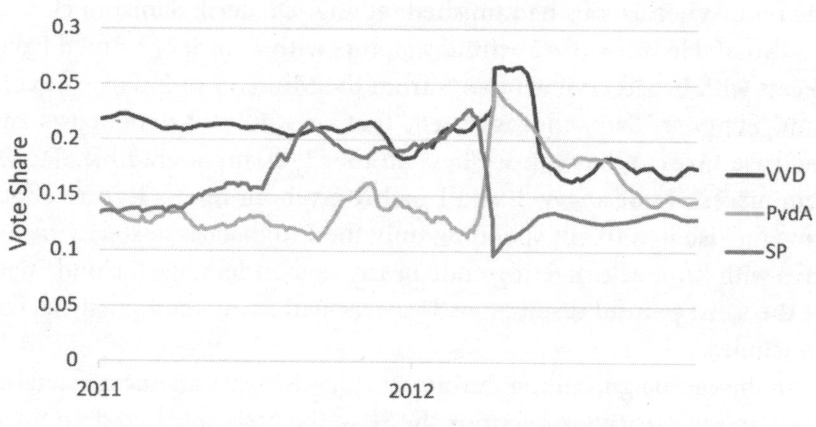

Source: peilingwijzer.nl

In that same week, Diederik Samsom received the CPB forecasts of
the economic outcomes of the Labour Party election programme. It
scored very badly in the CPB economic model. Growth and jobs were
what the social democratic campaign was going to be all about. 'Make
that recession and unemployment,' Samsom gloomily told his
campaign team.[110] Behind closed doors, he decided at the last moment
to turn around his campaign. 'We should not imitate the SP. I'm not
going to try to be a better Roemer than Roemer himself.' He ditched
the anti-austerity election posters and centred his campaign on 'telling
the honest story'. It was a plea against making empty promises in a
crisis, such as the pledge of VVD Prime Minister Mark Rutte that he
would stop sending money to Greece. But it also served as an empty
signifier of sorts, giving the Labour Party room for manoeuvre after
the elections.

In that crucial period, the economics professor and austerity critic
Bas Jacobs was invited to speak behind closed doors to the Labour
Party leadership, in a small room in the Dutch parliament.[111] Armed
with a large number of graphs and the latest insights from the IMF and
OECD, Jacobs urged the leadership to wait for economic recovery

110   Thijs Niemantsverdriet, *De vechtpartij: De PvdA van Kok tot Samsom*
(Amsterdam: Atlas Contact, 2014), 216–48.

111   Bas Jacobs, interview by the author, Amsterdam, 23 January 2023.

before making cuts. They certainly should not agree to tax increases for ordinary citizens, as these would nip the burgeoning recovery in the bud. When Jacobs had finished talking, Diederik Samsom cleared his throat. He was sitting behind a laptop, with a stack of printed Excel sheets with broad review reports from the Ministry of Finance next to him. 'Suppose,' Samsom suggested, 'that we still want to cut costs and increase taxes. What can we best do then?' 'Truly incredible,' Jacobs reminisces. 'I got angry. I said I hadn't given an hour's lecture about how unwise it is to cut spending only then to discuss austerity measures with him.' The meeting ended early and under a dark cloud. 'One of the most painful discussions I've ever had as an economist,' Jacobs concludes.

In the campaign, 'telling the honest story' became an unexpected hit. The Labour Party soon overtook the SP in the polls and ended up as the second-largest party, with forty seats – only one seat behind the VVD. At a rapid pace, Samsom began forming a new government with the VVD. During that process, it slowly dawned on people that Samsom had ditched his most important campaign theme: his critique of austerity. He had silently switched sides to join the budget hawks and now defended the need for austerity. There was one problem, however: he had not informed his own party.

'The about-turn came as a complete surprise to the parliamentary faction,' said Mariëtte Hamer, then Labour MP and later chairman of the Social and Economic Council.[112] 'The honest story' had been above all a criticism directed at the VVD. Now it was being used by Samsom to defend austerity. 'Of course, you never know what's going on in someone's head,' said Hamer. But nothing had changed in the Labour Party election programme until the government formation. There had been 'no debate on embracing austerity' within the party at all. Of course, people expected that the VVD would be given something, 'but not in the bold way in which it happened at the time'.

It was one of the fastest government formations in Dutch political history. The key decisions were made the day after the elections, when Rutte and Samsom met at the kitchen table of a The Hague residence of a prominent VVD politician. Former Labour Party leader Wouter Bos headed the negotiations, using the skills acquired from his new job at

---

112   Mariëtte Hamer, online interview by the author, 11 May 2023.

the Dutch consultancy giant KPMG. Bos wrote policy positions on pieces of paper for the most important policy issues. The reports of the broad review were again an important point of reference. The negotiators then took turns choosing cards. Preferences were traded, rather than compromised on. Rutte was the first to decide on the crucial subject of 'public finances'. He chose 'fiscal rigour'. In exchange, Samsom chose 'income levelling'.[113] In other words, the Labour Party decided to embrace austerity, as long as the pain would be equally shared. In a mere two weeks, the main issues were hammered out.

The Eurozone crisis had by then already reached a turning point – not due to the new government in The Hague but due to the new president of the ECB, Mario Draghi. In a speech to investors in London, he calmed market anxiety. 'Within our mandate,' he said, 'the ECB is ready to do whatever it takes to preserve the euro. And believe me, it will be enough.'[114] With those words, Draghi made clear that the ECB was willing to act as a lender of last resort. In one stroke, this ended market speculation on the fall of the euro – though it would take some time for that realization to dawn on Dutch politicians and economic policy-makers. According to Labour Party MEP Paul Tang, many did not understand how the financial markets and EMU worked: 'They didn't grasp the significance of what Mario Draghi did.' That there were such drastic cuts after Draghi's whatever-it-takes moment was 'quite remarkable' in his opinion, since the pressure of the financial markets was no longer there.[115]

The coalition partners consented to the earlier 12 billion in austerity cuts from the Spring Agreement, and a further 16 billion in cuts and tax increases of their own. As if that was not painful enough, an additional 6 billion in cuts had to be added in 2013, due to the economic damage caused by these cuts. When asked about these additional cuts on Dutch public television, Wouter Bos called them inevitable: 'As an economist I think it is unwise to cut back so much, but if you tell the rest of Europe – countries such as Greece, Italy and Portugal – that they have to play by

---

113   Tom-Jan Meeus and Derk Stokmans, 'Vannacht nog even bellen? Dwing de ander niet door het stof te gaan' [Should we call tonight? Never force the other on their knees], *NRC Handelsblad*, 3 November 2012.

114   'Verbatim of the Remarks Made by Mario Draghi', European Central Bank, 26 July 2012, ecb.europa.eu.

115   Paul Tang, phone interview by the author, 16 February 2023.

the rules and you insist on fiscal discipline, you lose all credibility if you don't follow the rules yourself.'[116]

Also at the European level, the Labour Party had turned the corner and rescinded its support for François Hollande's anti-austerity coalition. The Netherlands fell back into its traditional role of supporting Germany, while Hollande was isolated. The Labour Party Finance Minister Jeroen Dijsselbloem – a close confidant of Samsom during the election campaign and the government formation – became the face of European austerity policy as the president of the Eurogroup, the powerful body of finance ministers presiding over the Eurozone crisis. He made headlines in his clash with the Greek finance minister, Yanis Varoufakis, and for his disparaging remarks on Southern European countries: 'I cannot spend my money on booze and women and then ask for your support.'[117]

The Party's Over

The new Purple coalition of VVD and PvdA embarked on a series of painful reforms. It greatly reduced the number of civil servants, cut unemployment and disability benefits, increased the deductible on healthcare, cut back the Dutch social housing sector, lowered the mortgage tax deduction, increased VAT, stopped funding for sheltered workshops for disabled workers and ramped up its pursuit of benefit fraud. One of the larger operations was the devolution of domestic care, youth care and elderly care to the local level, which at the same time involved a large budget cut.

These measures were presented by the new government as a fundamental revision of the relation between state and society. In a prominent lecture, Mark Rutte praised the 1980s austerity policies of the Lubbers cabinets.[118] Ruud Lubbers had argued back then that retrenching the welfare state would revive civil society and boost voluntary initiatives

116   'Wouter Bos "als econoom" vindt bezuinigingen onverstandig' [Wouter Bos 'as an economist' finds austerity unwise], *Trouw*, 22 June 2013.

117   Paul McClean and Mehreen Khan, 'Dijsselbloem Under Fire After Saying Eurozone Countries Wasted Money on "Alcohol and Women"', *Financial Times*, 21 March 2017.

118   Mark Rutte, 'Nederland bij de tijd brengen: Verandering en zekerheid', H. J. Schoo lecture, 2 September 2013.

from ordinary citizens. The Netherlands would 'transition from a welfare state, which threatens to become unaffordable and oppressive, to a caring society where people look out for each other', Lubbers had suggested in parliament in 1982.[119] It was a nostalgic vision – a longing for the Christian civil society of the 1950s that the Dutch welfare state had displaced. Though the secular Rutte left out the Christian overtones, he presented his own austerity policies as a continuation of Lubbers's work, promising a society where people would not need the welfare state and could do more by themselves.[120] That same message was delivered in the traditional king's speech at the beginning of the political year. King Willem-Alexander famously announced that the Dutch welfare state would make way for a 'participation society' in which ordinary citizens would take on tasks that the welfare state could no longer fulfil.[121]

Despite predictions of quick economic recovery from politicians and central bankers, the Dutch economy continued to stagnate. Economic growth in 2013 stood at a meagre 0.2 per cent, and it was not until 2015 that Dutch GDP returned to where it had been before the 2008 financial crisis. Unemployment rose from 5.8 per cent to 7.4 per cent in 2014 – not as dramatic as in Southern Europe, but still a painful recession. Surprisingly, the new government presented a united front on austerity. Rather than blaming the bankers, the government now tried to convince voters of their own responsibility in bringing on the financial crisis. Speaking at the annual Den Uyl lecture only months after the 2012 elections, Diederik Samsom reframed the economic crisis in dramatic fashion:

The party's over. We entered the new age consuming like there was no limit. We dragged flatscreen- and Nespresso-luxury into our houses. Cars became longer, the station wagon, then higher, the MPV, then wider, the SUV, and then we got two. The sky was the limit. While partying, we missed the change that occurred just after the turn of the millennium. Living large, we postponed the end of the party a little

---

119   Parliamentary records, HTK, 1982/83, 647.
120   Rutte, 'Nederland bij de tijd brengen'.
121   'Troonrede 2013 – Toespraak – Het Koninklijk Huis', speech, Ministry of General Affairs, 17 September 2013.

longer. Until Lehman Brothers fell, dragging the entire financial sector behind it, contaminating the real economy and unleashing the euro crisis. A groggy generation woke up from its intoxication. As if someone turned on the fluorescent lights just as the party was well underway. Still blinking from the harsh lights, we have stood there looking at each other for the past few years. Who did it? Who ruined the party? The reckless credit card holders in the United States? The Greeks with their phony budgets? The real estate tycoons and perfidious banks in Spain? Ideally, we would like to throw the culprits out, turn the fluorescent lights off, the music on, and go on partying. But, ladies and gentlemen, that is an illusion. Yes, one culprit has turned on the lights. More than one, even. But we had really used up the beer and crisps ourselves. The party is over. And now we have to clean up. A bit like you used to do when you had thrown a secret party and quickly needed to get rid of the mess.[122]

Until this moment, culpability for the financial crisis had rested squarely with the financial sector, which had taken on irresponsible risks while awarding itself lavish bonuses. The fact that the bill for the financial crisis was now being passed on to ordinary citizens caused widespread anger. After mobilizing on this issue during the 2012 election campaign, Samsom now switched gears and diverted blame to ordinary Dutch citizens, in an effort to build support for the coming austerity measures. It was a remarkable development on the Dutch left. Rather than attempting to translate public anger against the financial sector and free market policies into support for left-wing measures, the centre-left came to the defence of the financial sector. GreenLeft leader Femke Halsema wrote an essay on why it was wrong to vilify Wall Street bankers, suggesting that we all have secret fantasies to live lives of excess.[123] Finally, the Labour Party minister of social affairs, Lodewijk Asscher, lambasted the critiques of austerity advanced by economists like Krugman and Stiglitz and politicians including Jeremy Corbyn in the UK:

---

122   Diederik Samsom (PvdA), 'Den Uyl Lezing door Diederik Samson', DNPP Repositories, 10 December 2012, dnpprepo.ub.rug.nl.

123   Femke Halsema, 'De wolf die in ons huist' [The wolf that resides in us all], *De Correspondent*, 21 January 2014, decorrespondent.nl.

We have to put an end to the debate on austerity. The truth is as follows: we cannot pretend to offer people better living standards, better education, better healthcare if the budget is a mess. It would be like a father with large debts, addicted to gambling, who comforts his children by promising that they will go on holiday next summer. The children will know better . . . Progressives have to be serious about budget discipline and economic competence.[124]

There was now a political consensus on austerity among the parties in the political centre. In fact, the new government presented itself to the public as heir to the consensus politics of Arend Lijphart. Reading out the government policy statement in parliament, Rutte placed his government in the tradition of the Great Pacification of 1917, the Wassenaar Accord and the Lubbers cabinets of the 1980s.[125] On the insistence of the Labour Party, the government actively sought the support of social partners in fine-tuning its austerity measures. When the economy started to recover in 2017, the government triumphantly proclaimed that this was the logical result of its austerity policies.

Academics of the consensus school soon hailed this as a new 'success story' of Dutch consensus politics. They wrote of an 'economic success that resembles the acclaimed Dutch "miracle" of the 1990s'.[126] Again, Dutch consensus politics was contrasted positively with the dominant model of majoritarian politics: 'While in majoritarian and presidential politics, like Britain and France, crisis management easily polarizes national politics, the consensual model of the Netherlands offers an alternative, wherein the government "shares political space" with societal stakeholders and builds different (centrist) majorities behind feasible reform proposals.' But economic data from the CPB, the IMF and the OECD did not support such a reading.[127] In fact, the austerity policies of

124   Lodewijk Asscher, 'The Future of the Left', 1 September 2015. See also Merijn Oudenampsen, 'Decline of the Dutch Left', *NLR Sidecar*, 16 March 2021, newleftreview.org.

125   Parliamentary records, HTK, 2012/2013, 21–3, 4.

126   Anton Hemerijck, Johannes Karremans and Marc van der Meer, 'Responsive Corporatism Without Political Credit: Social Concertation, Constructive Opposition and the Long Tenure of the Rutte II Cabinet in the Netherlands (2012–2017)', *Acta Politica* 58, no. 1 (1 January 2023): 162.

127   CPB, *Middellange-termijnverkenning 2018–2021* (The Hague: CPB, 2016); CPB, *Macro-economische verkenning 2014–2017* (The Hague: CPB, 2016); CPB, *Centraal economisch plan 2016* (The Hague: CPB, 2016).

the two Rutte governments had cost the country somewhere between 7.5 per cent and 10 per cent of Dutch GDP. If the government had simply sat on its hands, the leading economist Bas Jacobs wrote, it would have garnered far more income from unhampered economic growth than it did through six years of damaging cuts and tax hikes.[128]

Economic success was in fact limited, and so was corporatist consensus. The centre-right and the centre-left certainly agreed on austerity and tried to involve social partners in policymaking once more. But the trade unions were clearly opposed to austerity. The FNV claimed in 2012 that austerity was 'economically unsound' and would 'exacerbate the crisis'. The biggest problem was declining consumption caused by 'low consumer confidence, problems in the housing market, rising unemployment, wage restraint and, above all, tax increases'.[129]

Before the new government entered power, labour relations had been at an all-time low. 'We have been horribly swindled in the last decades after making deals, with politicians cherry-picking from corporatist agreements, like that on pension reform, leaving workers continuously at a disadvantage,' complained FNV leader Ton Heerts bitterly during the last days of the first Rutte cabinet. The main offices of the Employers Federation (VNO-NCW) and that of the Ministry of Economic Affairs sit across from each other on the same street in the centre of The Hague. Heerts suggested that the employers had secretly dug an underground tunnel from their office to the ministry and to the official residence of Prime Minister Mark Rutte, 'doing business with the government without us'.[130] 'It isn't that strange that we don't have that much to gain from negotiating in the Social and Economic Council,' Heerts concluded.

Due to the differences in opinion over austerity, the new VVD–PvdA government that entered power later that year did not manage to change this dynamic fundamentally. To the degree that trade unions were involved in policymaking, it was not because they agreed with the general direction of government policy but rather because they sought to limit some of its more harmful effects.

128   Bas Jacobs, 'De rekening van Rutte', *ESB* (blog), 20 September 2016, esb.nu.

129   Cited in Boumans, 'Did Trade Unions Reinforce the Neoliberal Transformation?', 146.

130   Marike Stellinga and Jos Verlaan, ' "Ik zit hier niet omdat het goed ging" ' ['I'm not here because things went well'], *NRC Handelsblad*, 25 August 2012.

Leading scholars of Dutch labour relations argued that the polder model of the 1990s was increasingly falling apart. The power balance between labour and capital was tilting ever more in favour of the latter.[131] Wage levels lagged behind productivity, the number of flexible and part-time contracts continued to increase, negotiations in key sectors were deadlocked leading to the exclusion of the largest and most left-wing union, FNV, while corporatist advisory bodies, such as the Social and Economic Council and the Foundation of Labour, had an increasingly marginal role in policymaking. In response, the FNV gradually abandoned its non-confrontational style of trade unionism and moved back to the left on socioeconomic policy. The union annulled its wage-moderation strategy in 2015 and adopted a (Keynesian) wage-led growth position, while at the same time making the fight against flexible contracts its first priority.[132]

A final nail in the coffin of the consensus narrative was that the second Rutte cabinet was one of the most unpopular governments in Dutch post-war history. Left-wing voters were especially disillusioned. When elections were held in 2017, the Labour Party suffered the largest defeat in Dutch political history, losing twenty-nine of their thirty-eight seats in parliament.[133] Labour Party leaders reacted defensively. Dijsselbloem said he still believed 'we have done what was necessary', what was 'responsible and good for the Netherlands'. The only problem was that they had failed to convince their supporters: 'We lost them somewhere along the way.' He concluded bitterly: 'We have been punished for saving the country.'[134] Diederik Samsom offered a similar reaction. After stepping down as party leader, he said in an interview that he was still unable to point to one decision that he regretted or would not take again. His government, he declared defiantly, had been 'a blessing for the country'. Samsom blamed the election defeat on the oversensitivity of the Labour Party base and said that 'at every

---

131   Paul de Beer and Maarten Keune, 'De erosie van het poldermodel', *Mens en Maatschappij* 93, no. 3 (1 August 2018): 231–60.

132   Boumans, 'Did Trade Unions Reinforce the Neoliberal Transformation?'

133   While the Labour Party originally had forty seats in 2012, two Muslim MPs left the party in 2015 due to a controversy over integration policies for ethnic minorities. They founded the Islamic party DENK.

134   Jule Hinrichs and Ulko Jonker, ' "Wij hebben de afgelopen jaren al het land gered, nu gaan we de partij redden" ' [We have saved the country these last years, now we will save the party], *Financieel Dagblad*, 29 May 2017.

compromise they would lie down crying in the corner'.[135] In the two elections held since then, the Labour Party failed to recover, and the broader left vote share dwindled to a historic low of 30 per cent of the electorate.

135   Marike Stellinga and Thijs Niemantsverdriet, 'Samsom: PvdA had kabinetsbeleid feller moeten verdedigen' [Samson: PvdA should have defended government policy more forcefully], *NRC Handelsblad*, 4 August 2017.

Conclusion

Politically, the Netherlands has long been considered something of a special case. It acquired an international reputation as the consensual counterpart to the more competitive and politicized Anglo-American model – a country where, in the words of the late Peter Mair, politicians of various stripes 'treat one another with a marked degree of mutual tolerance and accommodation, and in which opposition is pacified rather than excluded'.[1] It is a system in which politicians tend to depoliticize the most important political conflicts rather than foregrounding them. As a result, Dutch scholars have long considered the neoliberal turn, with its polarized 'battle of ideas', to be an Anglo-American phenomenon, something culturally alien to Dutch political mores. The Dutch market-based reforms of the 1980s came to be seen as a consensual alternative, marking the birth of the polder model.

This book breaks with the established consensus narrative and shows that there has been a neoliberal turn in the Netherlands – although it took a distinctive form. The Netherlands saw a highly depoliticized and technocratic version of neoliberal reform. There was no Dutch equivalent to Margaret Thatcher's bold aim to 'change the heart and soul of the

---

1   Arend Lijphart, *Patterns of Democracy: Government Forms and Performance in Thirty-Six Countries* (New Haven, CT: Yale University Press, 1999); Peter Mair, 'The Correlates of Consensus Democracy and the Puzzle of Dutch Politics', *West European Politics* 17, no. 4 (1 October 1994): 97–123.

nation' or Ronald Reagan's famous dictum that 'government is not the solution to our problem, government is the problem'. Instead, the Dutch prime minister, Ruud Lubbers, depoliticized the reforms and soberly ushered in an era of 'no-nonsense politics'. Initiative was outsourced to senior civil servants at the Ministries of Finance and Economic Affairs. The neoclassical economists leading these ministries were wary of Keynesian economics at quite an early stage. They proved receptive to the international ascendance of neoliberal ideas – in particular monetarism, public choice, new-classical economics and supply-side economics.

As a result, the Dutch neoliberal turn has taken a very different shape than the dominant Anglo-American experience of neoliberal transformation. The locus classicus of that Anglo-American trajectory is the rise of monetarism under Thatcher.[2] The idea is that a fundamental change in economic policy requires a politicized battle of ideas in the public realm: the established Keynesian policy elites dominated the institutions, and the neoliberals challenged those institutions from the outside. Politicians, journalists and neoliberal think-tanks took the lead in promoting new economic ideas and attacking the old guard. When Thatcher assumed power, she gradually replaced the established Keynesian policy elites at the Treasury with her own appointees, all avowed monetarists. From this experience, a universal theory of neoliberal transformation has emerged, seen as applicable in all advanced liberal democracies.[3]

While there was a contest over ideas in the Netherlands, it adhered to an opposite logic. In the Netherlands, it was not the participants in the politicized public debate who initiated the shift, and the public officials who then followed suit; it was the other way around. Senior economic policymakers pushed for extensive socioeconomic reforms of a highly political nature at an early stage, while politicians and journalists played a more secondary role, outsourcing initiative to technocratic policymakers and depoliticizing the reforms in the public debate as being 'realistic', 'pragmatic' and 'no-nonsense'. Hans Daalder, the founding father of Dutch political science, argued that the Dutch political system offered obvious

---

2   Peter Hall, 'Policy Paradigms, Social Learning, and the State: The Case of Economic Policymaking in Britain', *Comparative Politics* 25, no. 3 (1993): 275–96.

3   Colin Hay, 'The "Crisis" of Keynesianism and the Rise of Neoliberalism in Britain: An Ideational Institutionalist Approach', in John L. Campbell and Ove K. Pedersen, eds, *The Rise of Neoliberalism and Institutional Analysis* (Princeton, NJ: Princeton University Press, 2001), 193–218.

incentives for politicians, journalists and academics to present ideas as non-ideological – as instances of pragmatism, objectivity or realism. Daalder called this 'depoliticization-out-of-political-interest'.[4] In a country of political minorities, framing one's ideas as non-ideological allows one to build coalitions with other parties while appeasing one's own base with the compromises reached. This means that depoliticized discourse often serves as an artificial façade in the Netherlands. The result is a highly technocratic neoliberal turn, with a leading role for senior bureaucrats.

In a theoretical sense, this book contends that, in the Dutch case, it is not so much corporatism that proved decisive but rather the role of bureaucratic elites, as put forward by scholars such as Theda Skocpol and Margaret Weir. Their contention in *Bringing the State Back In* was that government is not just a neutral, passive arena in which interest groups negotiate policy.[5] Government is an actor in its own right – and policymakers can take the lead in diagnosing political problems and offering policy solutions. The state bureaucracy has a powerful institutional infrastructure to produce ideas, and the administrative biases it contains can help explain political change. This renewed focus on the state seems warranted in the Netherlands, as the ideas underpinning the Dutch policy shift of the 1980s did not originate in corporatist institutions but in the ministries in The Hague. To be clear, this is not an argument about the brute power of administrative elites per se but about their role in shaping economic policy ideas in times of crisis.

Of course, we should not overstate the autonomy of bureaucratic elites from societal pressures and interests – particularly those of Dutch business. Skocpol and Weir underlined the relative autonomy of bureaucratic elites, in opposition to Marxist perspectives on the state as an instrument of economic elites. In the Netherlands, heteronomy is very much the norm. The Ministry of Economic Affairs traditionally conceives of its role as representing Dutch business interests and acting as a mediator with political elites. The ties between business elites and senior economic policymakers at the Ministries of Finance and

---

4   Hans Daalder, *Politisering en lijdelijkheid in de Nederlandse politiek* (Assen: Van Gorcum, 1974), 34.

5   Margaret Weir and Theda Skocpol, 'State Structures and the Possibilities for "Keynesian" Responses to the Great Depression in Sweden, Britain and the United States', in Peter B. Evans, Dietrich Rueschemeyer and Theda Skocpol, eds, *Bringing the State Back In* (Cambridge: Cambridge University Press, 1985), 107–63.

Economic Affairs have historically been close. Senior civil servants have routinely moved from government to sit on the boards of the largest Dutch companies, while prominent business leaders have often been appointed to head ministries. The Wagner Committee, which prepared the policy shift for the Lubbers cabinet, can hardly be described as proof of the autonomy of civil servants.

This book does not wholly reject the consensus narrative, but it locates that consensus in the 1990s rather than in the 1980s. In a 1989 campaign speech, the Labour Party leader Wim Kok decried the unilateral and authoritarian approach of the previous right-wing coalition governments led by Lubbers. He stressed that reform needed broad support. From the third Lubbers cabinet of Christian Democrats and social democrats onwards, the Dutch government placed a renewed emphasis on corporatist consensus. This return to consensus politics remained mired in controversy at the beginning of the 1990s, with right-wing parties and leading commentators complaining of a 'sluggish state' and seeking to abandon Dutch corporatism whole. But by the mid-1990s, with the Labour Party as the largest party, the polder model suddenly became a matter of pride. It was founded on a new social-liberal compromise that had begun with the landmark 1992 report of the Social and Economic Council, 'Convergence and Corporatism'.[6] The compromise achieved was continued wage moderation and labour market flexibilization, with a shift towards a more market-based, active welfare state rather than its wholesale replacement with a so-called 'mini-system'.

To what degree has the Dutch neoliberal turn been a success? To what extent has the Netherlands become a more neoliberal country? The complicating factor here is there is no such thing as 'pure' neoliberalism. As the economic geographer Jamie Peck has argued, neoliberalism can only ever exist in impure form.[7] The main reason for this is that the utopian vision of a frictionless free market is unrealizable in practice. To the extent that the neoliberals have been victorious in their battle of ideas, their victories have always been partial, Peck writes. The historical reality is that of 'failing forward' rather than of a cleanly implemented free market revolution. As a result, neoliberalism manifests itself in a variety of

---

6   SER, *Convergentie en overlegeconomie* (The Hague: SER, 1992).

7   Jamie Peck, *Constructions of Neoliberal Reason* (Oxford: Oxford University Press, 2010).

national contexts in messy, hybrid forms. It is forced to share the stage with other traditions of political and economic governance – social democracy, corporatism, development economics or Soviet planning. At the same time, however, liberalized and privatized activities soon turn out once again to require new forms of regulation and state intervention.

This idea of neoliberal reform as 'failing forward' seems to fit the Dutch case well. Despite all the rhetoric of a Dutch miracle, by the end of the 1980s the dominant sentiment was that the reforms of the past decade had achieved limited success. It is true that wages had been moderated, Dutch business was competitive again and the growth of public spending had been halted. Even so, the Dutch economy had fallen seriously behind. In 1988, the OECD ranked the Netherlands among the worst-performing economies in that decade.[8] Unemployment remained stubbornly high, Dutch economic growth fell short and public debt had doubled in a decade to 80 per cent of GDP. In absolute terms, the Netherlands experienced the slowest growth in GDP per capita among all European countries in the 1980s. These experiences prompted a shift to a Third Way policy mix in the 1990s. When economic recovery set in, this became the new policy consensus. Neoliberal aspirations – such as Frits Bolkestein's 'mid-Atlantic model', Frans Rutten's 'mini-system' or Pim Fortuyn's vision of a fully liberalized labour market – ultimately remained out of reach. At the same time, within the more moderate limits of the social-liberal consensus of the 1990s, market-based solutions came to be widely accepted. The result was a more gradual trend towards marketization, without the privatization blitz that Thatcher had introduced in the UK in areas such as housing and public transport.

In the same period, the Netherlands became a leading fiscal hawk on the European stage. There is a common understanding of the European Union, and in particular of EMU, as structurally neoliberal. But from the Dutch perspective this was not inherently true. In fact, EMU and the European budget were seen by Dutch economic policymakers as new sources of government largesse. In a dynamic that suggests a more bottom-up European policy development, Dutch economic policymakers suggested bringing Dutch budgeting rules to Brussels. The Netherlands allied with Germany in establishing the Stability and Growth Pact. The European fiscal norms, in particular the 3 per cent

---

8   OECD, *Economic Outlook* 44 (December 1988).

budget norm and the 60 per cent threshold for public debt, were built on the economic and intellectual legacy of the 1980s.

During the Eurozone crisis, the Netherlands was once again a leading voice, insisting on austerity and structural reform. Both the Budget Memorandum and the Central Planning Bureau made the case for austerity while referring to the Dutch experience of the 1980s: 'Experience teaches that often a large crisis is necessary before far-reaching reforms can be implemented to boost growth.'[9] All too soon, though, the negative impact of austerity led to a double-dip recession. Rutte had to cut even deeper to stay within the 3 per cent norm, resulting ultimately in an estimated €50 billion in cutbacks and tax hikes between 2010 and 2017. This proved to be a spectacular exercise in economic self-harm, but leading politicians argued that the Netherlands had to discipline itself in order to have any credibility in disciplining others.

Ultimately, it was not the financial crisis but the coronavirus pandemic that brought an uncertain shift in Dutch fiscal policy. A series of Dutch politicians boldly announced the end of neoliberalism. Whether such a transition is indeed taking place is difficult to say. After becoming the country's longest-serving prime minister, the neoliberal Rutte has left the stage of Dutch politics. The last elections saw the unexpected rise of Geert Wilders's right-wing populist Freedom Party. While often depicted as a reaction against neoliberal globalization, its relationship to neoliberalism is complex.

Dutch right-wing populism emerged in the 1990s as a radical offshoot of the Dutch neoliberal turn. In the decade that followed, Wilders switched tactically to a more centrist and ambiguous economic position. In the 1990s, it was the shared consensus on economic policy and the profound depoliticization of socioeconomic issues that helped pave the way for a politics focused on cultural conflict. While neoliberal ideas have lost some ground in economic policymaking circles, the reality continues to be one of solid right-wing majorities. While the generation that presided over the neoliberal turn is now receding from public life, the legacy of the neoliberal turn continues to cast its long shadow over the future of Dutch politics.

9   Coen Teulings et al., *Europa in Crisis: Het Centraal Planbureau over schulden en de toekomst van de eurozone* (Amsterdam: Balans, 2011), 147.

Index